PSYCHOANALYTIC EMPATHY

PSYCHOANALYTIC EMPATHY

Stefano Bolognini

Translated by
Malcolm Garfield

Editorial Consultant
Anthony Molino

Free Association Books

First published 2004
by Free Association Books
57 Warren Street W1T 5NR

© 2003 Stefano Bolognini

All rights reserved. No part of this publication
may be reproduced, stored in a retrieval system,
or transmitted, in any form or by any means,
without the prior permission in writing
of the publisher.

This book is sold subject to the condition
that it shall not, by way of trade or otherwise,
be lent, resold, hired out or otherwise circulated
without the publisher's prior consent in any form
other than that supplied by the publisher.

British Library Cataloguing in Publication Data
A catalogue record for this book is available from the British Library

Produced by Bookchase (UK) Ltd
Printed and bound in England

ISBN 1 853437 23 9

Publisher's Dedication

This book is dedicated to R. M. Young who founded Free Association Books in 1983. His vision and flair in the early years resulted in the publication of many books which have now become classic psychoanalytic texts, providing the inspiration and material resources for this translation.

CONTENTS

Preface	9
Introduction: *The Psychoanalyst's Theoretical Models, Harmony and Consistency*	13

Part I: Historical Review

1. Romantic Empathy	25
2. Freud and Empathy	31
3. The Pioneers	36
4. The Fifties: the Rediscovery of Empathy	41
5. The Kleinian and post-Kleinian Conception of Empathy	54
6. An Italian Contribution: Savo Spacal and 'Comparative Analysis'	59

Part II: A Contemporary Prospective

7. The Analyst's Internal Attitude: Analysis *with* the Ego and Analysis *with* the Self	69
The ego, the self and the unconscious	70
Some characteristic modalities of analytic contact	73
8. Empathy and Countertransference: the Analyst's Affects as a Problem and a Resource	82
Aldo the heartless executive	85
Observations on the case	92
9. Empathy and Sharing: a Necessary Distinction	94
Sara, a case of contagious defeatism	97
A session with Sara	97
Reflections on the case	99
Sharing as a therapeutic factor	102

The Relationship between Sharing and Empathy	103
Sharing is a precursor of empathetic understanding	103
Sharing and its vicissitudes	104

10. The 'Kind-Hearted' Versus The Good Analyst:
    Empathy And Hate In Countertransference 107
    Empathy and adequate negative countertransference 111

11. Empathy and Empathism 118
    The Empathic posture between 'concordance'
    and complementarity 119
    Alessandra, a refined young lady 122
    'Empathising' as a task or claim 126
    An analytic journey: from emotional desert to empathy 130
    Conclusions 133

12. Empathy and the Unconscious 136
    Topographical aspects structural aspects 137
    Problem areas 140
    Anna with the clenched-tooth smile 144
    Discussion 149

13. Empathy and Fusionality 153
    Leopold's rage 161

14. Natural Empathy and Psychoanalytic Empathy 167

Conclusion 175
    Mr P.'s leave-taking 177
    A session with Mr P 178

Bibliography 180
Index 190

PREFACE

Freud described empathy in Jokes and their Relation to the Unconscious (1905) as a conscious or unconscious process of putting oneself in the other's shoes. He believed that the psychoanalyst's empathic response to the patient was the sine qua non condition for establishing a positive transference. For Freud empathy is the foundation upon which the psychoanalytic relationship is built, and is a part of everything positive that an analyst does. Freud never varied in his view of the central role empathy plays "in our understanding of the alien (or other) self of other people" (1907a), but his appreciation of the power of the transference and it's impact upon the analyst's person led him to caution colleagues on the use they made of their feelings.

Empathy is a one of those concepts that may be too easily taken ignored or misunderstood. By creative use of our imagination we tap the recesses of our experience to find within ourselves an approximation of what we think another person might think and feel. However, identifying the source and nature of empathy and defining its use in the psychoanalytic endeavour are elusive tasks.

Psychoanalytic Empathy is evidence that Stephano Bolognini is up to the task. While Bolognini reinforces Freud's caution about the use of empathy, his intellectual and emotional exploration of the concept amplifies the complexity of empathic attunement. Bolognini's internal processing of the subject of empathy gives his critical review of the literature and his clinical presentations a ring of authenticity. This book is accessible to the newcomer and will challenge the veteran. It makes an original and valuable contribution to psychoanalytic theory and deserves to be a reference on the subject of psychoanalytic empathy for years to come.

It is not an accident that this psychoanalytic book about empathy is written by an Italian. From my experience of listening to and discussing psychoanalytic papers presented by Italians at regular British-Italian Conferences, I have been struck by a passion and irony Italians bring to psychoanalysis along with a capacity to learn from and appreciate many theoretical models while not idealising any single framework. Stephano Bolognini has these qualities.

In Part I Historical Review, Bolognini traces the concept of empathy from its philosophical origins in German Romanticism through Freud and the early psychoanalysts to its 'rediscovery' in the 1950's, which coincided with the changing views of counter transference. He is well placed to understand and articulate a variety of historical and contemporary psychoanalytic views of empathy from the self-psychologists' emphasis on contact with the patient's wounded narcissism to the Europeans' focus on the complexity of the patient's defensive system. Of particular interest is Bolognini's account of the Italian analyst Savo Spacal's (1990) paper Empathy and countertransference as constituent parts of psychoanalytic understanding. However, Bolognini disagrees with Spacal's view that empathy is the same thing as a concordant disposition. Bolognini believes that empathy is far too complex an intra- and interpersonal event for the clinician to be able to consciously adopt an empathic 'attitude' or 'approach'. He maintains that if empathy is restricted to concordance with what is ego-syntonic for the patient, it loses its value as a psychoanalytic concept. Stephano Bolognini's curiosity about empathy was initially stimulated 20 years ago by his analytic work with patients and he continually returns to this source. Six of his analytic patients are at the centre of his inquiry like markers that guide a ship through dangerous water. This is particularly apparent in Part II A Contemporary Prospective, which speaks to the psychoanalyst, psychotherapist and mental health practitioner at the level of their 'here and now' experience with patients and clients. Typically, Stephano Bolognini begins with the analyst and reminds us that we cannot decide to be empathic. The analyst does not 'turn on' empathy. However, awareness of a loss of internal contact, a feeling of being uncentered, and not analytically integrated is a signal to begin finding one's self again through a process of self-empathy, which repairs and reintegrates his or her personal and professional internal objects. Bolognini proceeds to map out the topography of the analyst's internal attitude and makes clarifying distinctions between the ego, the self and the unconscious and the elaborates some characteristic modalities of analytic contact.

From Freud onwards psychoanalysts have acknowledged the inter-relationship between empathy and countertransference. Stephano Bolognini's caution, like Freud's, about the recognition and use of empathy arises out the influence of the countertransference. The analyst's affects provide access to empathy and the countertransference, but, as Bolognini points out, affects are highly complex, only partially made conscious and are notoriously unpredictable. Some affects may arouse unconscious conflicts within the analyst, and negative affects may undermine the analyst's narcissistic ideal. As usual, Bolognini does not immediately formulate a solution to these difficulties, but counsels patience and takes the reader into his own work with a patient he calls Aldo. Bolognini's honest and open account encourage the reader to follow his lead and look within the analyst patient relationship for personal insight into the often perplexing problems raised in the consideration of empathy.

There is, as Bolognini writes, a necessary distinction to be made between sharing and empathy. Although sharing may be a precursor to empathy, or a recognition of empathic feelings, Bolognini's concern is that sharing may become an end in itself to the extent that it pre-empts the process of thinking through the impulse to share a piece of the analyst's internal world. In this respect, sharing does not coincide with Bolognini's view of empathy as a privileged condition that enables the analyst to feel with the patient and to think about those feelings with the patient. Meaning that is arises from within the analyst conveys to the patient a sense that the analyst has 'been there' with him.

Empathy is often associated with an analytic atmosphere that is blissful, cloying and fusional and may become confused with positive feelings that are compatible with sympathy. The danger inherent in sentimentalising the content of empathy is that the analyst may fail to empathise with negative aspects of the patient's personality, such as his sadism, deceitfulness or manipulation, which, nevertheless, may represent a part of the patient's make-up at anytime in the analysis. Bolognini specifically addresses the risks of 'empathism', that is, an understanding based on overlooking the obstacles to understanding.

Stephano Bolognini has an openness that supports doubts and tolerates uncertainty about others' views as well as his own, which gives the reader the confidence to resist premature conclusions. He does not proselytise or promote. Rather, he is an explorer who allows himself to wander in unknown territory without superimposing someone else's map. As he says, the concept of empathy "... seems to be surrounded by a simplistic, indulgent and confusing aura attributed to it by those who are sometimes apt to identify it quite simply with a placid atmosphere, full of 'motherly' sentimentality. True empathy, on the other hand, requires - as we shall see- above all separation and differentiation, attention and an ability to keep theoretical thought in operation."(p. 8-9).

Stephano Bolognini's exploration of empathy grew out 'certain rare and privileged moments' that combined emotion, imagination and reflection in such a way that both he and his patient were able to fully comprehend what was happening. Bolognini writes with respect, and more than a hint of awe, for the psychoanalytic process, the patient and, indeed, the subject of empathy. It is Bolognini's humility and modesty toward his journey that draws the reader in. We move from the detachment of an intellectual study of empathy through uncertain ground, waiting and doubts toward a deeper understanding of the 'delicate terrain' of empathy and a greater appreciation of those rare and privileged moments.

Donald Campbell

INTRODUCTION

The Psychoanalyst's Theoretical Models, Harmony and Consistency

> For every complex problem,
> there is always a simple solution. Which is wrong.
> G. B. Shaw

When, in the early 1980s, I began to concern myself with the concept of empathy, I was driven by two motivations which now, at a distance of some twenty years, appear clear to me. One reason was linked to my clinical experience; at certain rare and privileged moments, I had benefited from a felicitous combination of emotion, imagination and reflection, which had enabled both the patient and myself to fully comprehend what was happening. As a subjective, relational, and clinical experience, it was unforgettable.

The other was the scientific one of trying somehow to identify this phenomenon better, to trace its contours, record the circumstances conducive to its appearance as well as the internal and external conditions which favoured it, in the obscure hope – which turned out to be largely illusory – of reproducing the phenomenon intentionally and in experimental conditions. Such was the firm Galilean view of science I had had drummed into me by my medical studies! I cannot deny it: my *arrière-pensée* was to go to the very heart of psychoanalysis and snatch up the technical secret that would lead me straight to the otherwise infrequent miracle of profound change.

Even at the time, I was able to smile at these clearly omnipotent expectations, but I soon realised that I was far from being alone; throngs of gold prospectors (searching for psychoanalytic gold, of course; you don't get rich in our profession) had gone before me, with varying fortune and, predictably, doubtful results. Yet, all of them had clearly worked with passion in the quest for the meaning of an experience that had moved them so deeply.

In the years that followed, I read and listened to everything I could on this theme and I hope I have set forth the most worthwhile and useful ones with a view to furthering our knowledge. Reasons of space have restricted me in many cases to fleeting citations of works which deserved fuller treatment. Nevertheless, I hope I have mapped out the subject sufficiently to enable the reader to locate the paths he[2] considers most significant. Present-day psychoanalysis, as I never tire of repeating, is extremely broad-based and stimulating, and if you have some good maps, a solid basic cultural training and a lively subjective instinct for research, it may lead you to surprising discoveries.

Naturally, one should be curious and keep an open mind on new developments, whilst at the same time maintaining one's critical faculties and scientific rigour. In compiling this text, I cannot say whether I have always managed to fulfil these criteria to perfection. I only know that I have not allowed myself to be intimidated by the criticism I heard on more than one occasion at conferences, stating that empathy did not constitute a 'psychoanalytic' concept. Whoever levelled this extreme criticism ignored the fact that the term can be found in the classic psychoanalytic literature and that its use – as we shall see – in psychoanalytic works over the last fifty years has been increasingly frequent. Curiously, this objection was never raised so promptly and with such conviction as regards other concepts in the realm of psychoanalytic research, such as 'field', 'relationship', *'ulteriorité'* etc., which fortunately have been introduced and studied with little opposition and with profitable results.

My impression is that this *a priori* rejection of the concept of empathy was a local, occasional and somewhat limited phenomenon, which may have been induced by certain initial misapprehensions. One of my declared intentions in writing this book is to clear up these possible misunderstandings.

I have attempted to explore the concept of empathy, rather than to emphasise and promote it. I have tried to understand what various authors mean by it and then to develop further thoughts on the subject. I have sought, first and foremost, to demystify the facile and superficial meaning often assigned to this term. It seems to be surrounded by a simplistic, indulgent and confusing aura attributed to it by those who are sometimes apt to identify it quite simply with a placid atmosphere, full of 'motherly' sentimentality. True empathy, on the other hand, requires – as we shall see – above all separation and differentiation, attention and an ability to keep theoretical thought in operation. In a word, it requires the ability to put a name to things even at very close contact. And I firmly believe that this has a great deal to do with psychoanalysis, that it is definitely something deeply within it.

I also want to warn the reader that what he finds in this book is psychoanalysis in evolution, psychoanalysis in movement (at least, that is what I hope). My training is classical and there is nothing I wish to repudiate of it; quite the contrary, like most of my colleagues, I look upon it as a precious legacy to be added to in the course of time and with experience. Like many of us, in fact, I have encountered along my psychoanalytic path a multiplicity of very different situations: I have been a member of two psychoanalytic Centres (Venice and Bologna) of different theoretical inspiration; I have worked with groups, both in the private and public sectors; I was for a time a hospital psychiatrist as well as an analyst, a member of the Committee for Serious Pathologies of the Italian Psychoanalytic Society for six years, and have acted as scientific secretary for that Society for four years, being thus placed in contact with the many theoretical currents featured in the highly variegated fabric of Italian psychoanalysis in general and the ten national psychoanalytic centres in particular; I have had continuous contact (both officially and otherwise) with colleagues from France, Britain, Argentina and North America and I am currently on the Working Party on Theoretical Issues of the European Psychoanalytical Federation. All of which means that my overall view, though undoubtedly subjective and open to discussion, is by no means devoid of interesting suggestions for keen observers of the complex field of contemporary psychoanalysis.

Let us take some very elementary observations as our starting point. First of all, we should note that our clinical experience puts us in contact with a variety of patients with different characteristics, needs, degrees of development and possibility for change. We also note that the same patient can go through very different phases in the course of treatment. In any one session, there is a succession or alternation of moments, functional levels and ways of relating between patient and analyst which differ considerably[1].

The various clinical circumstances may at least 'evoke' models of the mind and relationships of a correspondingly varied nature without actually 'requiring' them. Are we really convinced that the 'true' analyst is clinically and theoretically consistent? Does he continuously use only certain theoretical models and functions? Does he interact uniformly in the psychoanalytic relationship (for example, both in the treatment of a conflictual but fully-coherent patient, and for a patient with a serious risk of dysfunction)? Reading between the lines in clinical reports, we frequently get the impression that implicit micro-theories have been integrated into the psychoanalyst's basic theoretical position, generating micro-provisions with their own importance in the session (for example, in the way of putting forward an interpretation). Moreover, I think it happens quite often that, while reading various respected authors, we realise – with a certain amount of scientific embarrassment – that from one moment to the next we find there is something true in the most divergent of theories. This is not due to the reader's gullibility (as Gino Zucchini puts it, like Manzoni's Don Abbondio, who, in his timorous and wishy-washy way, agrees both with Lucia and the 'bravos', disconsolately acknowledging: "... you're right ... and you're right as well ..."). Rather, we appreciate a certain degree of realism, intuition and coherence – to differing extents – in the different theoretical models proposed.

It would be much more reassuring to feel oneself protected by a unique revealed truth, make use of a 'passe-partout' good for all occasions. This is not my case and I know I am in good company.

Anyway, there is a corollary to this statement: in certain cases knowing how to maintain a temporary suspension, when faced with the apparent irreconcilablility of different models, may lead in time to a better understanding of when, how, where and why a particular model is pertinent and suitable, what its sphere of application and its heuristic limitations are, how different models with intriguing similarities may overlap or be brought together (a classic example of this are the Freudian concepts of perception and representation compared to Bion's alpha and beta elements, with their relative clinical implications) and so forth. A conscious suspension of the sense of incompatibility when assessing different models is quite another thing to the split use of various models by the analyst himself. Some psychoanalysts work with coherence and satisfaction according to unitary theoretical and relational models with which they feel comfortable and through which they can cope with a variety of very different clinical occurrences.

At one time, psychoanalysts of this type formed the majority (especially in the classic Freudian and Kleinian areas); nowadays this is no longer so, at least, if one considers 'absolute' models excluding all forms of integration. However one judges the situation, many factors make it improbable or extremely rare for our candidates to be restricted to a 'monocultural diet' nowadays. One factor is the complexity of the sundry training programmes of the schools of psychotherapy and training institutes (with the partial exception of the fairly unified French system); another is the enormous growth in the number of psychoanalytic publications (making available even in less acculturated places a vast range of scientific proposals, the psychoanalysts' "plankton", as Musatti called it), and finally ever more frequent contacts and exchanges among colleagues from different countries and different schools of thought.

Nevertheless, there do remain certain basic characteristic connotations. Many of us, for example, are able to tell after reading only a few lines of a paper – even without citations – with a certain degree of precision, the writer's school of thought and sometimes even where he trained, his authorities and in some cases the personal psychoanalytic 'pedigree'.[3] But nowadays, scientific papers increasingly reveal the gradual hybridisation – sometimes successful, original and interesting, sometimes not – which an analyst faces during training. On occasion, we witness the 'thriving of hybrids': a well-known biological phenomenon whereby new combinations of originally distant genetic elements produce specimens which are in many ways superior to their forebears. At other times, we encounter a hotchpotch of mismatches, badly pieced together leading to incongruities.

One rather surprising case is that of the joint integration of elements from Lacan and Winnicott (a truly difficult combination, as Joyce McDougall vividly reminded us at a conference on Winnicott, held in Milan in November 2000), which produced interesting results in certain sections of the Asociación Psicoanalítica Argentina (APA). More generally, Kernberg, Mitchell and others have offered rather organic examples of the integration of various models. In Italy no-one has expressly carried out anything similar, but mention should be made of Giuseppe Di Chiara, who, more than anyone else, showed a broader and more appreciative view of really different theoretical and clinical contributions.

"Working with Freud ... Klein ... Bion ... Winnicott ... Kohut ... etc.": the repetition of these phrases puts me in mind of idealising polytheism or, depending on the maturity of the individual therapist, shelves full of items on offer at the 'psychoanalytic supermarket', or even – more opportunely and at a more advanced stage – a sense of the 'extended family'. It is almost like saying: these are my psychoanalytic parents, I recognise them in myself and do not deny them but actually appreciate what I have received from them. But the instruments and models proposed by my uncles, aunts and cousins, or sometimes even by my neighbours, may prove to be useful and interesting in certain circumstances. Naturally, the analyst's critical and selective faculties are kept in trim so that he may 'acquire' or discard the items encountered. This does not necessarily lead to the betrayal of one's original stock, nor to a loss of identity, but the acknowledgement of the complexity and richness of the psychoanalytic field and the opportunities it offers after a century of work, thought and debate.

Let there be no misunderstanding: betrayal and loss of identity may well occur, both internally and externally. There may be highly ambivalent, or even downright negative transference toward the masters of psychoanalytic thought, just as exists toward parents. There also exist patchworks, pastiches and schizoid concepts in which the congruous theoretic subject is unrecognisable. I am attempting to describe the various possibilities in order to rid contemporary training complexities of negative or positive fantasies which are too rigid and simplified, and which are somewhat stereotyped.

In the end, 'working with' one or more authors, or unitary or diversified models is not always, necessarily and only either something good or something bad. What is more important is how we manage to do it. We will explore this theme further in dealing with 'harmony' below.

Eclecticism is often subject to well-founded criticism (see the controversy between Greenson, 1974, and Rosenfeld, 1974; see Semi, 1988b), when characterised by superficiality and poor elaboration, taking fast and furtive possession of models, somewhat uncritically, with little comparative work, integration and overall coherence. In actual fact, over and beyond this degenerative form of eclecticism, a sense of complexity, articulation and personalised integration in one's models would appear to form part of the internal attitude of the present-day analyst. It smoothes the natural passage to relations between the models themselves and prevents cultural relativism. One example of this is the fact that no recently trained analyst would dream of making use of only one model exclusively to understand idealisation.

It is widely accepted that there are various types of idealisation, with different dynamic significance and functions, requiring different technical choices and giving rise to very particular developmental prospectives. It depends on whether the idealisation concerns the crevasse of splitting, the protracted effort of reactive formation, cohesive solidarity with an object-Self, or the subjective creation of a support for potential knowledge and growth. We know that certain malign idealisations should be analysed actively, that others should be tolerated until the right conditions are created for their natural lysis, that others may be greeted as signs of progress and so on. This is one of the many cases where the comparative knowledge of various models, combined with clinical sense and experience, may provide the analyst with a more complete instrument of work.

I remember an esteemed colleague of mine was once asked at a conference to specify whether he was Freudian, Kleinian, Bionian or goodness knows what else. He lost his temper and replied in a way which at the time I considered a little pompous. "I am first and foremost a psychoanalyst," he said. With the passing of time, however, I re-appraised his statement; it now seems to me to establish an attitude of research, reflection and clinical verification in opposition to the simplistic sticking on of labels.

INTRODUCTION

HARMONY AND CONSISTENCY

Like most of us, I have known psychoanalysts of every variety. Some are culturally monolithic, others flexible; some are as if 'possessed' by a theory, others have received it and cultivated it lovingly, others still have not yet espoused it exclusively, but are able to use it fruitfully and combine it with other theories and models. It is interesting that some psychoanalysts seem scientifically and technically '*harmonious*', while others are not, regardless of whether they follow one or more theories. Sometimes, we observe that the declared ideas, models, and styles of thinking and working may be truly consistent with the nature and effective way of being and working of those who propagate them (perhaps in books and articles); sometimes, it is otherwise. For example, I have listened to admirable seminars on the importance of the constant presence of the object in the primary relationship, by someone who would then disappear periodically for a month without batting an eyelid.

In other cases, I have had touching confirmation, from patients themselves, of the methodological consistency, care and sensitivity of colleagues with whom they had had consultation or stretches of treatment, in agreement with what transpired from their written reports.

But, more generally, harmony may be correlated with something which is still more internal and substantial, and which is sometimes clinically identifiable. One very precise element of disharmony, for example, may be perceived in those who find themselves in a state of projective identification with an object from the internal world: the analyst 'becomes' (as it were) his own Teacher. We then perceive a loss of contact with vast areas of the self, a tendency to conform too academically to the model, and a consequent lack of creative originality. There follows rigidity and a tendentially paranoid disposition towards critics, who partly represent the analyst's own unaware and unexpressed critical potential, free to consider and therefore feared. In such cases, orthodoxy may sometimes lead to one going off the rails towards fundamentalism.

Besides, we all know that, roughly speaking, the child who turns out right is the one who – having grown up – leaves his parents and goes beyond them, while recognising a great deal of them in himself. However, he is also able to dialogue with them, can separate from them, and has matured thanks to profound introjections; he knows how to interrelate as a separate being. He is not a devotee, an initiate, a replicant, a uniformed tin soldier, an alter boy. At the opposite extreme, the iconoclastic one, I think the psychoanalytic superego in our relationship with our patients, is not a 'Jimmy Cricket/know-all' to crush with a hammer blow; rather, it is a 'third party' to keep in the game through an internal dialogue which, in time, will gradually reach an equal footing, as experience and effective competence is acquired. Good natural development may consist of the growth of a *personal dialogue with the authors*, where the analyst acknowledges, criticises, and is willing to accept partial introjections which deserve to be experienced; always in conditions of separateness, without confusion, but with respect and acknowledgement of the internal objects, and not persecutory intimidation by them.

The mental models proposed by various authors are not religious truths, but tools for understanding which may be useful for our work, like the tools used by craftsman, technicians, researchers and artists.

Naturally, we do not have to acquire them 'lock, stock and barrel', but the overall coherence of the authors' theories should be respected. When we internally consult an author, when 'we work with him', we should respect his thought, without bending it into imprecise formulations or theoretical compromises to which he is extraneous, merely to justify with an authoritative *'ipse dixit'*, arbitrarily reworked and amended, certain hastily put together and inappropriately argued technical choices.

To sum up, the authors and their models should be studied honestly and well in order to use them with cognisance and perhaps even to take them a stage further. Thus, in one's own private workshop, to produce useful alternatives to Freudian metapsychology, one must first have studied, understood and truly assimilated it: otherwise, it is simply a way of avoiding, not a way of proceeding beyond. With a solid basic knowledge, it makes sense to venture forth with team spirit, but inevitably in a personal way, into the fascinating landscape that contemporary psychoanalysis offers us, a land of inexhaustible fertility.

A final word on the basic cultural choice which characterises the pages which follow. Making no secret of my *esprit du corps*, I will openly privilege accounts of contributions from fellow analysts past and present, while at the same time acknowledging the competence of certain poets and philosophers. In my opinion, those who share the vicissitudes of psychoanalytic relations in the field on a daily basis integrate personal experience, scientific theory and clinical practice in a way that finds no paragon in any of the neighbouring fields of human thought. Often (though not always) the words of poets and philosophers give one the impression of rising out of solitude; those of psychoanalysts (again, not always) arise from encounters. The analyst's encounters are with patients, but also colleagues, and above all with the masters of psychoanalytic thought, interlocutors who are constantly present somewhere deep in their inner world, albeit with alternating degrees of intensity and frequent rotations. In psychoanalytic thought, we always dialogue with someone.

INTRODUCTION

1   Berti Ceroni (1997) has proposed the concept of 'relational sequences' to describe the alternation of the functions carried out at different times by the analyst with regard to the patient's needs, in agreement with Bollas' (1987) criterion whereby psychoanalytic work should vary according to the immediate emotional situation of the session. According to Berti Ceroni, the analyst is hampered "when he puts too much emphasis on one or other function, becoming inflexible and reducing his working potential to the theory selected. For example, adhering rigidly to the projective identification function of containment may result in a paralysis of the couple in situations of containment not symbiosis (...) By contrast, it is well-known that an analysis carried out mainly on an oedipal register with high quality of symbolisation may result in the sudden breaking out of deep-seated fusional and symbiotic needs, giving the analytic couple the impression that little or nothing had been accomplished."

2   Throughout I use the masculine pronoun when referring to both analyst and patient. This, however, is a stylistic choice and should be taken to include both genders. It is only in the interest of clarity that this wording has been followed.

3   As Giannakoulas (2002) notes: "Psychoanalysts incorporate, introject and internalise aspects of the technique of their own – generally lengthy – analysis and training. These internalisations may insinuate themselves into the patient's analysis as a subjective structure, like a dogma, and change a personal vantage point into a clinical test. It may create a tradition with all the solidity of a legend, often complete with its own analytical family-tree." Clearly, these observations should be read in a deconstructionist way (Bolognini, 2002b), allowing us to understand the internal theoretical and clinical attitude of each psychoanalyst and each psychoanalytic author. They should not be used to encourage generalised relativism in a destructive way.

PART I
HISTORICAL REVIEW

1
ROMANTIC EMPATHY

Although the word *empathy* was coined by Titchener in 1909 as the translation of the German term *Einfühlung* (feeling in) for his *Experimental Psychology of the Thought Processes*, the term made its first appearance in a work printed in 1798: *The Disciples at Sais* by the German romantic poet Novalis.

Let us first consider the background from which the term *Einfühlung* ('empathy') emerged and the meaning it originally developed. Though closely linked by the common root of *pathos* (feeling), its meaning was so different from that accepted in present-day psychoanalysis that it deserves a special presentation. Significantly, the concept of *Einfühlung* emerged at the end of the rationalist century of the Enlightenment, in a very particular cultural and human atmosphere, characterised by the enthusiastic rediscovery of emotional registers by a number of intellectuals, poets and philosophers. Drawing on their close circles of friendship and the sensations of instinctive and visceral understanding, they believed they were experiencing together a memorable age for the spirit: the age of Romanticism. The chronicles of the time conjure up, in the aristocratic salons and the austere lecture-rooms of the universities of Leipzig and Jena in the decade from 1790 and 1800, the creative crucible of Romantic culture which brought into continual contact Goethe, Schiller, the brothers Schlegel, Hölderlin, and the philosophers Fichte and Schelling, as well as Novalis himself. The ties of personal friendship which existed between them made their meetings and exchanges particularly fertile, giving rise to those forms of *'synphilosophieren'* and *'synpoetisieren'* (thinking together, writing poetry together) which was the life-blood of early German Romanticism.

The leading spirits of the Romanticism in Jena were united by a close-knit web of personal relations and common interests, making possible the remarkably fecund exchange of ideas and thoughts as well as the mutual inspiration of genial insights through conversation and the exchange of letters.

"It is surprising to think how lively and direct contacts must have been at a time when the means of communication which are nowadays thought indispensable for any kind of cultural life simply did not exist." (Cisotti, 1982).

The point about the importance of personal relations in the context of a cultural group (be it artistic or scientific) is inevitably striking for psychoanalysts. Among my memories of secondary school, I recall a particularly colourful lesson given by our German teacher who had cultivated an intense passion for the Romantics. She related every possible detail of this creative environment with its frequent contacts and intense friendships. Many years later, whilst reading Ernest Jones' biography of Freud, I found myself making a spontaneous link between those two historical environments, early German Romanticism and psychoanalysis, which shared the same features of frequent encounters, a wealth of correspondence, the sense of discovering something new and profound, but most of all the enthusiasm of supporting and giving life to a common 'thing' ('*die Sache*' as Freud put it).

The analogies between the two movements, however, finish there and it would be straining things to look for others. Observing the contents and work-styles of the two would only reveal obvious and natural differences. Substantially, it would appear that the Romantics experienced and shared a fundamental feeling which, in present-day psychoanalytic terms, would undoubtedly be referred to as 'fusional': '*sicheinfühlen*', man's feeling at one with nature, experiencing the force of nature as if it were the strength of his own soul[1]. The external macrocosm was perceived as mystically corresponding to the internal microcosm. And in this cosmomorphic prospective, which inclines toward the myth of '*homo magus*', Novalis wrote: "Nature can never be understood by those who do not have an organ of nature, an interior instrument which generates nature and secretes it, by those who do not recognise and cannot spontaneously distinguish nature in everything, those who, with an innate desire to generate interior and multiform affinity with all bodies, do not involve themselves through their feelings with all natural beings, almost feeling themselves into each of them" (*The Disciples at Sais*, 1798).

As Rumi (2000) notes, Novalis' subject who not only identifies with the objects of nature, but is capable of 'feeling into' them and recognizing himself in them. This 'feeling oneself into' (*hineinsfühlen*) was to be taken up by the philosopher Theodor Vischer (1846) in his concept of the formation of the symbol, which in his opinion arises from the co-penetration of human subject and natural object.

The critic Kamla (1945), in his introduction to Novalis' *Hymns of the Night*, spoke of 'magical idealism', by which he meant "the absolute omnipotence of the ego, which thinks, believes desires and wants, over and above the body and the whole external world; thanks to this magic, thoughts may become things, and things thoughts."

Romantic empathy thus corresponds to a mental style which privileges feeling over thinking, makes massive and also poetic use of the projective functions, producing magical, grandiose, total and fusional experiences. It therefore takes little account of the separation between objects and the subject (hopefully with controlled regression for artistic purposes). Undoubtedly this was the heyday – speaking in literary terms – of a sort of *te deum* against Reason: it was an era characterised by delusions, megalomaniac grandiosity and pleasures full of yearning, exasperatedly self-centred, always on the verge of degeneration into euphoric exaltation, like the visionary Messianism (the *Christustendenz*, for example, which Goethe attributed to Schiller).

Notwithstanding this, literary historians all agree that the age of Romanticism was a period of great creativity, a thriving emotional and imaginative harvest ripening in seasonal harmony and cultivated in an atmosphere of sharing, conferring on mankind new depths and shades of meaning. It is therefore no surprise that the history of medicine traces back to this period the beginnings of a new relationship between doctor and patient. Von Engelhardt (1984, 1992) notes that the relationship between physician and patient, according to doctors influenced by Romanticism, consisted of a rather special blend of objectivity and subjectivity, asymmetry and symmetry. The main point, however, was the imperative of *Sympathie*: in order to progress in scientific knowledge, the doctor had to be driven by a personal interest in the patient. Thus Schubert (*Briefe "über das Studium der Medizin"* (1805) maintained that "an internal and loving interest in the sufferings of one's fellow man speeds up the healing process rather than slowing it down".

The concept of profound interchange in relations also appeared in the work of Hufeland (*Über Sympathie*, 1811), who believed that the 'sympathy' which ties man to nature and his fellow men is the "dependence of the life of the individual on the life of the totality", with an infinite series of mutual influences, beneficial for some and not for others: "Just as the sick make healthy subjects into sick ones by means of sympathy and change their form of life into a pathology, so we see, on the contrary, the way weak, old men living in the midst of strong young ones, by the same laws of the world described above, become healthier and stronger."

Von Engelhardt states that at that time personal relations did not mean only sensitive acceptance and comprehension by the doctor of the feelings, ideas and life conditions of the patient, but also a collective relationship with the community of ideas: the idea of Nature, the idea of mankind, the idea of Metaphysics and Transcendence. This was why Justinus Kerner, a doctor of Romantic persuasion, not only treated his patients individually but also by 'empathically' giving them hospitality with his own family at Weinsberg, near Stuttgart (we do not know with what results for the patients themselves, nor for the internal equilibrium of the family), for the sake of this healing principle of 'diffuse' empathy.

Bound up with these potent and colourful artistic and philosophical roots, the concept of empathy was characterised by a massive predominance of projective functions until the start of the twentieth century. In 1906 – before Freud made use of the term in his scientific work – the philosopher Theodor Lipps used the term widely in *Aesthetik*. According to Lipps, aesthetic experience should consist of projecting human emotions onto the aesthetic object, in other words in "giving inanimate things meaning and passion", as Vico states. Clearly inspired by Romanticism, the philosophical movement which cultivated the aesthetic of *Einfühlung*, whose exponents were Lipps, Gross, Volkelt and others, recognised the basis of the artistic creative process in the identification of the subject with the object, the act of entering (as indicated by the prefix *ein*) such that the "object, of itself cold and inert, becomes animated, warmed and humanised by the feelings of the artist, who transforms it into a work of art" (Abbagnano, 1993).

This process of osmotic identification of the subject with the object, by means of a 'projection of oneself', gives rise to a work of art of which the artist's feelings would be the form and the object the material, presupposing a sort of identity of nature of the two, in a philosophical atmosphere of pantheistic mysticism.

Dilthey's reflections on *nacherleben* (re-living) are also pertinent to the theme of empathy: "Experience which is more emotional than intellectual, where feelings provoke other feelings with nothing else as an intermediary but the facial expression itself (...) Guided by the expression of the other person, I re-live (*nach-erleben*) his experience in my conscious mind, and this is the essence of understanding: reproducing is the equivalent of re-living" (Egidi Morpurgo, 2001). Dilthey concerned himself with the communicability of subjective experience and – as Egidi Morpurgo notes – with expression as the source of the experience of others.

Correale (1999), drawing on Edith Stein's work of *Zum Problem der Einfühlung* (1917), pondered in particular the vitalistic aspects of this cultural atmosphere, pointing out that in this opening up of a correspondence between internal life and external life, empathy produces "in every case this reciprocal activation of vital affective forces between subject and object, which is perceived as beauty by the subject himself." Correale appreciates in these concepts "the activation of a force which re-opens a powerful drive toward the future and toward the world" and emphasises its powerful physical and sensorial component, thus grasping, in my opinion, one aspect of health, a mutual interflow between subject and object for the mutual induction of sensorial energetic surplus which becomes available and is then brought into play again together in the quest for new configurations of meaning.

Is there not something in all this which calls to mind the 'enrichment of fields' put forward by intersubjectivism? Naturally, there is no avoiding the possible analogies between this process of artistic creation and the primary processes of the formation of self, as concerns the 'ingredients' and the projective contributions actively provided by the mother right from the very first moments of the dyadic relationship, in the active aspects of the function of *reverie*.

Similarly, the baby's faith in its own omnipotent capacity to create the object, enhanced by the mother's skilful confirmations (Winnicott, 1971), seem to come into play in the matter of artistic creativity. But overall, if we refer strictly to the historical development of the concept of *Einfühlung* and its effective origins, we have to conclude that the prospective of extension-projection-osmosis between human beings and things[2] was far from our present-day meaning of empathy. It was the refined but difficult task of psychoanalysis to integrate understanding with feeling reciprocally, by honing down delicate and sensitive instruments capable of perceiving the inner life of human beings, in a situation of conscious separation.

It is fascinating for us to find similarities in philosophical or artistic thought which may contain anticipatory suggestions; with a little adjustment and a change of terminology, these may prove to be insights which anticipate later psychoanalytic acquisitions. Yet, I do not believe that in the frenzy to show off our transcultural and interdisciplinary nature at all costs we should underestimate the originality, specificity and – why not? – the sheer hard work involved in our acquisition of knowledge. It springs from a terrain which is far harder to work than that of philosophers, that of clinical practice and relational experience. This is important to bear in mind. As I will attempt to show in the following chapters, the gradual refinement of the concept of empathy (still an ongoing process) has been slowly acquired generation after generation, session by session, through psychoanalytic work as well as through its successive theoretical elaboration, in the extended psychoanalytic community.

The Romantic roots (and to some extent the philosophical current of *Einfühlungaesthetik*) may be seen as a rich 'pabulum', a terrain of culture, a precious source for further developments and so forth. At the same time they were also a remarkable projective melting pot, and I want to stress the considerable efforts of those who have contributed to gaining a greater knowledge of intra- and interhuman events, from Freud onward.

1   According to Freud (Totem and Taboo, 1913), "... primitive man transposed the structural conditions of his own mind into the external world ... which he was aware of by what is known as endopsychic perception". The Standard Edition Vol. XIII. p.91. See also Petrella (1993).

2   G.W. Pigman (1995) notes that *Einfühlung* originally implied the perception and understanding of the non-human.

2

FREUD AND EMPATHY

Freud turned his attention on a number of occasions to the intrapsychic aspects of the psychoanalyst, such as his free floating attention for example. Through his self-analysis Freud had acquired valid internal channels of communication with the preconscious and, if his clinical material is anything to go by, we can assume he had a good empathic capacity.

G. W. Pigman (1995) in his essay *Freud and the History of Empathy* with its wealth of detail, makes certain fundamental observations:

1) Freud was familiar with the work of Lipps and mentioned it in two letters to Fliess (dated August 26 and September 27, 1898), showing, as well as his enthusiasm, a little anxiety at the idea that Lipps ("whom I suspect is the most lucid mind among contemporary philosophers") had somehow preceded him in the field of metapsychology.

2) The reason why so many English-speaking analysts are unaware of the importance Freud attributed to the concept of 'empathy' lies in the fact that the Standard Edition translates only three of the twelve mentions of *Einfühlung* as 'empathy', and never translates the verb *einfühlen* – which appears eight times – with 'empathise'. Pigman maintains that Strachey must have had some fundamental reason ('a rationale') to avoid the word empathy ('a vile, elephantine word'). On the other hand, he appreciates the decision taken by the current translators of the French edition of Freud's works (Bourguignon et al., 1989) to keep to a strictly literal translation for hundreds of key terms.

It is interesting to note that the Italian translation suggests '*immedesimazione*' for *Einfühlung*, which not only avoids the term '*empatia*', but also gives rise to a further complication. Whether intentionally or not, it entails not using the more current term *'identificazione'*, which, as we shall see, is inappropriate and does not coincide with empathy, but rather is often seen as its opposite.

3) In 1905, in *Jokes and their Relation to the Unconscious*, Freud uses the word empathy to describe the process of putting oneself into the other's shoes either consciously or unconsciously, and he was to continue to use the term with this meaning for the rest of his life. He never used it as Lipps did to refer to 'aesthetic empathy' toward objects, but in the sense of comprehension between two human beings.

4) Pigman rightly places great importance on an extract from *The Start of Treatment* (1913), in which Freud advises the analyst not to begin interpreting until the relationship between patient and analyst has become solid. To achieve this, the analyst need do no more than give the patient time: "If one exhibits a serious interest in him, carefully clears away the resistances that crop up at the beginning and avoids making certain mistakes, he will of himself form such an attachment and link the doctor up with one of the imagos of the people by whom he was accustomed to be treated with affection. *It is certainly possible to forfeit this first success if from the start one takes up any standpoint other than one of sympathetic understanding [einfühlung]*, such as a moralizing one, or if one behaves like a representative or advocate of some contending party- of the other member of a married couple, for instance" (1913c, pp.139-140) (my italics).

Empathy becomes a *sine qua non* condition for the analyst, in order to establish positive transference and access to interpretation.

5) In his exchange of letters with Ferenczi on the occasion of the presentation of *The Elasticity of Psychoanalytic Technique* (1928), Freud confirms that empathy concerns almost everything an analyst should do in a positive direction. However, he worries that some analysts may, for the sake of 'act-cum-empathy' suggested by Ferenczi, justify arbitrariness, excesses of subjectivity and so forth. Later, I shall return to this point.

6) Pigman provides us with a great many complex thoughts on one of Freud's most famous remarks about *Einfühlung*, to be found in the chapter on "Identification" in *Group Psychology and the Analysis of the Ego* (1921), in which Freud states that the members of a group identify with one another by means of a process which psychology calls "*Einfühlung*", and which "plays the largest part in our understanding of the alien (or other) self *[Ichfremd]* of other people" (1907a).

With reference to Freud's use of 'ichfremd' in other passages, Pigman notes that Freud uses the alien self of others not to imply alien to us because it belongs to another; rather it refers to the internal parts of others which are alien and unknown to their own egos.

Thus, empathy would not enable the analyst to understand the part of people which is unknown to themselves. In my view, Pigman has tracked down something of great interest here, which we will come back to later in the book. Pigman concludes his careful exploration of Freud's relations with the concept of *Einfühlung* – for which we should be grateful – with some broader considerations: "One might be tempted to characterise Freud's attitude towards empathy as ambivalent, and perhaps it is. I think, however, it would be more accurate to say that he adopts an intellectual attitude because he is ambivalent about emotions, suspicious of their place within the analyst." (Pigman, p.252)

Some years earlier, Schafer (1983) also concerned himself with this corner of Freudian theory. Without explicitly using the term, Freud formulated several important pieces of advice connected with empathy. For example, solutions should not be formulated until the patient is so close to the solution that it would take but a short step for him to reach it himself; it is essential to maintain a certain flexibility with regard to the level on which the analysand will function at different times in the treatment. In Schafer's view, these statements bear witness to the importance which Freud implicitly attributes to an empathic type of approach.

This is an interesting observation, which is not in my opinion supported by either the scientific texts or Freud's letters. In fact, rather the opposite view would tend to emerge from them. Freud was always very worried about and for many years even diffident toward the emotional reactions of analysts toward their patients. And this fear must have included the '*pathein*' of empathy.

Robert Fine, in his *History of Psychoanalysis* (1979), writes that in private Freud left no doubt that his major worry was about excessive involvement. In a letter to Jung dated 31 December 1911, Freud wrote: "C. told me a great many things about you and Pfister (. . .) I deduce from all this that you and Pfister have not yet acquired the detachment necessary for the exercise of the profession. There is still a tendency to impose oneself and give much of oneself with the intention of giving something in exchange. May I, venerated old master that I am, warn you that with this technique you end up making false calculations and that one must remain inaccessible and insist on the receptivity aspect? We must never allow the poor neurotics to send us crazy. The article on 'counter-translation', which I feel is necessary, should not be printed, but copies should be distributed amongst us."

The meaning of the letter is undoubtedly complex and, what is more, it refers to a private communication between Freud and the patient, whose content we do not know. We do not know, for example, how Jung and Pfister tended "to give much of themselves." Freud speaks of "the detachment necessary for the exercise of the profession" and says that "one has to remain inaccessible", that "we must never allow the poor neurotics to send us crazy," and that the article on countertransference must be distributed in copies among analysts, but not printed. To tell the truth, he also tells them "to insist on the receptivity aspect", but it is quite probable that here by receptivity he meant a technical position of passive waiting, which mainly consisted of avoiding as far as possible the analyst's experiencing strong feelings, which, at an internal level, would complicate the work of deciphering, translating and reconstructing the material. He was also concerned to avoid word getting out about these risks.

Perhaps, at the time, Freud focussed more on *'erklären'* (explaining, understanding, clarifying), than on *'verstehen'* (participatory comprehension) (Jaspers, 1913).[1] Or perhaps Freud's cautious attitude was instinctively aimed at protecting the fragile seedling of psychoanalysis from contamination by one of the great ailments of the empathic function which were later to be described by Greenson in 1960: the loss of control of empathy (the other being inhibition of the same)?

We should not perhaps criticise the fact that, in those pioneering times, Freud could legitimately be suspicious and even rigid toward all that an analyst might feel for a patient. Countertransference was, in fact, unexplored territory and the minds of the analysts, probed at the most for a few weeks of didactic analysis, were no less so. At the time, Freud had hard and fast reasons for taking up such a position. It was Freud in 1909, for example, who had been, figuratively speaking, obliged to wipe Sabina Spielrein's tears after the sensational countertransference episode with Jung.

We might wonder whether the 'necessary detachment' and 'inaccessibility' which Freud expected of the internal attitude of his co-workers might not have frightened off more than one researcher, in the heroic times at the origins, as regards directing theoretical attention to the inner sources of empathic comprehension. Undoubtedly, Freud felt justifiably concerned about lack of emotional control among his followers when in 1915 in *Observations on Transference Love*, he wrote: "Besides, the experiment of letting oneself go a little way in tender feelings for the patient is not altogether without danger. Our control over ourselves is not so complete that we may not suddenly one day go further than we have intended. In my opinion, therefore, we ought not to give up the neutrality towards the patient, which we have acquired through keeping the counter-transference in check."

Given that, in this case, Freud was not talking about empathy, but countertransference reaction, what did he mean by this advice?

Not to feel emotions as they presented themselves and therefore, as Albarella and Donadio (1986) hypothesize, to establish a sort of strengthening of the defences to stop the emergence of the repressed provoked by contact with the patient? To diminish the *'pàthos'* of the encounter in the psychoanalytic situation for defence purposes?

Quite frankly, I would say so. I also think that his advice did not arise from technical or basic theoretical assumptions, since in 1912, in *Advice to Doctors in Psychoanalytic Treatment*, he hoped that the analyst would be really, and in the full sense of the word, receptive: "He must turn his own unconscious like a receptive organ towards the transmitting unconscious of the patient. He must adjust himself to the patient, as a telephone receiver is adjusted to the transmitting microphone". Rather, it arose from a realistic perception, on his part, of how the psychoanalysts of the time (through no fault of his or theirs, but due to the physiological immaturity of a new current) were lacking in their capacity to maintain a true and profound psychoanalytic attitude in the presence of the inner upheavals induced by genuine receptivity. Nowadays, we know that this capacity is the result (always relative, and anyway in need of constant care) of a long, necessary and careful experience of personal analysis.

Alongside this, we should not forget a positive ideal in Freud's thought: the neutrality of observation. Generally speaking, it seems that Freud tended to encourage the observation of certain elements of the inner life of the analyst: memories, connections, images, words. In any case, he gave pride of place to representational elements over emotional ones, as if being surprised by the former were methodologically profitable, and by the latter, dangerous.

Freud had wished to 'master' countertransference (1910, p. 200); twenty-seven years later, in *Analysis Terminable and Interminable*, he showed himself to be far less optimistic, pointing out, in the contact with the patient's unconscious, the danger of a pathogenic influx that made it advisable for the analyst to repeat personal analysis every five years.

With his great perspicacity and the wisdom gained from clinical experience, Freud had probably understood the inadequacy of the psychoanalytic equipment of the time against the *mare magnum* of countertransference. To make navigation safer in that vast sea, he pointed to the Pillars of Hercules: the comprehension of psychoanalytic material was to be hoped for more through association, deciphering and translation, than through dangerous identifications with the patients or their internal objects.

Besides, a remarkable amount of scientific and institutional work, exploration, discovery and creation had been accomplished. It would have to fall to his pupils and the pupils of his pupils to proceed along that way, shedding light on the 'black hole' of the analyst's feelings, a dark forest full of hidden dangers, populated by alluring sirens and fleeting phantasies.

---

1 For more on Jaspers' position on *Einfühlung*, see the excellent essay by Vanna Berlincioni and Fausto Petrella (2001).

3

THE PIONEERS

In 1926, in an article with the rather striking title *"Okkulte Vorgänge während der Psychoanalyse"* (Occult Processes during Psychoanalysis), Helene Deutsch courageously touches upon the topic of the communication that may occur between the analyst's unconscious and that of the person under analysis, drawing attention to the fact that the processes of development will have been similar for both and that, consequently, each one's impulses, desires and structures may well become tuned into the other's, leading to an 'identification'.

Deutsch of course could not yet call upon a conceptual apparatus capable of articulating the insight in terms of a two-way psychoanalytic exchange, but she was already able to give the following thoughtful description of what, in her view, takes place in the empathising curer: "The affective psychic content of the patient, which emerges in his or her unconscious, becomes transmuted into an inner experience of the analyst's, and is recognised as belonging to the patient only in the course of the analyst's subsequent intellectual work."

If we examine this description, dividing it into two parts, in the first ("the affective psychic content . . . becomes transmuted into an inner experience of the analyst's") we have a formulation that is absolutely and surprisingly modern, which focuses on the receptive responsiveness of the analyst.

In the second part ("is recognised as belonging to the patient only in the course of the analyst's subsequent intellectual work") it is suggested that, in order to attain to this responsiveness, the analyst must succumb to a certain amount of regression (in the service of the ego), resulting in a degree of crepuscular pre-confusion between the self and the other. The "analyst's intellectual work" would thus consist in a clarifying re-emergence of this sort: "Wait a moment! I am feeling this because I am identifying with him, but in fact it is the patient who should be feeling this! (Or, who "is making me feel this!")[1]

Berger (1987), commenting on the passage in question, notes that Deutsch did not specify whether the different positions (participant and critical observer) could be experienced simultaneously by the analyst, who would thus feel fusion and separateness at one and the same time. This is an important point, but it seems to me that, for her times, Deutsch had already ventured surprisingly far into the terrain of the analyst's inner stance: the temporary relinquishing of the functions of active control of the ego in the psychoanalytical session, which she advocated, went beyond fluctuating attention and led to an introjective sampling of the other's experience.

Deutsch stressed how the analyst's empathy often consists of a partial identification – which she called 'complementary'[2] – with an infantile object of the patient: perceiving what is happening on the emotional plane within himself, the analyst is in a position to reconstruct what occurred at an earlier period with the first infantile objects, and, aside from the temporal framework, what continues to happen at a deep level with the internal objects of the patient, as the deeper relation reinstates itself through the transfer and counter-transfer.

In this connection, Deutsch also pointed out that the unresolved childhood conflicts of the analyst can lead him or her to 'fix upon' some of these, initially partial, identifications, inasmuch as they may be in some respects gratifying; in this way a complete identification could ensue, thereby no longer allowing the object to be understood and leading the analyst unconsciously and repeatedly to 'act out' a certain role.

This, in my view, is an extremely important piece of technical advice, especially in relation to the period, since it already hints at the inadequacy of the term 'identification' where empathy is concerned, and it proves to be of value in the clinical context, since it describes a virtually ubiquitous phenomenon that enters into the framework of 'classic' countertransference.

Two years later, in 1928, it was the liveliest, the most 'affective', of Freud's followers, Sándor Ferenczi, who turned his attention, in an original contribution, to a possible participatory inner stance on the part of the analyst. It is from him, in the already cited article "The elasticity of the psychoanalytical technique", that we receive a simple and succinct definition of empathy: empathy "is the capacity to put oneself in another's shoes". Of course, this definition, however effective from a stylistic point of view, leaves a number of open questions: what does it actually mean "to put oneself in another's shoes"? Are there different ways in which it may be achieved? Which structures and functions of the person are involved in this process, and how? And so on.

The fact remains, however, that from as far back as 1918 (Psychoanalytical Technique) Ferenczi had considered this aspect of psychoanalytical activity to be fundamental: "Without a sensibility of this kind [the analyst] could not understand the patient's psychic conflicts". Or again in the same work (a veritable mine of ideas) we find a passage concerning the different positioning of the analyst and the patient in relation to psychic levels – conscious or unconscious – in the experience of understanding: "If, with the help of the knowledge obtained from the dissociation of many minds, but above all of our own, we have succeeded in forming for ourselves a picture of the possible or probable associations of the patient, of which he is still completely unaware, we, not having to contend with the same resistance as the patient does, are able to imagine, not only his thoughts but also his tendencies, about which he is unaware."

Personally I attach considerable importance to this passage, because it already presents a significant example of ego-dystonic empathy with respect to the patient: analyst and patient are not "in accordance", they are asymmetrical, and it is precisely this that allows the analyst to give the other self-knowledge that the other lacked.

Ferenczi also attempted an outline description of the analyst's inner stance: "I should like to mention, as a problem that has not been considered, that of the metapsychology of the analyst's mental processes during analysis. His cathexes oscillate between identification (analytic object-love) on the one hand, and self control or intellectual activity on the other. During the long day's work he can never allow himself the pleasure of giving his narcissism and egoism free play in reality, and he can give free play to them in his fantasy only, for brief moments."

Further on he continues, with a tone of persecutory concern: "There is no doubt that many – and not only beginners, but all who have a tendency to exaggeration – will seize on what I have said about the importance of empathy to lay the chief emphasis in their handling of patients on the subjective factor, i.e. on intuition, and will disregard what I stated to be the all-important factor, the conscious assessment of the dynamic situation."

Ferenczi thus reminded practitioners of the need to ensure that both feeling and thinking remained operative (which we can connect, jumping ahead to the present, to the fine statement in Riolo [1983] on the relationship between reverie and semiosis: "The receptive-dreaming position and the investigative-rational one represent the extreme points of a mental spectrum that we should keep as wide as possible").

Ferenczi was aware how much effort was called for on the part of the analyst, and in a nearby passage he commented: "In the course of his day's work, he [the analyst] can never abandon himself to the pleasure of releasing his narcissism and egoism in reality, and in fantasy he can do so only for brief moments (. . .) This overload of tension, which in life almost never comes about in such measures, sooner or later will require the institution of a specific hygiene regime for the analyst."

Which inner resources can the analyst call upon as he or she undertakes this difficult and tiring task?

One answer came a few years after Ferenczi's writings, from across the ocean, when Robert Fliess, in *The Metapsychology of the Analyst* (1942), claimed that the analyst's "work ego" gets partially restructured for the purpose, releasing itself from some of the pressures of the superego in order to better fulfil the professional activity; this allows the work ego to open itself to a field of lived experiences, fantasies, feelings (usually repressed) that is much wider than normal, in turn leading the analyst to be more capable, freer, as well as more receptive and reliable in the psychoanalytical relations than they are in their personal extra-analytical relations.

In order to explain the dynamic of empathy, Fliess conjectures that 'trial identifications' are produced in the analyst. His dynamic description of empathy contains the idea that a person who uses empathy toward an object introjects it temporarily and projects back onto the object what he has introjected. It is this that enables him to perceive 'from within' as well as 'from outside'. The introjective identifications that permit the analyst to know the patient 'from within' involve risks: those of falling too deeply into states of regression, of undergoing crises in their own narcissistic equilibrium, or of handling object relations from unsustainable positions of identification.

According to Fliess, the analyst's work ego would become capable, in time, of fostering a special, temporary displacement of cathexis between the ego and the superego, where the critical self-observation function of the latter is used to recognise the instinctive material which has been acquired temporarily through identification with the patient. Thus, thanks to this habit of self-observation regardless of the degree of awareness of the material observed, the superego broadens the ego's perception.

It can be seen, then, that the realignments of cathexis between the ego and the superego do not reinforce the censoring functions of the latter, but lead to a sort of working alliance between their relative claims; there is a psychoanalytical superego that protects the ego and works alongside it in the analysis, assisting it.

I consider Fliess' contribution to be historically very important: it is the first to contain a real attempt to supply a dynamic description of an empathetic process, in which the author tries seriously to consider what is really involved in "putting oneself in the other's place".

The concept of 'work ego' was to be taken up and developed in 1983 by Schafer, who renamed it the 'second self' of the analyst, and who amplified it with a further description of the beneficial 'work superego' which, "prohibiting, through the training and the identification with the instructors, intimacy of an erotic or hostile nature that would be contrary to the technique, releases the tension to which the operations of the ego are subject and expands its limits".

Schafer's fundamentally important contribution will be discussed in depth more than once in what follows, in keeping with my intention in this historical survey to adhere, as far as possible, to a chronological exposition: the principle restricts the possibilities for synopsis but is, I feel, useful in highlighting the progressive movements of psychoanalysis towards this end point of the deep intra- and interpersonal contact between separate individuals.

1   Rosenfeld was later to take a closer look at this important but difficult part of analytic work especially in Chapters 1 and 8 of *Impasse and Interpretation*.

2   The concept of 'complementary countertransference', which Racker (1953, 1958) later formalised and developed so masterfully, may to some extent trace its origins to Helene Deutsch's 'complementary identification'. For a closer examination of the analyst's receptive functions, see the excellent contributions by Carloni (1988, 1998) and Borgogno (1998, 1999).

4

THE FIFTIES: THE REDISCOVERY OF EMPATHY

There are notably few contributions in the psychoanalytic literature specifically dealing with empathy until the second half of the 1950s, at which point one encounters a surprising proliferation.

Renata de Benedetti Gaddini (1984) has drawn attention to this historical trend, comparing the alternating appeal of the concepts of 'empathy' and 'insight' on the basis of frequency of citation: before 1955, in the index of the *Psychoanalytical Quarterly*, only one citation is to be found for 'empathy' and no less than 42 for 'insight'; between 1967 and 1980, on the other hand, there are 23 references for 'empathy' and only 6 for 'insight'. Among the various possible reasons for this transition, De Benedetti notes the fact that, as the decades passed, analysts found themselves working with patients different from the classic neurotic personality types, patients at times with primitive ego functions, and who had not therefore developed adequate communicational abilities (see Fries, 1968).

It was the North American psychoanalysts who dealt with the subject in depth, in a series of studies in which, alongside an at times painstakingly scholastic descriptive metapsychology, they introduced examples of clinical sequences of great emotional intensity, with a lively atmosphere at the relational level. The present chapter, on the rediscovery of the concept of empathy in the second half of the century, is devoted to them; the contributions of the five most original and creative authors on this subject will be summarised and their distinctive features highlighted.

In this survey we will deal in turn with the conceptions of Christine Olden on maternal empathy as the outcome of the progressive renunciation of sensual fusion with the baby; the work of Roy Schafer on psychoanalytical empathy as an introjective process that allows the analyst to constitute an inner image of the patient, and to relate to that; the observations of Ralph Greenson on the topical positioning of empathetic phenomena, and the clear distinction between them and processes of identification; the horizons opened by Heinz Kohut towards the functions of the object-self and the *mare magnum* of narcissistic vicissitudes; and the construction of the network of connections and of communication that Ping-Nie Pao describes as being fundamental in order to come to be in empathy with severely troubled patients.

This chapter is thus devoted to authors who have dedicated works specifically to the topic of empathy; naturally, in the same years there are elements in the work of other analysts that are of great interest in relation to the subject with which we are concerned, but they were put forward in the context of wider-ranging studies: the contributions that also touch upon our topic will be discussed in a later chapter.

In *Notes on the Development of Empathy* (1958), Christine Olden argues that the sensibility of one person towards another can only be called empathy when it is not at the service of narcissistic needs, but of mature object relations, which entails awareness of separation and absence of confusion.

Olden presents the clinical example of a mother who does not understand her daughter because she identifies her with herself; the mother's completely unconscious starting assumption was that whatever her daughter needed was what she herself needed, or what she herself wanted.

"I can't understand why Jane was so afraid to ring the neighbours' bell; I am not afraid." (p.506)

Or "Jane will never drive a car; I can't!" (p. 506). In addition, she managed, equally unconsciously, to make the daughter want what she wanted; she was utterly convinced, by virtue of her narcissistic confusion, that she understood her daughter deeply and satisfactorily.

Jane, for her part, had developed decidedly conformist behaviour patterns, inasmuch as she tried systematically to guess what was expected of her.

The basic model of this type of mother-daughter relation is 'incorporation', in the functional sense described in Greenson (1954):"The aim of incorporation is satisfaction without regard to the object. In this sense it indicates neither hatred or love" (p. 506).

This mother, and other analogous cases described by Olden, had maintained the primitive narcissistic mother-daughter fusion with their offspring, and this allowed them vicarious gratification of their frustrated instinctual needs, thanks to the projection of themselves in the child: "This case demonstrates that psychic immaturity necessarily precludes true empathy in the mother, which in turn, is a prerequisite for the development of empathy and social abilities in the child" (p. 512, Olden).

In the second part of the work, Olden emphasises the importance of the sublimation of maternal sexual impulses, for the development of empathy: this is the most original aspect of her contribution.

The physical-psychic mother-child fusion is a sexualised condition, replete with sensual gratifications for the mother as much as it is for the baby; with regard to the mother it is desirable for this situation to evolve by way of ". . . the transition from the earliest physical satisfaction to satisfactions in a more sublimated form where purely narcissistic pleasure is replaced by the joy and intellectual stimulation of watching a new personality emerge and develop . . ." (p.515 Olden)

(This aspect, where the author is referring to the mother-baby couple, could of course be applied to the analyst-patient couple, in the sense that the capacity to convert any positive instinctual drives that are mobilised in the counter-transference into the technique of psychoanalysis, thereby making it useful for the development of the patient, is certainly an important quality for anyone who practises this work.)

Empathy is thus, for Olden, a fruitful identification of oneself with the person who is growing, so as to better understand their evolving needs, but it is made possible only at the price of suffering a loss: that caused by the first, physiological phase of fusion. Without this renunciation, and without sublimation, there can be no real empathy.

The renunciation of fusion is difficult and painful, and the capacity of the mother to be interested in the progress made by her child is put to the test when the child shows objective signs of independence.

"You know what the baby did today?" asked one of Olden's patients with satisfaction, " he crawled all over the floor into the room, away from me"(p. 515, Olden).

Calmly reflecting, another mother reported: "It could be that you renounce complete possession of the baby more easily if these first months were a satisfactory experience, if you are satiated and feel free to go on to different joys with your child".

This aspect, about the acquisition of separateness as an indispensable prerequisite for the possibility of achieving empathetic contact with the other was subsequently taken, further developed and highlighted by Giuseppe Di Chiara (1982), who maintains that "in order for the analyst to fulfil his function to best advantage, he must be capable of achieving the greatest possible degree of closeness and of separateness. In simple language: be capable of an intense inner intimacy, together with reserve; affectionate abandon and careful discretion".

Stefania Turillazzi Manfredi (1994) also felt it was useful to specify that "empathy implies a relationship between two objects that are, and are experienced by whoever feels empathy, as separate", being based above all "on an already advanced development of an inner world of objects and of representations of self". The importance of these considerations, dating from several decades later, further reinforces the impression that Olden, with great insight, had focused attention on a crucial aspect of the problem.

Roy Schafer (1959) speaks of 'generative empathy', taking up the adjective used by Erikson (1959). 'Generativity' is the seventh of the eight 'evolutionary stages' in the life of man, according to Erikson, and normally it is attained in middle age; it is constituted by an interest in founding and guiding the next generation, and in assuming the responsibilities of a parent.

Schafer gives the following definition: "Generative empathy may be defined as the inner experience of sharing in and comprehending the momentary psychological state of another person. Specifically, what is to be shared and comprehended is a hierarchic organization of desires, feelings, thoughts, defenses, controls, superego pressures, capacities, self-representations and representations of real and fantasised personal relationships." (Schafer, p.350)

It is based on an interplay of introjective and projective mechanisms that is subtle and relatively free from conflict and occurs at the conscious and preconscious levels. It is distinguishable from the secondary process in its pure form, and is characterised by a rediscovery and an affective reinvestment of memories and future prospects, by its intuitive quality, and by the adaptable use it makes of the primary process.

We should remind ourselves here that it was in fact Schafer, in a later and much better known work (*Aspects of Internalisation*, 1968), who – echoing Freud – emphasised the prevalently unconscious nature of identification; in particular, when a person identifies with another, he or she is not aware of it, the identification persists for more than a short period of time, and a large part of the self is substituted by the other (and is thus not at all the same as empathetic identification, which is conscious and preconscious, transitory and non-substitutional – if anything it is most often 'in accordance' with parts of the self; this gloss is my own: Schafer later seems to contradict himself somewhat in this work).

Schafer writes that generative empathy presupposes in the analyst the recognition and the protection of the individuality and the separateness of the object; the object is introjected and, at the end, returned.

"Observation of countertransference reactions suggests that the recognition and protection of the object's separateness involve some combination of motherly care, fatherly workmanship and command, fraternal allegiance, filial reparation, and sensuous intimacy of an intrusive and receptive nature. In his empathic functioning, the therapist is in certain respects mother, father, sibling, child, and lover of the patient as well as, through introjection, the patient himself. [...] Ordinarily we work with partial empathy, which in no way minimizes either the extraordinary precision partial empathy may achieve in picking out specific areas of greatest momentary tension or its therapeutic effectiveness." (p. 355)

In Schafer's view, the analyst constructs for her- or himself a non-simple, temporary, inner image of the patient's world, as he or she gradually acquires familiarity with the patient's associations, expressive characteristics, history, present situation and future prospects.

In building up this image, reproducing the inner world of the patient in his or her own inner world, the analyst comes closer to a position from which he or she becomes able to fantasise as the patient does and to experience the same feelings.

This comes about through a series of partial introjections, emotional reactions, and rediscoveries of memories concerning herself or himself and the object.

It is followed by re-exteriorisations and projections onto the patient, subsequently measured against reality, to test the correctness of the image that has developed.

"The hypercathected internal image is thereby increasingly enriched, focused, hierarchically organized, and stabilized. It becomes a substructure within the analyst's ego, which means it does not need to be re-created anew on each occasion of stimulation but remains steadily available. It may be said, therefore, that an identification with the patient gradually takes place. Optimally, however, this identification remains segregated within the ego as an object of actual or potential contemplation" (p. 356).

This point, as I was saying, could be a matter for discussion, for it apparently amounts to an identification (and thus a largely unconscious phenomenon) that is however 'observable', though it does not seem clear what would be involved.

Reading Schafer's 1959 study, one is in any case impressed, not only by the painstaking reconstruction of the weaving of psychological fabric, which enables him to represent the vicissitudes of the inner relations with patience and precision, but also by his recourse to elaborate and 'capacious' spatial representations of the inner world of the analyst into which the patient is accommodated.

In a certain sense, in the work of Olden we can represent empathy to ourselves as the fruit of the mother's renunciation of concrete sensual symbiotic gratification, leading to the creation of a greater inner (as well as external) space between the mother, who sublimates, and the child, which is freed. With Schafer the emphasis falls on a process that moves in the opposite direction: taking as a given the awareness of separation, it is an introjection that ushers in an inner relation, that is welcomed in the mind of the analyst: "en-pathia".

Schafer was to return to the subject, further elaborating his point of view, right up to the collection of essays from 1983 (*The Analytical Attitude*); my comments here, however, refer specifically to his article dating from 1959.

The year after Schafer's work, saw the publication of Ralph Greenson's contribution, *Empathy And Its Vicissitudes* (1960). Greenson is, in my opinion, an unusual author, because he combines a notable capacity for placing the clinical material within a theoretical framework with a high level of emotional authenticity and an at times transparent sincerity in communicating emotions; amongst other things, he was one of the very few authors of his time to relate his own practice, thus enabling the reader to feel a participant in the clinical experiences to which he repeatedly refers.

No surprise, therefore, that an author of this sort should choose to consider empathy, writing a monograph on the subject. Greenson sees empathy as emotional knowledge, the sharing and experience of the feelings of another. This sharing is temporary, and concerns the quality of the feelings, their degree and their quantity. The analyst allows part of himself to enter the patient and undergo his experiences as if he were the patient. Thus, the analyst sees what happens within himself while undergoing those experiences.

For Greenson empathy is essentially a preconscious phenomenon, unlike imitation or mimesis, which are conscious phenomena (as well as being limited to outward behavioural characteristics of the person).[1]

It is also clearly distinguished from identification, unlike in Schafer's perspective. Greenson notes that identification is an unconscious and permanent phenomenon, the end of which is the defensive avoidance of anxiety, a sense of guilt or object loss, whereas empathy is of use in feeling and understanding these inner conditions. I will select and summarise the more significant considerations formulated by this writer:

1) Empathy requires the capacity for controlled, reversible regression, involving not only the functions of the ego, but also of the object relations. It is very similar to the creative experience of the artist as described in Kris (1952).

2) Empathy cannot be taught, but, anyone wishing to carry out scientific work, must have learned everything that can be learned on the subject.

3) Empathy and theoretical knowledge complete each other.

4) In order for empathy to be able to yield fruits, it is necessary for the analyst to have a plentiful supply of personal experiences to draw on as this makes it easier to understand the patient.

5) Empathy is a way of re-establishing a contact with a lost love object: the misunderstood part of the patient.

6) Analysts who have overcome a certain tendency towards depression

seem to attain to a greater capacity for empathy. Obsessive characters can never abandon themselves to the empathetic relationship, while characters dominated by impulses will tend to slip from empathy into identification, which will lead them to 'act out' with the patient.

7) The analyst must have a thoroughgoing familiarity with his or her own unconscious processes so as to be able to accept, with humility, that probably the patient's anomaly is, or has been, also present in them.

8) The analyst must be receptive: it is better to let oneself ultimately to have been misled, following the patient's productions, than prematurely to refuse them as false.

The capacity to suspend judgement, to the very limit of credulity, is what makes empathy with the patient possible, and will eventually lead to an understanding of the underlying movements.

With regard to this aspect, Greenson reminds us of the passage in Jones (1957) testifying to the fact that Freud did not consider himself to be a great *Menschenkenner* ('connoisseur' of persons), which may have acted in favour of his empathetic disposition: just think of the credit he was willing to confer on recounts of infantile seduction.

Scepticism, then, but of a well-intentioned kind, and always directed towards an understanding of the deeper meanings within the deformations of reality mentally elaborated by the patients.

Those conversant with psychoanalytical literature automatically associate the concept of empathy with the contributions of Heinz Kohut (1971, 1977, 1984), which are organically incorporated as the keystone of an impressive theoretical edifice, albeit one that has drawn justifiable objections to certain of its tenets: from Schafer (1983), on treating the individual as largely pre-conflictual; from Kemberg (1975), on the lack of an adequate differentiation between pathological narcissism and normal developmental narcissism; and consequently on the failure to vary technique in relation to the differing imbrication of narcissistic and instinctual vicissitudes from one case to another.

Without for the moment entering into the merits on each side of these conflicting views, extremely interesting though they are, I will note how the tragic dimension of the human condition is traced back by Kohut to a primary failure of empathy in the parents in the first stage of infancy, which is responsible for a early loss of cohesion in the self: the need to reproduce the mirror-like narcissistic transfer with objects having a function and meaning analogous to that of the parents is destined to remain the dominant note in the individual, who, at a deep level, will experience the successful recreation of a similar transfer substantially as the equivalent of acceptance on the part of the parents.

Only empathetic understanding on the part of the parents or their subsequent equivalents can, in the case of these subjects who lacked the primary predisposition to organise the specular relationship, make the apparently inadequate regression acceptable; if the specular relation is not organised, and if the physiological establishment of an idealised parental imago thus comes to be lacking, what can result is a hyper-investment of the primitive stages of the corporeal (autoerotic) self and of the archaic stages of the grandiose self, with a consequential fixation on them. The analyst inherits the parents' role in the vicissitudes of these needs, which are constitutive of the self.

Kohut sees empathy as a cognitive way to perceive complex psychological configurations; to enjoy another's disposition to empathy produces a growth in the subject's own capacity for empathy. The expansion of empathy in successful analysis is always genuine. He adds that the mobilisation of archaic narcissistic structures and their working through, within the area of both the idealised object and the grandiose self, lead to an increase in empathic capacity. In the case of the grandiose self, on the other hand, it leads particularly to empathy towards oneself.

Kohut maintains that the development specifically of an empathetic sensibility contributes towards the decision to become an analyst, and that it constitutes a useful professional skill, provided that it is kept under the control of the ego: the analyst must not only have free access to empathetic understanding, but must also be capable of abandoning the empathetic stance.

If not endowed with empathy, the analyst cannot perceive and gather the elements that he or she needs; but if they do not know how to go beyond empathy, they cannot establish hypotheses and theories, and ultimately they cannot arrive at an explanation of the observed data.

For this reason, Kohut repeatedly refers to the need to replace the empathetic behaviour with appropriate activities using the secondary process, to evaluate the psychological data that has been acquired and to place it in a logical and realistic framework.

It is probable that this insistent preoccupation in the case of this author is connected with the fact that he had devoted himself, courageously and with some originality, to the discovery and analysis of archaic levels of development of the self, levels that contain – deep-frozen in the unconscious – bizarre and megalomaniacal psychical configurations.

The analyst who has to enter into empathy with patients who may harbour within themselves crazy, absurdly grandiose primitive phantasms (Walt Disney, the great magician of fantasy would surely have defined them as 'plausible impossibilities') is necessarily obliged to have recourse to a proportionate extent to secondary processes; for it is this natural balancing of forces that allows the analyst to work, moving in empathy with the patient among these monstrous formations, without losing the sense of his or her own internal reality, as well as enabling him or her to understand the sense and the function of each choice made at the level of technique in this situation.

Kohut nevertheless points out that it is not infrequently the case that aspiring analysts are unable to feel sufficient empathy with patients on account of an inhibition of a secondary type, due to a defensive reaction typical of a personality tending to obsessiveness, when faced with a deep-seated, residual animistic conception of the world.

The belief in magic and the animistic tendencies that are not analysed by the psychoanalyst remain repressed (or, more often, split): such is the price paid for strict avoidance of an unrestricted empathetic disposition.

If I may be permitted, I will conjure up a personal psychoanalytical phantasm that may take its place within the inner laboratory shared by psychoanalysts, ready to be brought forth in the course of our everyday professional activity; if, as I was saying, Olden made us see the creativity inherent in a deliberate holding-back from fusion, and if Schafer made us understand the usefulness of our being open to partial, progressive introjections of the inner world of the patient, Kohut basically requires us to undertake a further task, at both a human and a professional level, one that it would be absolutely unthinkable to ask of non-psychoanalysts: it is the requirement patiently to make it possible (with a farsightedness dependent on our specific form of knowledge), for the patient's 'inner dinosaurs', derived from the grandiose self, to become unfrozen and to appear on the surface, without overpowering us. Analysis has taught us that it is only by letting them come back on to the stage of the conscious world that they can be transformed and can evolve.

Furthermore, Kohut invites us to understand the patients' need to not be faced too soon with an interpretation that unmasks the idealisation of the object; more than others, he gives us the means to appreciate the utility and appropriateness of certain phases, certain aspects of the psychoanalytical situation, which otherwise could have induced some to outbursts of indiscriminate interpretation and to a basic lack of confidence in the validity of the prognosis.

Kohut teaches us, in some sense, to let the analysis 'take its course': as far as possible to respect the primitive transfer and to support it with empathy and trust, accepting its apparent absurdities, counting on the integrating effects of this way of proceeding.

In his book *The Analytic Attitude* (1983), Roy Schafer interestingly develops some of the considerations on this theme that he had already put forward in his previous works. He sketches a portrait of the informed, disinterested, empathic analyst, listing some of the factors that are conducive to "relatively secure and complex" empathic activity.

The analyst is less involved at the personal level than are the other people very close to the patient, inasmuch as the psychoanalytical relation is not where the patient's principle needs are concentrated (apart from the need to feel himself capable of working well).

The analyst is not expected to respond openly, as people are required to in normal social life.

Through his 'training', the analyst has adequately come to terms with his or her own regressive levels of operation, and the erotic and aggressive drives associated with them have been integrated.

The analyst knows that, with the termination of the analysis, the intense and peculiar intimacy of the relationship will rapidly diminish, and he is protected by this awareness during the experience of the relationship itself.

Thanks to these factors, explains Schafer, the analyst is less prone to ambivalence and anxiety, has less need to be loved and appreciated, to be satisfied or vicariously victimised and so forth.

Schafer goes on to discuss the positive orientation of the analyst's second self (the work-self), a concept for which he feels partially indebted to Kohut (whose psychology is constantly orientated towards growth) and to Freud (1922), whose discussion of the ego's struggle to be predominant moved in a similar direction.

The 'positive orientation' consists in the fact that, by empathising, the analyst assumes that whatever the analysand does or feels is essential in the extremely adverse circumstances which prevail in the unconscious or the psychic reality.

By way of 'adverse circumstances', Schafer cites those described by Freud in *Inhibitions, Symptoms and Anxiety* (1925): total loss of the love object; total loss of love; castration; archaic punishments of the superego. These phantasies of danger generate the inner anxiety of infantile impotence. To these Schafer adds other basic dangers: paranoid terror, depressive impotence, fragmentation of the self, loss of the self in the de-differentiation of self and object.

If the analyst works with a tragic vision of human development and existence (Schafer, 1970), succeeding in initiating an inner contact with the universal element of these phantasies (unconsciously, we are all members of a humanity in danger), he will be able to empathise with the person under analysis, whose passage through the analysis is conditioned by the need to defend himself from these basic dangers.

Other components of a 'positive orientation' are: being inclined to presuppose the coherence and potential intelligibility of what the person under analysis produces; a capacity for anticipation, that is, for predicting certain psychoanalytical events with the help of a grid-like set of updatable reference points (the fruit of the growing knowledge of the patient, of personal psychoanalytic experience, and of supervision); learning to recognise attacks on the state of empathy; and that which Schafer apparently considers to be the most important component of the 'positive orientation': the capacity to maintain a long-range view of the analysis as a whole.

It is thus a matter of achieving prolonged empathic activity in extended contexts. Keeping an empathic approach over an extended period is a sign of great tenacity. Also very interesting are the fine distinctions he proposes when examining the relationships that exist between empathising and imitating, which lead him to conclude that empathising in psychoanalysis cannot generally speaking be imitative, as both Freud (1921) and Fenichel (1945) contended.

Schafer stresses the cognitive, creative aspects of empathy rather than those linked to imitation: he upholds a vision of the transformational nature of empathy, according to which by empathising, we reflect or imitate something which we have already forged, and in so doing we forge it further.

Ping-Nie Pao's contribution specifically on the subject of empathy is to be found mainly in his 1984 work *Therapeutic Empathy in Schizophrenics*, through which we can become familiar with the atmosphere of the work undertaken by this great psychiatrist (as well as psychoanalyst) in the famous Chestnut Lodge institution, treating patients with serious psychotic conditions.

In the closing statements of this article, Pao makes us share his inner position, so full of drive and creative optimism, and to my mind he discloses its origin when he describes a couple of particularly good and generative inner parental objects. He recalls that during his training period, he was full of reverential admiration for Harry Stack Sullivan and Frieda Fromm-Reichman and the way they managed to induce most patients to abandon their schizophrenic language. Through their example, he believed it would be possible for future generations of analysts to reach such heights.

Starting out from this basic confidence, nurtured by the idealised couple of (psychoanalytical) parents, Pao avers that the capacity for empathy is potentially present in every human being, and is then naturally assisted or inhibited by the initial mother-child *transactions*.

According to Pao, empathy is not due to the actions of one person alone. The two people involved in the experience (one who wishes to understand, the other who wants to be understood) both must, to some extent, take an active part. Together, step by step, they form an ever more intricate network of interconnected communications, composed not only of a continual exchange (verbal and non-verbal) between the two, but also through mental interactions active within each of them. These mental interactions are aimed at keeping up the exchange.

Pao reminds us usually one of the participants can decide without difficulty to interrupt the from...to exchange, even if the other would like it to continue, and he cites in this connection the well-known concept of attack on the bond (Bion, 1959), on the basis of which the patient can actively bring about the rupturing of the emotional contact.

Naturally, it is very difficult to build up this with schizophrenics and when a communication breakdown occurs, it may be permanent. The patient may never again make an effort to want to be understood: "you have made to many mistakes with me, therefore you will never understand me." These are serious risks, but, Pao stresses, hope is an important mitigating factor; a future-orientated openness that I would like to set alongside the considerations – which seem to me likeminded – in Schafer (1983), where the author points to tenacity and the capacity to maintain a far-sighted view of the analysis as a whole as being the prime requisites if the psychoanalyst is to keep his or her role in operation even in the most discouraging stages of certain particularly difficult treatments.

According to Pao, in establishing an empathic network of communication during treatment of neurotics, the analyst tends to use above all verbal exchange; with psychotics, on the other hand, non-verbal exchange can become significant to a large extent. In any case, once this network of communication is set up, the analyst is gradually absorbed by both levels of exchange (verbal and non-verbal), as well as by what occurs in his mind as an effect of this exchange: at such times, the analyst is totally unmindful of other stimuli.

Pao argues that, although it may be innate in some people to possess the capacity for empathy, the use of this potential can be learned, but cannot be taught. Anyway, it takes a long and patient effort to construct the network of empathetic communication step by step; in my view this is an important point, on the one hand because it provides a depressingly realistic reference model for the time-scale for what can be achieved, in terms of building up the empathic function, over and above the immediacy of intuitions; on the other, because it presents something very different from the "magical" and spontaneous achievement of an interpersonal understanding often conjured up in the minds of aspiring therapists who have not yet submitted to analysis their own illusions of omnipotence and their own unconscious expectation to reproduce, just like that, the enchantment of the state of fusion.

There have been other contributions specifically on the subject of empathy, in addition to those summarily presented and reviewed above; I will not omit to refer to them in the course of this work, but I have preferred to reserve a privileged space for those that, in my view, have been historically influential and whose characteristics, from the theoretical-clinical point of view, are clearly marked.

I would like to recall the essential points of these contributions:

The refusal of an undifferentiating state of fusion and the acquisition of the sense of separateness in Olden.

The introjective constitution of the object image and the establishing of a relation within the analyst, discussed by Schafer.

The locating of empathetic processes at conscious and preconscious levels and the clear distinction of them from processes of identification in Greenson.

The empathic function of the analyst as *'pabulum'*, as a terrain for cultivating the self and the self-objects of the patient, in Kohut.

The long effort involved in constituting the network of communications that enables the from ... to exchange to take place, in Pao.

These points, for me, are milestones marking the course of theoretical-clinical developments, and they bring us to the heart of our work as psychoanalysts.

1   The reference to 'imitation' requires mention of the work of Eugenio Gaddini (1969) who used the term to indicate a pathological aspect of the identification process, on a primary level of experience which is activated, for example, in psychosomatic complaints and feelings of hypochondria. Imitation is not only an extreme form of defence against internal death, but also an obstinate reinforcement against individuation and integration on a higher level of psychic functioning.

5

THE KLEINIAN AND POST-KLEINIAN CONCEPTION OF EMPATHY

Not unlike other components of the psychoanalytical movement, the Kleinian school has known phases in which it flourished and expanded and others largely given over to withdrawal behind internal lines, in the face of partial rejection on the part of the international 'establishment' of member groups; overall, however, its presence among these groups has been continuous and firmly based.

And if, on the one hand, the theoretical/technical divergences from the other strands continue to be evident and in some respects unbridgeable, on the other, it should be recognised that many Kleinian conceptions have in fact become an accepted part of the set of cultural notions that every contemporary analyst brings with them: just think of the use – it takes diverse forms, admittedly, but is by now ubiquitous – of the concept of projective identification, which is the one that most interests us in the context of the present discussion (without forgetting all the theoretical apparatus connected with ideas of scission, persecution, PS <-> D positions and so forth, which are more and more often re-utilised without reference to the historical sources, implying that it is taken for granted that they have been assimilated into the collective theoretical patrimony).

This chapter sets out to acknowledge this reality and the very considerable theoretical indebtedness it entails; in the case of our subject matter this debt is inescapably evident. Indeed, the Kleinian school has formulated an original and coherent theory of empathy of its own, despite having used the term itself only on very few occasions, and it is for this reason that I feel it certainly merits specific mention here.

As Hinshelwood (1989) notes in his *Dictionary of Kleinian psychoanalysis*, for Klein (1955) empathy is the product of a "normal projective identification". We find further specification in the classification of different qualities of projective identification provided by Rosenfeld (1969, 1987), where he distinguishes communicative projective identifications from evacuative ones.

For Rosenfeld (1987) communicative projective identification is a benign process, and its basic characteristic is that the object in which the projection is directed does not become greatly modified by the projective process; moreover, he thinks that a similar type of projective identification in any case plays a part in the process of object investment.

Rosenfeld's contribution is, to my mind, notable in two specific directions: when, with great clinical perceptiveness, he describes the way in which the weightier and more intrusive projective identifications disturb the analyst's functioning and the capacity for understanding, making it necessary for care to be taken in perceiving and recognising the intrusive elements (one is at first only aware of inner tension); and when he deals with the problem of giving interpretations "which have an emotional meaning for the patient", a somewhat specific issue, which I will discuss in Chapter Seven.

In conclusion, then, Rosenfeld also belongs among the numerous analysts who consider the experience of self-immersion to be indispensable to the analyst's work. He states that an essential precondition for psychoanalytic treatment is the analyst's entering sufficiently into contact with the patient's thoughts and feelings so as to be able to feel and experience personally what is happening to him.

Also definitely of interest for our study is the contribution, pre-dating that of Rosenfeld, made by Roger Money-Kyrle (1956), on the "normal countertransference" (*Normal Countertransference and Some of its Deviations*), in which he writes: "Now, to a parent, a child stands, at least in part, for an early aspect of the self. And this seems to me important. For it is just because the analyst can recognize his early self, which has already been analysed, in the patient, that he can analyse the patient." (p. 359).

For Money-Kyrle, identification during the session can assume two forms, introjective and projective, both of which are to be found in empathy, in the analyst's partial identification with the patient. In the normal progress of the analysis, the analyst undergoes a continuous, rapid alternation between introjection and projection: "As the patient speaks, the analyst will, as it were, become introjectively identified with him, and having understood him inside, will reproject him and interpret. But what I think the analyst is most aware of is the projective phase—that is to say, the phase in which the patient is the representative of a former immature or ill part of himself, including his damaged objects, which he can now understand and therefore treat by interpretation, in the external world." (p. 360).

All in all, Money-Kyrle describes as 'normal' a psychoanalytical situation that could rather be defined as 'ideal'; indeed, he goes so far as to anticipate the completion of the virtuous circle of this sequence when he observes that, if the analyst's interpretations are successfully attuned, the patient will be induced to produce further comprehensible associations and so on, and the analyst's feelings of countertransference are limited to that sense of empathy on which intuition is based.

Every analyst will surely have experienced at some points in his or her life a positive series of this kind, and has no doubt taken great pleasure in it; unfortunately – I add with the regret that follows disenchantment – "it is not Sunday forever", our work almost never proceeds in this smooth, linear fashion, and most often we advance discontinuously and with difficulty in our process of understanding. Nevertheless, Money-Kyrle's description is not to be discounted: it retains its value as an orientation, provided it is not taken in an overly idealistic way as if it were an absolute criterion for discriminating between good and bad psychoanalytical work.

Bion's concept of reverie (Bion, 1967, 1970) is of great importance; it designates the maternal function of receiving, containing, elaborating, modifying and returning, in a transformed state, the child's projections and projective identifications, thus performing the work of transforming beta (sensory) elements into alpha (elaborated) elements and contributing in this way to the formation of the child's mental apparatus: this complex functional activity allows mothers (and analysts) to attune themselves to the sensory and proto-mental elements of children (and patients), facilitating their progressive mentalisation.

Bion's theoretical contribution is too extensive and important (at the same level as those of Klein, Winnicott and Kohut) for a extended description to be attempted here; instead I will refer the reader to a couple of excellent studies (Grinberg, Sor and Tabak de Bianchedi, 1972; Ferro, 1992) in which its great wealth of conceptions is presented and in some instances developed. I will limit myself to noting the fact that reverie, a fundamentally important factor in the alpha (mentalising and transforming) function of the mother, has a founding and constitutive role in the formation of an analogous function in the mental apparatus of the child, and it is "first of all an interpersonal event rather than an intrapsychic and personal one" (Borgogno, 1992); the mind, for Bion, is extended and relational, whereas for Freud and for Klein it is largely intrapsychic.

Moreover, reverie may be taken to represent a mental state open to the reception of all 'objects' deriving from the loved object (Bion, 1962), and thus represents an interactional event through which the mother expresses her own love outside the physical channels of communication (Rumi, 2000).

For Bion, the greatest obstacle that the analyst has to face in the session is the fear of his or her own feelings and emotions, together with the defences called upon to elude this fear: it is this that can hamper or even prevent empathetic listening.

Grotstein (1994) describes empathetic communication between two people as a process in which the subject carries out a partial and limited projective identification which the object receives and accommodates within his or her own inner reality through introjective identification. When, on the other hand, the projective emission is very strong, the object is occupied by the countertransference.

Already in his previous book (*Splitting and Projective Identification*. 1981) this author had explicitly stated that, in its positive meaning, projective identification makes it possible to understand what happens in another person, and in its most sublimated form underpins empathy.

Grotstein, taking his lead from Bion, also formulated what is, I believe, an extremely important reminder of the fact that the analyst must – by means of the interpretations – bring the patient to feel empathy towards those aspects of the self from which he withdrew at a much earlier stage; to achieve this, it is necessary to work through and to diminish the hostility contained in the objects and in the split-off parts, decisive in determining the scission.

Grotstein also merits mention for the capable and impassioned way in which he made sense, at a theoretical level, of the needs that patients have to share experience, whereby projective identification is used as a means of communication: "How else can a beleaguered patient know that his analyst understands that he suffers that experience which the patient lacks the words to describe? That is why I have come to the belief – and insist upon the definition – that all projection is projective identification, from the vantage point of the projector. We each are projectors and ultimately wish the other to know the experience we cannot communicate or unburden ourselves of until we have been convinced that the other understands. We cannot be convinced that they understand until we are convinced that they now contain the experience." (pp. 202-203).

It should be made clear, to avoid misunderstandings about the meaning of the 'rhetoric of sharing' that I will refer to later, that these notes are not to be taken to be exhorting the analyst to offer himself voluntarily as a sort of St Sebastian figure, ready to let himself be shot through with the patient's projective identifications: rather, they are an attempt to give a meaning to interpersonal events that are encountered in any case, the underlying dynamic of which needs to be understood, apart from the conscious intentions involved.

Taking up the ideas of Klein and Bion, Grotstein reaches the paradox that "... it can be said that the existence of projective identification ultimately depends upon the receiver of it. The more empathic the therapist object is with the patient's projective identifications, the less projective and identifying they are and the more they become communications which can have self-transcendent meaning for the patient." (p. 206).

It was an Italian analyst, Antonio Di Benedetto (1998) who was to complete the line of thought limned by Grotstein in this passage, by formulating the concept of 'projective pro-identification': a natural disposition of human beings (which analysts, with the fruit of experience, act upon and further refine) to be receptive to projective identifications, as a physiological requirement for those who perform functions of mental nurturing in relation to those who need to be helped to grow, and in the desperate – although often unwitting – search for a transformative object (see also Chapter 12).

6

AN ITALIAN CONTRIBUTION: SAVO SPACAL AND 'COMPARATIVE ANALYSIS'

In this chapter I will refer to a paper by Savo Spacal[1] entitled *Empatia e controtransfert come parti constitutive della comprensione psicoanalitica* (Empathy and countertransference as constituent parts of psychoanalytic understanding) which contains a number of truly valuable considerations. After a brief account of the work, I will go on to criticise the restricted meaning the author applies to the concept of empathy. This, however, does not detract from the value of his contribution, which is exceptionally clear and rich in clinical experience.

Spacal reports the two principle distinctions between empathy and countertransference, formulated by Berger (1987):

1) Empathy: an emotional state experienced by the therapist mutually with the patient as *subject*.

Countertransference: an emotional state experienced by the therapist mutually with an *object* in the patient's inner world.

Spacal then notes that these two definitions correspond substantially to Racker's (1957) concepts of 'concordant identification' and 'complementary identification' (with the object projected by the patient onto the analyst).

2) Empathy arises from a non-conflictual sector of the analyst's personality.

Countertransference, on the other hand, arises from a conflictual sector.

The second distinction is more closely linked to the experiential sphere, whereas the first is nearer to a psychoanalytic vantage point.

Spacal goes on to report a series of clinical examples which enable him to get to the heart of the matter. He distinguishes situations in which he achieved an understanding of the patient through empathic activity ("having, figuratively, chased after the patient throughout the entire session, I finally got the impression that I had reached him. The final thoughts could have belonged to both of us"), from other situations when it was possible to use countertransference reactions advantageously, and where, from the start, "projective identification was a necessary and automatic consequence of the analyst's empathic limitations."

In another case, Spacal illustrates "the way the analyst may commit serious errors by seeking to put aside his own countertransference reactions in the hope of mitigating the persistent tensions inherent in the analytic relationship", and thus losing the authenticity of his empathy in his efforts. In this case, he points out "how the quest for empathic communion with the patient may also lead the analyst to deny an unpleasant and traumatic situation, and in the end to use the same mechanisms the patient uses to try to mitigate the impact with psychic or external reality."

But the clinical case which is most worthy of mention concerns the singular relationship between Mrs Z and her identical twin daughters X and Y. Given the exceptional quality of Spacal's account of the clinical material, I will not attempt a paraphrase. Here is the full text:

> Mrs Z's husband was frequently away from home on business from the time of the twins' birth on. Mrs Z had established a very different relationship with each of her twin daughters. Her relationship with X was marked by great intimacy and emotional fusion. Mrs Z saw herself in her daughter and identified the daughter's characteristics with her own. The other twin Y was something of an outsider to her: Mrs Z certainly did not neglect her basic needs, but she was unable to identify with her subjective experience. I do not intend to go into greater detail about her behaviour or provide a psychodynamic explanation. Instead I will describe the images which X and Y had of their mother at the start of their adolescence.
>
> I should add that, thanks to psychotherapy and certain circumstances, Z was able to improve her relationship with her daughters remarkably. She reduced the fusional tendencies in her relationship with X and her emotional detachment from Y, and often had the impression that she got along better with Y than with X. Despite these changes, the twins developed a completely different relationship with their mother, which reflected the difference in the image of the mother which each had created. X felt she was intimately similar to her mother and that much of her life was a continuation of her mother's. Her key interests were the same as those which her mother either expressed openly or cultivated in secret. X felt she could understand her mother and

accept her almost completely. She knew how to deal with her frequent moments of crisis and could help and console her. Her moods, frame of mind and even her somatic reactions were the faithful copy of the mother's mental and psychosomatic states.

Despite the fact that X had soon developed a remarkable capacity for introspection, this did not allow her even the least detachment from her mother's conditions, because of her persistent need to share her mother's experiences, by which she was often overwhelmed. X's fusional experiences, evidently, were not yet sufficiently mature to be of use in understanding the mother's experiences empathically.

Y's position was at the opposite extreme. By her attitude, she gave the impression of being completely unable to comprehend the mother. At difficult moments, during Z's frequent periods of depression, Y was seen to be impatient and irritated. She felt she was being deliberately neglected by her mother. Her mother's inconsistencies seemed to her to be the result of her falsity and selfishness. She thought she had no traits in common with her mother and did not share her interests.

In view of the relationship that Z had established with her daughters from their birth, I believe that the twins' attitudes, very briefly described above, are hardly surprising at all. At first appraisal, it is understandable that X, who had had more maternal care, should show more understanding toward her mother and identify herself more completely than Y, who had never been completely accepted. Such a consideration is hard to refute. One could add that X's excellent understanding of her mother was due to her capacity to empathise, whereas Y's inability to understand arose from her lack of identification with her mother. I believe, however, that it is possible to go more deeply into the matter.

We should perhaps ask ourselves how X and Y oriented themselves in their relationship with their mother and how they judged her behaviour and her frames of mind. When the mother was depressed and needed looking after, which of the two twins was able to understand her better? X, who saw in her mother a helpless being, in need of care and consolation, or Y, who regarded her mother's behaviour as aggressive and arbitrary? I do not want to spend too long on the matter, but would only suggest that the daughters' attitudes to their mother are based on two fundamentally different 'methods of understanding'. X shows a tendency to identify with the mother's subjective experience, without being aware of it and exceeding the usual limits of empathic knowledge. Y, on the other hand, shows persecutory aggressiveness provoked by the mother's accusatory weeping and complaints. We might say that both X and Y only half-understand the mother. Using the technical definition, we could state that X identifies with her ego-syntonic subjectivity and Y with the ego-dystonic aggressiveness and sense of persecution. Unlike the attitude that an analyst might have, both X and Y have a reflex reaction, X as regards her empathic immersion and Y whose experience is a 'countertransference-type' persecutory reaction. What both lack is the mediating introspective function capable of filtering their experiences and modifying their chaotic feelings so that they may be combined in more rationally knowable form.

We cannot exclude the possibility that the twins, at some time in the future when the turbulent phase of adolescence has passed, may improve their understanding of their mother considerably.

Probably, however, the starting point for their judgement will continue to be different: of a predominantly empathic nature in the case of X, and of a reactive nature ('countertransference') for Y. This applies not only to their relations with their mother but also more generally, in a broader social context.

This splendid clinical material prompts me to make the criticism I mentioned at the start, which I will expound in more detail in my final comment on Spacal's work: does identification with the conscious subjective experience of the other (i.e. X with her mother) constitute empathy? Can that way of 'concordant harmonising' be defined as empathic? I believe Spacal himself provides the elements for a negative response: X's relationship with her mother was "fusional", lacking the capacity for detachment. And here we must refer to the work of Olden (1958), who showed that separateness is a necessary condition for empathic recognition.

Spacal says that "both X and Y only half-understand the mother". There is no empathy in X, because she fails to perceive the mother's aggressiveness and her ego-dystonic sense of persecution (the elements Y experiences by reflex but without reflection). In my opinion, true empathy is far more complex; it covers a wider spectrum including all shades of colour from the darkest to the lightest; above all, it constitutes a progressive shared and deep contact with the complementarity of the object, no less than with his ego-syntonic subjectivity.

In the 'methodological discussion' which follows, Spacal identifies two epistemological and methodological approaches in the psychoanalytic literature: one concerning countertransference and the other which he terms empathic. To illustrate this, he cites respectively *Impasse and Interpretation* by Rosenfeld (1987) and *The Psychology of the Self: a Casebook*, edited by Goldberg (1978). He then adds that – in his personal opinion – countertransference and empathy should not be regarded as methods of investigation in themselves, but as emotional positions. He believes that in normal clinical practice, analysts tend to direct their introspective attention toward both the empathic aspect and the countertransference of their own experience.

At a practical level, however, Spacal points out that analysts often find it hard to understand whether they are in an emotive countertransference frame or an empathic one, and that this difficulty in distinguishing between the two conditions is a kind of dysfunction of the introspective capacity, *due to the intensity of the emotional reaction.*

According to Kernberg (1988), empathic listening is particularly difficult with borderline and psychotic patients, whose intense communicative dissonance and divergence may give rise to confusion or psychic dissociation in an analyst, intent on following empathically their experience. In such cases, the analyst must concentrate on self-analysis for therapeutic purposes as regards the patient (Bollas, 1987). Spacal agrees with Kohut (1984) and Goldberg (1978) that it is impossible to adopt an empathic attitude with such patients. I do not entirely agree. I believe that it is impossible to maintain a 'concordant' posture with these patients, but I also think that 'concordant identification' and empathy are not the same thing. If we hope to enter into empathy with a psychotic patient by 'concordance' with his subjectivity, which is of its nature already fragmented and moreover represents only a small part of his psyche that is as precarious and erratic as a leaf in the wind, we shall be in for a quick disappointment: just when we believe we are holding his hand in ours, we are dismayed a moment later to find we have nothing more than a false stump; he has divided himself up and withdrawn into two or three different places, all 'elsewhere'.

I agree with Pao's view: empathy may sometimes come about after a long time with these patients, but it is not the result of an 'empathic attitude' (that is, of a concordant disposition as understood by the authors cited above). Rather, it is the product of prolonged, structured toilsome and complex efforts to understand, which may result from the patient construction of a network of interconnected communications, sufficiently continuous two-way exchanges, observation of a greatly expanded field and active mental interactions within each protagonist. In the same way, Rosenfeld is 'right' about his work of perceiving the projective identifications and seeking to render them reintrojectable by the patient. One can then, in my view, empathise progressively with seriously ill patients who resort to splitting or fragmentation, rather than by an approach based on methodical subjective 'concordance, which often turns out to be but a house of cards.

"The situation changes radically – writes Spacal – if the patient shows himself capable of self-observation, making good use of the method of free association (...) In this case, if the mental capacity of the analyst is not limited for reasons which depend on him, empathic contact will be possible without great difficulty."

In this case, we are concerned with patients who are less disturbed, whose communication is not greatly divergent. Spacal warns us that the tendency in these cases to base oneself exclusively on countertransference reactions may lead to errors in understanding the patient. He highlights two of the factors which lead an analyst to choose one cognitive approach rather than another:

a) membership of a given school of psychoanalysis;

b) the basic cognitive attitude used by an individual to approach his own intersubjective environment, a factor which is unlikely to be modified even by the best-trained analyst.

These two factors interact in the choice of patients by the analyst and may create difficulties where the theoretical formulation of the school of psychoanalysis to which the analyst belongs imposes a cognitive approach which is very different from the original basic cognitive tendency of that specific analyst. It is in any case essential for the analyst to have a degree of elasticity and readiness to move to and fro between the sphere of countertransference and that of empathy.

Assuming the existence of 'psychoanalytic pluralism' (Wallerstein, 1988), Spacal ponders the consequences (both practical and theoretical) of the preferential use of one or other cognitive method. He refers to the works of Rosenfeld (1987) and Goldberg (1978) cited above, and reveals that, on the basis of clinical material, the accent is placed, in the empathic approach, on describing the patient's experience, whereas in the countertransference one, the analyst's experience is emphasised. In the empathic approach, the issue of the analyst's experience is limited to the question of whether or not the analyst achieves an empathic attitude.

Another fundamental aspect is that the analyst's communications aimed at understanding try to harmonise with the patient subjectivity, whereas those aimed at interpretation tend to de-structure the patient's existing subjectivity.

Furthermore, those analysts who prefer to aim for comprehension appear to give greater importance to the concept of 'analysis as a process'. The empathic approach gives more room to the patient's initiative, to his activity of self-investigation, always backed by the support of the analyst. "It is left to the patient himself to achieve, thanks to the activity of free association, a regulated and controlled de-structuring of his own subjectivity (. . .) the danger comes, however, from the fact that important sections of the patient's psychic situation may remain outside his conscious perception."

On the other hand, the countertransference approach privileges the reintegration of the projected aspects of one's own psychic reality. This normally confers a greater sense of psychological depth on this type of analysis, whereas in empathically oriented analysis there is a risk of superficiality and stagnation.

On the subject of risks, it should however be pointed out that the destructuring caused by countertransference interpretation may be conducive to the fostering of a persecutory atmosphere, something which does not occur in the case of psychoanalysis carried out empathically.

As regards the working through, in the empathic approach it is a process which takes place in the patient's mind and it is also possible for the patient to have flashes of insight outside the sessions. In the countertransference approach, the working through takes place chiefly in the mind of the analyst and the patient's insight seems to be far more tied to the analyst's interpretations.

Spacal concludes his comparative exploration by focusing on two different spheres of transference which arise from the two different approaches in question. They are: a) a relational area of drives and objects, for the countertransference approach; b) the relational area of support and object-Self, for empathic approach.

In conclusion, in the empathic approach, "the patient tends to destructure his own subjectivity and increase his self-awareness considerably, given adequate analytic containment. These observations have reduced the role of interpretation as the main vehicle for the re-emergence of things repressed." In the countertransference approach, the analyst may exploit the introspection of his own subjectivity to the advantage of the psychoanalytic process, using elements of his own consciousness which, at first sight, appear to have no connection with the patient and which go to form that indispensable instrument for change: interpretation.

In this work, Spacal moves with care and balance through a comparative field which is both vast and sensitive. As already mentioned, I have one fundamental criticism to make: I do not believe that empathy is the same thing as a concordant disposition. To be honest, I do not even believe that it is legitimate to speak of an empathic 'attitude' or 'approach'. As I will explain in the second part of the book, I consider empathy to be an intra- and interpersonal event which cannot be programmed and I believe that the so-called 'countertransference' approach has, in various situations and with sufficient working through, no less likelihood than the so-called 'empathic' one of giving rise to situations of empathy.

Finally, I also think there exists a 'compulsion to empathise' whose unfortunate results in the clinical field are none other than the definitive loss of any chance of empathic contact. True empathy very rarely comes about only at the level of concordant resonance: human beings are too complex, the vicissitudes of human relations are too complicated to be recorded by an ear attuned to the subjective consciousness of our interlocutor; a similar perceptive disposition is almost always necessary, but very often not even that is enough. I have the distinct impression that this is above all a matter of terminology: the concept of empathy should not be restricted to concordance with what is ego-syntonic for the patient, otherwise it is true that empathy is no longer a psychoanalytic concept. Psychoanalytic empathy, as we shall see, is a more complex function.

1 On 10 March 1990, at the Veneto-Emilia Psychoanalytic Meeting held in Padua, this work by Savo Spacal, who had died only months before, was read in an intensely moving atmosphere. Spacal, of Slovene origin, had trained as an analyst at the Columbia Institute, New York and was therefore familiar with the work of North American authors. On moving back to Trieste, he was able to integrate his scientific background with the various contributions Italian psychoanalysis was producing at the time as well as incorporating from other schools of thoughts. His specific background made him naturally competent in the field of 'comparative psychoanalysis' (Schafer, 1983, Chapter 17, On Becoming a psychoanalyst of one credo rather than another)

PART II

A Contemporary Prospective

7

THE ANALYST'S INTERNAL ATTITUDE: ANALYSIS *WITH* THE EGO AND ANALYSIS *WITH* THE SELF

Traditionally, psychoanalysts have dedicated themselves to a careful, even meticulous study of the literature. Armed with this specific theoretical and semiological expertise, the analyst is able to play an active part in investigating, contextualising, deciphering and translating the elements of mental life.

On a more modest plane, in the privacy of their own self-analysis and later in their daily work with their patients, analysts practice the art of making contact[1] with their own inner world and with that of others. At the end of the day, if the analyst feels he has worked well enough, this sensation is usually accompanied by the feeling of having experienced the most significant encounters of the day 'from within' (perhaps in silent expectation, or discreetly acting as a witness). Psychoanalysts take many years to learn how to combine their ability to feel and think in an integrated way. In particular, the ability to feel, which enables us to help others to do so, is a hard-won achievement that needs to be appreciated, nourished and protected.

The hundreds of hours the analyst devotes to his work can involve unpleasant experiences, a chaos of negative or anti-emotional feelings (such as tensions, exhaustion, emptiness, intolerance, mental wanderings), and sometimes somatisation or a drying up of the rich representational vein. Such experiences afford practical insight into the delicacy and importance of our affects, without which our profession would be little more than the heroic effort of having to sit for hours, detached from a vast part of ourselves.

The analyst's hardest task is having to work even when he is aware of not working well. This is both necessary and even useful, since working badly is often closely related to the current analytic situation and is thus a suitable object for research, or perhaps an inevitable stage in the analytic process.

'Working badly' means not being in contact with oneself, and still less with the patient. In more theoretical terms, it means not functioning at a level of integration sufficient to allow one's own working ego to make contact with the self in order to recognise and work through its experiences during the analytic process. In the following pages I will attempt to define the accepted meaning of some basic concepts and then to outline some characteristic patterns of contact between various parts of the analyst and patient during the analytic relationship. Though lack of space prevents me from giving complete case histories, I will try to convey as closely as possible what we experience every day with our patients.

THE EGO, THE SELF AND THE UNCONSCIOUS

I will use the term 'ego' in the complex meaning proposed by Laplanche and Pontalis (1967): (1) a nucleus of consciousness and a set of active mental functions; (2) an agency which organises defences; (3) an agency which mediates between external reality, the id and the superego. However, I will use the term mainly in the first of these three senses and will specify when I refer to the other two.

The term 'self' is usually employed in a rather restricted sense. It is understood to mean that set of representations regarding the person himself when he is the object (potential or actual) of his own subjective experience. Unlike the ego, the id and the superego, which are dynamic components of the mental apparatus, the self is not a psychic agency, but a content of the apparatus, like the representations of objects. Since it is endowed with continuity in time, it appears to be part of the mind's internal structure, whose location therein is rather complex. Various and frequently conflicting representations of the self are distributed in the ego, the id and the superego (Kohut 1971). Bearing this in mind, the self appears to be partly conscious and partly unconscious.

Personally I believe a broader definition of the concept of the self would be more useful and closer to the truth. According to such a definition, the self would not correspond to the total personality *tout-court*, which is what Klein (1959) was basically suggesting, but to the internal reality (including object representations) which turns out to be a *lasting, characterising* and *constituent* part of a person's mental world, and which may be the object of his subjective experience.

I remember a book that was very popular in the 1950s: *Les carnets du Major Thompson* by P. Daninos. It contained a rather witty description of what would be revealed if an Englishman were 'opened up', and gave a long list of typical objects (bowler hat, portrait of the Royal Family, croquet ball, club membership card, college tie, etc. etc.), thus representing a sort of orbital part of the self (Wisdom 1961) which contains the internalised external object world.

The nuclear part of the self, on the other hand, is the part in which the elements that have most profoundly and authentically been the object of projective identification form a compact organic nucleus with the person's hereditary somato-psychic constitution. At this level any psychoanalytic work involving de-identification will inevitably be inappropriate and destructive, and we should speak of a deep identity (the equivalent of Winnicott's 'true self', 1965). Daninos, whose aim was to make light-hearted fun of the English, based his humour on a presentation of their 'orbital' objects as absolutely 'nuclear' ones. The result was to create a sort of over-simplified caricature. For the most part, the orbital 'objects' of Major Thompson's self were representations of concrete objects; however evocative they might be, dynamically they were without any life of their own. But since they were lasting, characterising and constituent, in my opinion they were still to be considered elements of the self. Many of the objects we find in our own and in our patients' selves are far more dynamic.

The overall picture formed by the internal objects, the nuclear self and their relations can convey a basic emotional atmosphere of the self, whose occasional fluctuations can be perceived in the patient's state of mind, in the contents of his dreams and the atmosphere of the session. The analyst can choose to observe this dream theatre or take an active part in it. In the first case he works mainly with the ego, in the second he also brings his own self into play. If he decides to follow this course, he can no longer count on emerging from his consulting room unchanged. To be able to accept this, he must have a well-founded faith in the integrity of his own identity.

There is a meeting between 'intermediate areas' (Winnicot, 1971) which goes back to the primary biological experience of being at the same time both two and one, with all the benefits and potential risks that involves, as well as all the equivalents and derivatives that will turn up later on the same basis in the social and cultural developments of our existence (see Chianese, 1997, pp 200 ff., for more on these aspects).

The analyst needs to have really worked through a *deep mourning: mourning for the archaic omnipotent illusion that he can exert so much control over his own affects as to be able to decide what they have to be.*

Thus at the beginning, the analyst's ego is asked to have faith in the efficacy of a rather paradoxical technique, which is reminiscent of the need to lean unnaturally forward when skiing or to enter the water in a certain way when learning to swim: traditionally the analyst is supposed to adopt a model of (freely) floating attention *(gleichschwebende Aufmerksamkeit)*, which lets him be surprised by predominantly ideational, mnestic or visual-representational mental contents. This traditional model is supplemented by a willingness to make internal contact which can transform the formality of the session into a personal emotional experience that can be shared[2].

Those psychoanalysts who over time develop an articulate and sensitive working ego are able to carry out wide-ranging, conscious and preconscious partial sameness (Bolognini and Borghi 1989) covering vast areas of their patients' egos and selves, and are able to avoid the trap of classically unconscious, anti-affective and anti-analytic identification.

I now wish to discuss the further theoretical problem of the intersections between self and conscious/preconscious/unconscious system and, respectively, self and psychical agencies. In order to do this, I will refer to a popular literary character, Guareschi's Don Camillo, a country priest who often addresses his remarks to the figure of Christ on the cross. What is the most accurate description of the Christ to whom Don Camillo speaks? Does it represent the superego or an object of Don Camillo's own self? Firstly it should be pointed out that this Christ is not an unconscious element: Don Camillo walks up and down before him, often stopping to speak to him, though he sometimes tries to slip away. But the level of their conversation is preconscious, since it is quite surprising for the subject.

We readers are amused and at bottom quite grateful to Don Camillo for not being too surprised by the sensational fact that this Christ speaks: we are not faced with the alienating horror of hallucination, if anything we are in the realm of Disney's plausible impossible, where illusion (Milner 1952) allows regressive access to the symbolic and the oneiric. Thus, as we read, we identify with Don Camillo, and – through a sense of humanisation – we experience the fact that an initially unconscious portion of the superego finds preconscious channels of communication with the ego and that this *lasting, characterising, constituent* scene progressively comes to form part of Don Camillo's self.

The Christ becomes less and less a part of Don Camillo's unconscious, though it retains a root which enables it occasionally to surprise us and become an object endowed with its own original autonomy. It becomes more and more a preconscious and conscious experiential element of the self, without losing its natural superego qualities.

I do not think it is a matter of purely academic definitions. Apart from the legitimate need to establish terms and generally accepted, valid concepts, there exist different technical approaches. These derive from the different vantage points. Indeed, if we stress the superego aspect, the classical technique seems to favour the conscious 'identification of the agency superego (or, similarly, in other cases, the id) and a maturation of the patient's central ego, which makes him sufficiently free, responsible and able to 'drive his own chariot' by providing agency-interlocutors and making tentative explorations into the unconscious: in a predominant perspective of knowledge, growth, and emancipation of the ego-persona. If, on the other hand, we stress the aspect of the '(superego) object of the self', then what seems to become more important is the process of representation and relational internalisation which brings about an enrichment of the internal world and the predominant perspectives are the integration and the profound experience of the recognition of the self. Experience teaches us that in a good analysis these two processes of development are destined to meet and combine harmoniously, in spite of whatever the various prominent theorists of technique might say. The result is a person with a *valid ego* and a rich *self*. However, at the end of an analysis, the internal proportions are not always so harmonious, and, in my opinion, this provides particularly stimulating material for discussion.

SOME CHARACTERISTIC MODALITIES OF ANALYTIC CONTACT

The situations I am going to describe should not be considered the product of an inflexible attitude to analytic functioning, since I think that – like many colleagues – I have experienced and re-lived various stances, at different times, in relation to the way certain analyses have proceeded and to the fluctuation of the internal levels of integration, which amount to a sort of internal meteorology.

However my order of presentation indicates a gradient of integration 'in progress', which broadly corresponds to the development of the way a psychoanalyst works.

CONTACT BETWEEN THE ANALYST'S EGO AND THE PATIENT'S EGO

ANALYST (concluding) "... So clearly that slip of the tongue you made, whereby you would have preferred not to miss yesterday's session, reveals in fact the other side of the coin to us".
PATIENT "It's true, it's very convincing; it's just that I don't feel it".
ANALYST (scientifically): "All the same, you made the slip and we must take account of it when trying to reconstruct what happened".

PATIENT (very seriously): "Of course, it's a very useful piece of information, and we'll have to bear it in mind".

Apart from the work on the patient's classic slip of the tongue or a 'badly timed' attempt at systematic reconstruction (i.e. outside the area of the emotive relation at that precise moment), the most frequent initial level is this: by chance the analyst becomes aware of an incongruous element (a fantasy, memory, sensation, a simple visual representation, etc.) that interrupts the continuity of conscious meaning of his secondary process, and with a set of active ego functions searches for the meaning underlying the incident.

The analyst's unconscious, which has 'received' something from the patient's unconscious (Freud 1912), has found a gap in the web of censorship: the analyst, technician or scientist- who is working on the upper levels of the ego observatory snaps up the 'meteorite' – the unconscious element that has fallen into his lap and prepares to analyse it with the aid of all the technological tools at his disposal. Thus the 'meteorite' is discovered and studied in an environment – the conscious laboratory of the analyst's, and at times the patient's ego – which is different from its original environment (the patient's internal world). Initially, there is an air of chance happening about the scene, but, as a rule, its continuation is methodical. The elements that make up the 'meteorite' and the meaning of the discovery are used to reconstruct a comprehensible model of a portion of the patient's mental life and are transmitted from the *analyst's conscious ego to the patient's conscious ego*. At this level of perception and exchange, word presentations *(Wortdarstellungen)* come predominantly into play and their evocative power compared to 'thing presentations' *(Dingdarstellungen)* is relatively modest. In describing and investigating their situation, analyst and patient act as if they were locating themselves on a map: they see, for example, where Rome is, and how far it is from other cities, or what roads run through it, but they do not experience being in Rome, or getting to know the city by living there. Subjectively, one experiences a characteristic sensation of *bi-dimensionality,* because *one does not enter the internal world* and one shares a surface space. This is an informative and explicative way of working in analysis *(Erklärung)*, unlike experiential understanding *(Verständnis)*, which nevertheless has a valid *raison d'être* in certain situations: for example in situations of chance disorientation (not of confusion, because this structure's power to contain is very limited), in which a more distant perspective from the experience can prove advantageous. And, more generally, this way of working cognitively can still provide useful elements for a subsequent elaboration, when the conditions of internal contact become more favourable *for both*.

Of course, the *essentially active structure of the conscious ego* does not allow the experience of contact with the self which arises from a 'letting oneself exist in a thoughtful way', and the high level of activity itself gives rise to the attempt to force a way into preconscious channels which are blocked by an equally active force of the defensive unconscious ego. In the worst sessions, during the contact between the analyst's ego and the patient's ego, functions dealing with rarefied objects are at work: it is like pedalling a bicycle with a broken chain; analyst and patient develop sterile ideas, they talk just for the sake of it, the self is far away, the real relationship is hidden. What are the analyst's affects and his sense of self in such a situation? We might say that usually, in such cases, the analyst is 'dressed up as an analyst' in the sense that, since he feels remote from his own personal emotions, he defends himself by identifying with a stereotype based on the idealisation of a super-personal research (working ego ideal). The precious and complex concept of the 'therapeutic alliance' is also often inadvertently used to justify a certain distance from the actual experience of the relationship.

I would stress that by no means am I describing the work of a blundering analyst, clumsily malfunctioning at the level of the ego. Quite the contrary, this profile may apply equally well to one who is careful and professional, objective and intelligent. For example, the tendentially obsessive analysts described by Greenson (1960) might possess all these qualities, but may nonetheless not have the wherewithal to make empathic contact. There are many situations where a limited and limiting ego/ego contact can be established. Perhaps the most interesting is the situation in which analyst and patient unconsciously both fear and desire the nonexistence or insubstantiality of the limits: the impoverishment, rigidity and superficiality of the relational experience prevent a type of contact whose potential richness, freedom and depth seem to represent a danger to the structural organisation of both.

THE CONTACT BETWEEN THE ANALYST'S EGO AND THE EGO-SELF OF THE PATIENT

This way of functioning works mainly when the analyst is able to operate in a *relatively stable condition of preconscious receptivity, while maintaining his own experiential centre of gravity in the conscious ego,* in situations where the patient is more willing to establish a deeper and more complete contact and exchange.

The situation is akin to that of an Eskimo who cuts a circular hole in the ice and fishes through this hole with a line or harpoon. He thus draws something up from the submarine world into the open air – something which forms part of an environment that is biologically inaccessible to him. The Eskimo cannot be sure he is going to catch anything or what it will be (though with experience he can make accurate predictions according to the season of the year), but he knows that this is the way to fish. He does it automatically, and the act of fishing in itself is no longer anything special.

The analyst who finds himself in this situation achieves a *predominantly visual contact with the patient's internal world,* and is able to identify its configuration and unconscious and conscious developments with sufficient accuracy and objectivity. The analyst is also able to perceive the patient's projective intrusions, which he recognises as non-self-elements, and, by formulating dynamic hypotheses, he can trace them back to the patient's internal processes. We might say that a clever analyst is one who can objectivise and analyse extensive scenarios of his patient's dream life competently. Characteristically, what he cannot do is to *deal with what he observes in a creative way, in terms of psychoanalytic transformation, restitution and exchange.* This lack of emotional contact with his own self turns him into an artist without paints: *since he does not want to feel, he cannot make himself felt.*

The analyst's handling of the patient's projections provide the acid test for his internal attitude. If he only works with his ego, the analyst will tend over-hastily to focus on the patient's projections as such and mark them down as illogical, unrealistic dysfunctional anomaly of the patient's ego. He will avoid their use like the plague to reproduce within himself (even if it were possible) the dream conditions that the patient is experiencing and to recognise himself as an agent of potential transformation within the scene. Having identified the fantastic configurations that arise during the session, the analyst tends to offer a *saturating descriptive interpretation* of them, which acts like the fixing-agent on a slide: it will make them statically visible by blocking the profound processes that bring the ego and the self closer together, which require the creation of an atmosphere in which analyst and patient are brought together. To sum up, the analyst's observations tend to be objective, premature, verbose, orderly and conclusive.

This 'preserved' analyst is like an intelligent and observant child whose mother has deprived him of bodily contact and stopped him playing with supposedly 'dangerous' things, making him melancholic and phobic. This 'preserved' analyst observes his patients from behind a glass screen, frequently offering realistic, accurate interpretations, which nourish the patient's hopes of establishing contact. Such hopes never die, because it is almost as if the patient feels that the analyst 'can improve'. Once, while I was working more or less in this way, a patient who on that particular day was much more integrated than I was, pointed out this out to me with a certain resigned serenity: "Doctor, today you seem to be like one of the nobles in Manzoni's *The Betrothed* who personally waited at table on the poor, for the sake of Christian charity, but were careful never to sit and eat with them! ...". However I must make it clear that the contact configuration I have described concerns cases in which the analyst, defensively, cannot take part in the encounter with a great part of himself. There are other, completely different situations in which the analyst consciously decides to adopt an attitude of waiting, detachment and partial distance because this is tactically useful.

THE CONTACT BETWEEN THE ANALYST'S EGO-SELF AND THE PATIENT'S EGO

This occurs completely naturally at the beginning of many analyses, when the analyst's well-tested ability to establish empathic contact enables him to reproduce in himself a precise, useable model of the patient's defensive organisation (generally situated in the unconscious part of the ego) (Schafer 1959; 1983). This enables the analyst to understand what the patient can allow himself to think and experience at that moment, and it thus helps him to decide how to behave as an analyst.

The analyst uses the resonance of his own self (Kelman 1987) to identify, comparatively, the underdeveloped or inaccessible areas of the patient's self; but with his own self he also experiences the ways, levels and strength with which the patient's unconscious defensive ego habitually suspends, stifles or cancels the patient's own subjective contact with his own self (Bollas 1987). The analyst can often find this sameness quite disturbing. It is precisely this experience which at times prompts him to reflect on just how seriously ill the patient is, irrespective of how striking the external symptoms are. Extensive and profound contact with his own self enables the analyst to receive, experience and discern the parts of the patient's mental life (objects and functions) that have been split off and projected into him[3]. The analyst, who intends to help the patient's spontaneous and conflictual deep movements towards reintegration of ego/self contact, rarely possesses the boldness of a conqueror or an investigator's cunning. If anything, his distinguishing feature is *patience,* because contact with the patient's self is a sort of promised land. If it is lacking, this can be a source of frustration for a lengthy period, since deep down this contact is like a lost love-object (Greenson 1960), whose loss and difficult, toilsome rediscovery the analyst relives internally. The patient's conscious observing ego is usually the analyst's surface ally, helping to maintain the setting and the overall conduct of the analysis. *The patient's defensive ego,* the guardian of the unconscious and kidnapper of the self, is *the analyst's true profound interlocutor,* and often it takes years for a shift to come about in the analyst's mind from an antagonistic dialectic to a transformative treatment of this agency of the patient's, founded on representations and affects which are authentically and benevolently parental. This crucial shift in the analysis takes place when the analyst manages to make *experiential contact* with the patient's anxieties and resulting primary defensive processes, rather than limiting his efforts to deducing them in an 'engineered' way. At this stage, even the patient's most obscurantist and sabotaging parts begin to be treated and no longer fought against.

In these natural stages of analysis, the appearance of the configuration I call 'contact between the ego-self of the analyst and the ego of the patient', with its more or less complex developments is part of a correct process of development. In addition to these natural stages, there may also be substantially perverse presentations of this very configuration. This happens, for example, when the analyst allows himself to develop a high degree of involvement and emotional communication with very narcissistic patients, whose emotions refuse to take part in the encounter with splendid detachment, with a great deal of complacency and self-justification. In such situations, some analysts might let themselves go and offer an 'example of humanity' by showing and communicating their feelings, perhaps hoping to prompt the patient into doing likewise. But to do so is rather like diving masochistically into an empty swimming pool: a 'lyrical' analyst and a frigid patient (see also Lopez 1976). At the other extreme, a facile exhibition of ego/self contact on the part of the analyst dealing with a patient who is inhibited in this sense and narcissistically deprived, can arouse strong feelings of envy and humiliate the patient. In other cases, an analyst who is particularly attentive and who consciously perceives the patient's dynamic situation can find a way of stimulating a positive *emulation* in him, by making his own good ego/self relationship apparent to the patient in a form that does not disturb him (Bollas 1987). This deliberate delicacy could be considered an element of 'psychoanalytic behaviour'.

THE CONTACT BETWEEN THE ANALYST'S EGO-SELF AND THE PATIENT'S EGO-SELF

We cannot decide *ipso facto* to be empathic. When we feel internal contact has been lost, self-analysis becomes at the same time both a duty and an opportunity. 'Finding one's self again' is the reconstituting act needed for access to otherness, enabling us to recuperate the psychoanalytic functions de-activated by internal detachment. Milella (2001) calls this passage 'self-empathy': "When the self-empathy occurs during the analyst's work, he undergoes a diffused experience of reparation and integration of his personal and professional objects." When, on the other hand, we are well-integrated and manage to work empathically, we feel that, in joy or in sorrow, *everything is in the right place,* and we feel gratitude towards our teachers and our parents: having given us experience of contact, understanding and sharing, they have provided us with the means to recreate this useful and productive condition in our lives and work. I think there is much truth in what Greenson (1966) says: all in all, apart from being a science and a profession, from the human point of view, psychoanalysis is also a very fine way of living.

I think that from the very first meeting with the patient, some of the *psychoanalyst's basic affects,* like some basic representations, contain and nourish the psychoanalytic relationship. Subsequent emotional developments in the relationship – both positive and negative ones – are made possible and guaranteed by the basic affect, which is usually founded on the deep, grateful and admiring recognition of the fertility of the internal objects.

What goes on within the analyst when he is working at a good level of internal contact?

At his disposal, the analyst has a rich representational heritage contained in the self, and it is thus easy for him to represent the experience of countertransference to himself. I would say that to some extent the thing-presentations gain the upper hand over the word presentations[4], since, *when they combine, the latter adapt themselves to the former (rem tenes, verba sequentur).* Thus in the analyst's mind, experience generates the explanation.

The preconscious channels broaden and the exploratory functions of the ego (observing ego) can illuminate, deepen and make contact with parts of the id: *the analyst does not deduce,* but *sees more.* The fog of the patient's defences clears, he achieves insight, but extends his self too; at times, what he experiences becomes a part of him.

The primary process alternates with the secondary process, according to the model of regression in the service of the ego (Kris 1952), which underlies many forms of creativity. *Introjective processes prevail over projective ones ("en-*pathy") in conditions of conscious separateness which brings about (conscious and preconscious) sameness and not identification (which is mostly unconscious). *The patient's projective processes,* which are experienced by the analyst, are not always only the object of description, but more often they are *dealt with:* for example, sameness and the capacity for creative play permit interpretation in the sense of *being an interpreter* (consciously giving voice to a mute part of the patient), as well as in the sense of providing the ego with an interpretation. Through an articulate attitude which also uses *role-responsiveness*

(Sandler 1976), the analyst perceives the needs of the patient's ego and integrates them empathically so as to achieve a psychoanalytic self-representation.

The analyst's affects: 1) exist anyway, 2) cannot be decided, 3) are, or rather, can be instruments to work with.

We know for sure that since some of the analyst's affects are unconscious, they can disturb him and induce him to make technical errors. I have always been struck by the fact that certain conscious affects can also represent a hindrance (for example, a liking for a patient can cause the analyst to scotomise elements of negative transference or *vice versa*). I am even more intrigued by the idea that while the analyst is in a state of complete consciousness, certain affects of his can be employed for technical purposes.

The analyst's affects is the theme of the next chapter, but first I feel I owe the reader an apology. Re-reading these last few pages, I notice that the level of technical language has probably exceeded the safety limit, so to speak. To continue the theme, I could say that my ego has overwhelmed yours with abstractions. Not much has been heard of the 'self'. Perhaps we would do well to move back to the consulting room, at least for a moment.

PATIENT "I had a dream: I was a child, sitting on the steps outside my nursery school. There was a sparrow that was bleeding. It had hurt its head and couldn't fly any more. Along came the bird's wife, mother, girlfriend or whatever to help him. In the end, the sparrow managed to fly again. I saw this and felt joyful, happy and calm".

ANALYST (*moved*): "Who does that sparrow remind you of?"

PATIENT "Me". (The patient leaves, with a more profound look in his eyes).

1 As regards the relationship between 'contact' and 'empathy', certain authors, such as Di Chiara and Carloni, prefer the use of the former. Di Chiara (1982), in particular, feels it is best used in opposition to the concept of 'psychoanalytic detachment', to highlight the analyst's internal dynamic posture based on the experience of conscious separateness. He defines 'psychoanalytic contact' as the capacity to make contact with the psychological experiences of infancy, knowing how to experience and re-present things which happened in childhood. Carloni (1984), in his splendid work on touch, contact and tactics (*Tatto, contatto e tattica*), looks specifically at the metaphors for contact: "Just as we test and feel by physically touching, through psychic contact (which uses the sense of touch as well as the other senses, including the sixth and most important sense which we call empathy) we observe, feel and study the disposition of oth-

ers, structured and conditioned by individual vulnerability."

2. Some have gone further, describing not only sensitivity but also a specific internal spatial and functional *readiness* ('projective pro-identification') as a characteristic feature of the psychoanalyst (Di Benedetto, 1998).

3. On this matter, Mitchell's (1993) concept of 'self-reflexive responsiveness' is interesting. "Self-reflective responsiveness to the patient is an highly cultivated skill. It assumes that the mind of the analyst, like that of the patient, is characterized by shifting, discontinuous self-states and self- organizations; it presumes that mind is generated in interpersonal fields of reciprocal influence; it presumes that self-reflection is itself always, necessarily, perspectival and highly selective." (p.194)

4. Racalbuto (1994), I think, agrees with these observations. In the first chapter of *Tra il fare e il dire* he states: "It is true that the analyst must concern himself with the connection between 'things' and 'words' (for instance, by finding the words which give things 'soul'), but it is equally true that in certain cases it is the libidinously dense things which make words 'spring to life'."

8
EMPATHY AND COUNTERTRANSFERENCE: THE ANALYSTS AFFECTS AS A PROBLEM AND A RESOURCE

The problem of the analyst's affects in the course of his work runs through the history of psychoanalysis from its very origins on a clinical, theoretical and institutional level. There is little point here in reviewing the writings of Freud and his closest collaborators offering descriptions of the proper attitude of the analyst while practising his profession. However, we should note the initial need to present to the scientific community, potential patients and – just as importantly – the patient's family the professional figure of a therapist whose reliability depended to a great extent on his being emotionally neutral and proof against the usual relational vicissitudes, totally identified with the super-personal ideal of the quest for the truth, and free of the inevitable interactive complexities of ordinary human beings. This point of view later gave way (at first in the face of fierce resistance and then more resignedly) to an acknowledgement of the fact that things are not – and cannot be – as simple as that. The stylised straightforwardness of the conflict-free professional, so much the master of his own emotions as to be able to receive a variety of patients with imperturbable functional constancy, proved in the event to be highly improbable. In exchange for the loss of this illusion, in its first century of life psychoanalysis has greatly benefited by its increased knowledge about the containment, analysability and utility of the analyst's affects. First of all, it was discovered that perceiving their presence gave a natural sense of realty and truth to the analyst's work experience, which might otherwise be removed from reality, fictional, false and in any case impoverished, if carried out in isolation and emotional splitting. Moreover, the analyst's work is usually far more consuming and fatiguing when a great deal of energy is used up in defending oneself from contact with one's own affects, than when they are experienced directly (something which the layman finds paradoxical or hard to understand).

Secondly, analysts have gradually been reassured by the evidence that, if this contact is maintained and the affects experienced are somehow recognised, the risk of impulsive and reactive behaviour by the analyst himself is substantially reduced. The analyst's 'acting in' occurs more often in a context marked by repression, apathy and split detachment, than from sufficiently conscious experience of the affects.

Thirdly, it has been seen that if the affects are sufficiently distinct from their *a priori* transference components (for example, the analyst's overdetermined transference toward the patient on grounds of a physical, social, professional or gender nature etc.), those produced in countertransference by psychoanalytic contact may contribute – after adequate working-through – to the dynamic understanding of whatever provoked them.

These and other considerations developed by the psychoanalytic community as the result of years of reflection, now place us in a position where the analyst's affects may be treated not only as something which cannot be eliminated, but also as something precious to be held in great consideration, as a resource to be protected and an instrument of perception to be used with precision.

The analyst's mental hygiene, by which I mean an interest in keeping oneself personally complete and well-integrated, is by no means in contrast with ethical and technical worries about proper professional functioning. The analyst cannot set up real empathic contact with the patient's affects if he loses the corresponding balanced contact with his own, lapsing into anaesthesia or *emotional contagion* (Bolognini, 1991; for more on the concept of "emotional contagion", see the excellent study by Bonino, Lo Coco and Tani, 1998).

At the same time, in order to steer clear of facile idealisations, we should be aware of certain aspects which will undoubtedly curb our optimism and induce caution:

1) the analysts' affects, like those of all human beings, are neither predictable nor decidable, and therefore cannot be planned even for therapeutic purposes;

2) they are highly complex and their conscious liveability will always be partial (it is pure Utopia to suppose that there can be constant and complete contact between the central conscious ego and the affects and deep experiences of the self).

3) Over and beyond our theoretical acceptance, affects cause us continual problems, especially since the quota of negative affects will never measure up to the expectations of the narcissistic ideal on the basis of

which every analyst – to a greater or lesser extent – secretly loves to represent himself (Abend, 1986).

4) Finally, the analyst's affects, occasionally even more directly and embarrassingly than dreams, place him in touch with his subconscious, thus often highlighting his corresponding associative and representational difficulties, i.e. we experience the affects without knowing why or what they are connected to.

But a century of psychoanalysis has taught us to have patience and place our trust in the integrative processes which are powered along, despite a thousand obstacles, by the psychoanalytic functions of the mind. This trust allows many of today's analysts to bear sometimes even lengthy periods of the absence or incomprehensibility of affects, their apparent lack of sense or their degenerative transformation into tensions not aimed at the object, as we often find in the treatment of patients who are seriously ill. To my mind, this possibility to venture forth with a certain basic faith into the desolate territory of anaffectivity, in the tempestuous realm of nonaffectivity and, generally, wherever there is 'apparently little of the human', is largely thanks to the theoretical and clinical contributions of many generations of psychoanalysts. But I also believe that a good plant needs a good seed and that we should be grateful to Freud: though a positivist, medical doctor and neuropathologist, demanding scientific rigour, he avoided the use of the white coat (that powerful symbol of emotional asceticism and uncontaminabilty) in his psychoanalytic setting; he refused to be terrorised by Breuer's affective cataclysm with Anna O.; he used the telephone (1912) as a metaphor for transformative receptivity, and the mirror as a symbol of the reflection/restoring/objectivating function. But most of all, we should be grateful to Freud for his courageous but utterly human recourse to self-analysis, which has undoubtedly enabled successive generations of analysts to maintain healthy contact with their own humanity, even in very adverse, complex and potentially alienating conditions.

I shall now present a case history which well describes the complex vicissitudes of countertransference in psychoanalytic work. In the course of treatment, there were occasions when my working ego and the experience of my Self seemed to go their separate ways. At certain times I thought I had found the key to the problem in rational terms, yet, somewhere within me, I felt that it was not so. I know that I unwittingly identified with the patient's internal objects and parts of the self. The 'countertransference work' (Di Benedetto, 1998) consisted of realising this and using the experience and the knowledge thus gained about the nature of these objects and parts, together with the quality, tone and atmosphere of the relations between them. To my mind, the experience of countertransference is a necessary condition for entering the patient's inner world. I believe that it by no means guarantees empathy (if one remains identified through countertransference, one limits oneself to repeating the same internal scene, without being able to understand or interpret it). However, I would say that going through, and especially working through the countertransference experience may develop empathy which is both deep and far-reaching, and which is not restricted to ego-syntonic concordance. These considerations constitute the natural base-camp for the approach to and development of profound changes in the patient.

I share Tuch's (1997) view of the importance not only of understanding how others feel, but also why they feel the way they do, in relation to their characteristics and personal history, while keeping the sense of psychoanalytic work structured and complex.

ALDO, THE HEARTLESS EXECUTIVE

One of the first patients I had in analysis caused me a great deal of emotional ups and downs during the first few years of treatment, putting into perspective many of my residual illusions about the ability to adjust the analyst's affects to a given situation. However, it taught me many things. Most important of all, I learned that empathy is a complex, many-faceted and undecidable condition. This influenced the course of my subsequent work. Time, prolonged therapy and a lot of working through is required in order to make real contact with the patient in his entirety (and not merely with one specific aspect).

Aldo, an executive, showed up for his first meeting twenty minutes late. On the way he had made a somewhat ambivalent phone call to let me know that he would not be on time. In fact, he was bothered by the idea of having to "submit to an interview", and at the same time he was afraid of not being well received.

I was faced with a distinguished and energetic man of 42, well in command and sure of himself. Initially, he appeared arrogant, but liable to win me over because of some fleeting expressions lasting no more than a second, during which his eyes appeared to admit some difficulty and to seek understanding. Most of the time, though, that was not the case. He immediately told me that he had never heard of me and that I seemed to be too young, but that he trusted one of my renowned colleagues who had mentioned my name to him. I was grateful to my colleague even though I did not find it particularly pleasant to be placed in the Second Division.

Aldo the executive wished to start treatment to cure a deep sense of unhappiness and emptiness that he felt he had experienced from childhood, though he expected little from it. It had become increasingly more difficult to bear over the last few years and was accompanied by a general feeling of detachment and irritability towards his children. It was this that had struck him the most.

On the other hand, the focal point of his life was his relationship with his wife, a pleasant, affectionate woman, totally devoted to him. He would, in fact, have liked to have had her all for himself and saw his two children, a daughter of 12 and a son of 8, as rivals who wanted to take his mother away from him. Though his family was well-off, Aldo had had a particularly unhappy childhood due as much to his parents' total disagreement on everything as to his mother's bad-tempered character. The quarrelling between his parents seemed to have produced a discordance and a lack of association within aspects of his otherwise operational character. Aldo, an only child, had often as a boy enjoyed his father's company both at work and during his free-time, and had introjected some positive aptitudes.

Now he could realistically define himself as a man of success, wealthy, well-established both socially and professionally, physically active, a seasoned traveller and a shrewd businessman. Besides, he keenly cultivated his hobbies in the basement of his home: mechanics, carpentry and all sorts of do-it-yourself crafts. He was unable to share any of this with anyone except his wife. He had never had any friends due to his unbearable feelings of rivalry, envy, jealousy, of the need to stand out, to be unique, to crush the Other.

I had to endure his impatience with me from the very beginning. He studied me and weighed me up. Even lying down, he tried to keep me under his control and verify my real strength while moving between two diametrically opposed opinions of me. On the one hand, he tended not to think much of me due to my younger age and modest home (compared to his), and spoke candidly of this. Besides, my method did not appear to produce any appreciable immediate results, and so the idea that I was, professionally speaking a "dud", began to take shape. He could have got rid of me just like that, but then who would have helped him? The situation reminded me of those films where the gangsters cannot kill a prisoner as he is the only one who knows where the loot is hidden, or something of the sort. The classic line is: "Damn it! He's no use to us dead!..". On the other hand, he began in fact to have the overwhelming impression that I was an all-round person in perfect health, blessed with a prodigious general knowledge. The idealisation "worked" to create the necessary transformative object. This deeply disturbed his sense of Self. In a word, he could not tolerate the object he needed.

Aldo the executive's mother was suspicious to the point of stupidity. She had it in for one and all and trusted nobody, to the point of avoiding any possible contact, benefit or new discovery. It was this, much more than any conflict with an idealised father image and oedipal rivalry, that was the real *leitmotiv* of this analysis onto which "the shadow of the object" was indeed projected in a distinctive way. Now and then, he had an occasional streak of depression and called himself a "bastard". He would then describe how he had mistreated his family or an acquaintance, sadistically taken financial advantage of someone weaker, or hypercritically and polemically torn other people's remarks to pieces. Being intelligent, he was well skilled in these arts.

At the start of treatment, I considered him to be basically an alloplastic, psychopathically disturbed person, since he appeared to attack only me and psychoanalysis. After several months, I began in fact to understand the extent to which he also subjected himself to this form of harassment. As can be seen, my feelings towards this patient underwent clear variations both in a positive and a negative sense. They varied according to the different phases of treatment, and were especially dependent on the predominance of concordant or complementary countertransference. If I identified myself with the 'bastard' part of him or with the distrustful mother, fantastically, I became in a way his accomplice, a hired thug, involved in his dirty dealings to the detriment of third parties.

If I put myself in the shoes of these third parties, I would shake with anger against him. When he let me glimpse his aggrieved self, I felt sympathy with him and tended in the heat of the moment to forget the other side of the coin (which he had very convincingly revealed to me only a few minutes beforehand): this is an example of the ease with which one identifies projectively with an inner persecutory object.

In this kind of treatment both negative and positive emotions can create a problem. Negative emotions, usually a result of his criticism and hostility, fired me to respond in kind. But I kept myself under control, trying instead to organise my reaction into a method, or at least into analytical questions such as: why is he doing it? What is he defending himself from? What part of him or of his internal object is hostile to me? What part of him is in command at the moment, since he is totally part and parcel with it? Who is 'against' whom? etc.

At times, the analytic work was successful and my affects changed accordingly, as the patient recognised and worked through the fears and suffering that were the source of his hate. In a completely natural way, and without any deliberate effort, his growing contact with suffering led me to feel sympathy for him. On other occasions I felt an insurmountable difficulty in relating to him. One of his recollections made my persistent negative attitude more understandable. At the age of seven or eight, he would urinate from his balcony, aiming at the other children's toys strewn about the courtyard below. This scene was completely in tune with his scathing attacks, both sadistic and urethral, on my analytical toys/techniques. More generally, his 'dropping things down from on high' and thus denigrating objects with his hostility/urine, clearly represented his feeling of superiority and pleasure in degrading those who appeared happier and luckier than he was. Genetically speaking, we naturally associated all this to the distressful loneliness he experienced as a child, more than to his sense of inferiority (his mother distrusted the children who played in the courtyard and forbade him to go down and play). That jet of urine might even figure as an inappropriate and pathetic means of contact, as well as being the expression of his hate and envy towards those children then, and towards me now. Aldo the executive contributed to and agreed with this reconstruction, but the feelings I experienced toward him remained the same as before: hostility and resentment.

It got to the point where I ended up secretly blaming myself and regretting my testiness. Then a sudden change occurred when the patient, while recognising that at first it had most likely been a defence against suffering, paused to consider the strong narcissistic pleasure that was concentrated and fixed time after time in that operation. I must have felt his 'total honesty' in recognising that sadistic pleasure, because my clouded attitude towards him cleared almost effortlessly. As if to confirm my perception, this is what Aldo brought to the next session after a week's programmed absence on vacation.

In line with his character, Aldo the executive was a hunter. An acquaintance, who was much keener than him on the sport, had invited him for a week's hunting in Hungary. He accepted, despite the fact that he knew this would mean missing four sessions. He returned badly shaken. In Hungary, they had ventured to the banks of a lake with hundreds of wild ducks. Firing wildly with his automatic rifle, the friend set about literally massacring them. Apart from all else, this involved no skill, since the ducks were a stone's throw away, hampering each other in their attempt to take flight. The lake water turned red with blood but the friend continued shooting like a madman. "Stop it! Stop it!" Aldo yelled, but his friend, irritated, had just pushed him out of the way. Something had broken down between them, and more importantly – in him. I listened with intense emotion to his story, which was dramatic and fitted the events narrated. In this case, I chose not to make interpretations or comments: the patient was fully in contact with the various internal levels condensed by the scene; he was deeply disturbed, but not overwhelmed, impaired or occluded by the powerful sensoriality of it, and it was not the right moment to trace too many doodles around it. I actually had a clear perception that if I had intervened like a petty academic to formalise in some way 'the possible interpretations' of his story, I would largely have wasted a legacy of experience and insight which had sprung up naturally in that case and was directly available, as happens only in certain fundamentally important moments in one's life. The most obvious consequence of this unexpected experience was a renewed interest and care for his children.

As I mentioned earlier on, even positive affects were in a certain sense a problem during this analytical treatment. I will start with a general observation of which I am certain: in human relations, everyone, whether analyst or layman, tends to be deeply touched and moved 'lyrically' when a person who is normally bad-mannered, cold and cruel behaves well toward them. The gentleness of a violent person or the tenderness of a 'man of ice' hold an incalculable power of seduction, because they temporarily keep some of the basic anxieties of the person one is talking to at a distance, giving the illusion of having fortunately made a mistake in suffering or being afraid. The disillusions that follow (the ups and downs) create a tendency to be more distrustful than before.

Something similar must have happened to me with the patient in question. Following a period of emotional ups and downs, which took me a little beyond a balanced articulation of complex and realistic perceptions of both the positive and the negative, I was pushed towards the "entomological" pole (emotionally disassociated), which was precisely where the patient's mother was.

During analysis, Aldo the executive came out with an embarrassing recollection, followed by an observation-fantasy. He had noticed that after he rang the bell, I opened the security gate outside my front door just as he reached the landing below. Seeing my hand and arm emerge from the apartment to perform that ritual gesture reminded him of a period of mutual masturbation with a male-friend at the not so tender age of sixteen. Times had been hard and he said the practice had been a kind of 'consolation game for outsiders'. Once he started going out with girls, he had quickly forgotten those episodes.

On the one hand, I instinctively found this level of communication very positive from an analytical point of view. The fact that all this had come back to mind and that, in spite of his great embarrassment and shame, he was able to talk to me about it was a testimony of both his growing confidence in me and a certain basic trust in the analytical help he was receiving. However, made mistrustful (like his mother) by the previous disappointments he had caused me, I focused more of my attention on the potentially perverse and manipulative-resistant aspect of him in the masturbation scene, fearful of not being 'technical' enough on that occasion and of ingenuously relying too much on my positive affective perception, in my evaluation of that analytical development.

With hindsight, I am most grateful to my 'working super-ego' (Schafer, 1983), for recommending caution, a waiting period and self-analysis. Had I shown my distrust, I would probably have missed the opportunity to witness the progressive growth of the patient's trust in me and in analysis. Rather than being truly neutral and open to the perception of negative transference, I could have unconsciously sought revenge for the ups and downs I had continuously been subjected to in this case.

A certain need to control the other, *hic et nunc*, was brought out by that recollection and fantasy, but it proved not to be the main element. The analyst who was intimately contactable and concerned (the one who opened the front door to welcome him in) was a strange mixture of an external object and a twin narcissistic object, something in-between. The sharing of the 'Second Division' (the masturbatory aspect) temporarily allowed him to feel close enough to the analyst, reduce the difference and the distance between them (Bolognini, 1997a) and lessen his feelings of envy towards the analyst: a dynamic intermediate phase, preparatory to a relationship with an external object.

Overall, this story of 'gates opening and closing' (as a child, preventing him from playing with the other children in the court-yard, in analysis, opening up new possibilities of contact) reflected the difficulty and the preclusion of intrapsychic contact between internal zones. During the second part of the session, the patient felt confident enough to speak about his sexual relations with his wife, which, though good and gratifying, he tended to put off fearing a loss of vitality and lack of drive at work. This enabled us to work productively on his basic anxieties and his anal and phallic defences against them.

I will produce one last clinical note, as further proof that true neutrality in analysis does not lie in non-affectivity, but in a temporary suspension of judgement and in keeping oneself open to complex perceptions and unpredictable developments in the field and process of analysis.

Often, towards the end of a good treatment in analysis, the parents are discovered, accepted and sometimes reappraised. Occasionally, even a 'negative' parent can become progressively more human. By contrast, for Aldo the executive, the figure of his mother changed in time from a source of anger to a source of pain, forcing him into a genuine period of mourning. It became evident that this apparently cynical and insensitive man suffered greatly not only because his mother did not love him, but more particularly because she would not let him love her.

For quite some time I thought, in textbook fashion, that his good relationship with his wife and his bad one with his mother constituted an external manifestation of an internal split. As time went by, I was forced to change my mind. His mother suffered from atrocious back pain. To make matters worse, she had a staved-in bed, sloping to one side, which was clearly inadvisable. Aldo had urged her to buy a new bed, but the elderly lady (despite her wealth) had cut short the discussion by saying that it was a pointless and exorbitant expense. "She's been like this for the last thirty years", he told me, anticipating a possible query from me. The son then went out and bought his mother a bed as a gift, pleased with the idea of assembling it for her, since he was keen on carpentry.

He came to his next session shattered: his mother had refused his gift, insulted him and had warned him not to call on her again for a while. Aldo the executive, once so cold and cynical, began the session with tears in his eyes and a lump in his throat. A few minutes later, he burst into tears. I fully shared his feelings and no longer felt quite the 'lyrical' analyst. On the contrary, as an analyst I was well aware of all the work that had been done to reach this stage. I understood the economic problem of the narcissistic ('exorbitant') 'price' to be paid for the progressive reclaiming of his basic object relation. This was made possible by his conflictual catharsis in me and in the analytical experience. I also knew that reparation towards his mother, the desire to offer her a 'good bed', derived from his having received, in turn, 'a good-enough bed' in analysis, and with it the chance of accepting and treating his affliction.
Repairing the broken bed corresponded to an internal structure 'which was neither welcoming nor supportive' (like a bad mother), and perhaps also meant repairing the bad effects of a violent primal scene, i.e. the endless rows between his parents.

Over the weeks that followed, Aldo realised that he would have to accept the situation and make his way in life, leaving his mother behind him. He felt less anger and more pain. By recognising the object and the feelings it aroused in him, he identified with it to a lesser extent. In a word, he was becoming less of a 'bastard'. Emotionally, I was close to him without any intentional effort to be so (in fact, his name is written without the addition of 'the executive' in this last paragraph). There was no need for any author to prescribe "the use of empathy" as a method of analysis: it happened, and that was all. I felt like a witness as he kept vigil over his dead mother, very moved by being near him, sharing in his grief. There was no discontinuity, no incompatibility and no contradiction between the function of analyst and the emotional resonance of an ordinary human being, with sufficient maturity, understanding and capacity for respect.

Aldo's mourning also inspired a new sense of respect because it did not only concern his relationship with an external or internal object. It also involved a way of being, a component part of his self, from which a certain self-praising and self-legitimating narcissism was gradually withdrawn. And faced with the pain which accompanies profound structural change in the patient, the natural emotional response is respect; it is not a technical measure.

OBSERVATIONS ON THE CASE

The pioneers of psychoanalysis feared the interference of the analyst's affects in the proper development of the therapeutic process (a realistic assumption, since they were breaking new and unknown ground). Now, after a century of scientific learning and reflection, we are able to operate more freely and with less defensive recourse to affective isolation or emotional splitting, *due precisely to the fact that we are more aware of the complexities of psychoanalytical relationships and of our internal attitude.*

Again, this may appear paradoxical to the layman, yet caution, greater knowledge and respect of its complexity can lead to a fuller understanding in which affects constitute both an instrument for exploration and an important part of the general picture. In essence, we must neither disregard our affects, nor credit them with an all-embracing magical function.

I will highlight two points from the case history in which affects have a different function: one concerns the hostility and resentment I continued to feel towards the patient, despite his concordance with my reconstruction of the meaning and origins of his scathing, sadistic and urethral criticism (once, the jet of urine on other children's toys; now, his scorn and sarcasm towards me and my game/analysis).

With hindsight, after an adequate working through, I believe that the persistency of my negative experience was a valuable, unexpected and ego-dystonic indicator of a hidden obstacle: the patient's fixed narcissistic complacency. If it had not been recognised and further analysed, it would have made the work of reconstructing the link with the past sterile and superficial. In this case, the analyst's affects functioned somewhat in the manner of a stubborn hunting dog that disobeys his master's call and continues to search in a certain area because his nose tells him something important is there.

The other point concerns my diffidence regarding the patient's possible manipulative tendencies (the recollections and the mutual masturbation fantasies), in reference to the 'hand that opens the gate' of my studio. My mistrust was neither illicit nor strange, nor was it ego-dystonic. It simply proved to be mistaken and inappropriate, once the general picture emerged from developments and consequent experience. Quite the contrary, to my mind that mistrust was a good example of 'classical' countertransference with complementary identification, that is, with the analyst's unconscious identification with elements of the patient's internal object (Racker, 1953, 1958).

In the controversy between the advocates of 'total countertransference' (Heinmann, 1950; Racker, 1953, 1958; Pao, 1979, 1984; Searles, 1979; Di Benedetto, 1991, 1998) and the 'classical' school (A. Reich, 1951, 1960; Gitelson, 1952; Fliess, 1953; Arlow, 1985; Brenner, 1985; Pick,

1985; Semi, 1998), I would place myself midway. Countertransference can be a valuable source of understanding. Yet it would be over-optimistic to deny the risk of its being an obstacle, leading at times to truly misleading identification, in our haste to assume its relatively easy and immediate technical utility. It sometimes becomes possible, when – as Lichtenberg, Lachmann and Fosshage (1992) put it – the analyst consciously 'dons' the role that the patient expects of him. But more often than not, things do not work that way and the analyst lapses into an identification process which is unconscious by definition.

To a certain extent that is what happened to me: a 'mistrustful' identification with the maternal object of Aldo the executive, unable to accept a provisional condition of sympathetic twinship. Here, as we can see, the affect I had experienced was not, technically speaking, an illuminating "guiding emotion", but the misleading epiphenomenon of a repetitive event. From being intrapsychic (within the patient), it had become interpersonal; I had unconsciously become the maternal equivalent.

A certain amount of methodical caution and the continual working-through of countertransference have enabled us to understand the situation's significance along the way. Clearly, after this experience of countertransference I was better able to understand the deep structure of the patient's inner world. I believe that, as a general rule, the experience of countertransference is a necessary condition (though not by itself sufficient) to achieve empathy with the patient's internal ego-dystonic parts (Bolognini, 1995, 1997; Orange, 1995; Di Benedetto, 1998).

I hope that, through the two different points highlighted in this case history, I have managed to show fairly concisely that the analyst can neither eliminate his affects nor suppose himself capable of 'deciding' which affects will occur. He should neither idealise them as being always clarifying and therapeutic, nor fear them as always confusing and unscientific.

9

EMPATHY AND SHARING: A NECESSARY DISTINCTION

I am absolutely convinced that contemporary psychoanalysis runs the risk of succumbing to a 'rhetoric of sharing'; so much so that at a recent convention I permitted myself a comic gag, impersonating an 'empathy-advocating analyst' who calls his colleagues together in an imaginary battle against mental illness with the words: "Everyone to their compassion stations!" [*Translator's note*: 'compatimento' (compassion) rather than 'combattimento' (combat)]

This is still our problem: in psychoanalysis, all that is too intentional and programmatic runs a real risk of becoming an imposture, of running aground and sinking into the ridiculous. The nature of the sharing cannot, I believe, be decided upon *a priori*; still less can we decide on 'how' to share: I believe in the force of the unconscious and its unpredictability and irreducibility, no less than I do in the advances continually made by analysts in the art of navigating and crossing it.

But, just as in sea voyages, nothing ever presents itself once and for all.

Now, having stated these premises, the fact remains that it seems that the sharing of the patient's deepest experience is one of the new dimensions specific to psychoanalysis in our times; not the only one, and not necessarily applicable to every patient (each one has her or his own history and needs), but neither is it the least important: by now it has come to be understood that the transformation should preferably take place in a relational medium, and that the patient's mind is comforted and able to organise itself when the analyst is able to fulfil her function, competently and with humanity, precisely where the primary objects had been found lacking at the moment of need.

In effect, the psychoanalysts of today, willing as they are to share the intersubjective field (Baranger, 1993), seem to have less fear than the pioneers did of emotional involvement in the psychoanalytical session; this is due to the more extensive and far-reaching experience they acquire in training, which often translates into an increased capacity for inner articulation. They appear more inclined, or are at least 'resigned', in some ways, to love and hate, to fear and to hope, to suffer and to enjoy themselves with their patients; in short, to be transformed to some extent together with them, besides trying to confer an intelligible meaning on things.

This transgenerational lowering of technical defences has led to a natural enrichment and greater depth in the psychoanalytical field: the fact that, for example, a disturbing experience, a deformed element or even a simple incongruous detail tend to be welcomed, taken into consideration and treated in the session as something to be shared and worked on by the set of the two minds together, prior to officially establishing, and prematurely labelling, their individual provenance ('treat' projective identifications before 'attributing' them)[1], has allowed significant changes to be produced in areas that were once inaccessible, being fraught with persecutory feelings or because they were too fragile from the point of view of the narcissistic balance.

These technical changes geared towards co-penetration, sharing and collaboration are also the consequence of the increasingly frequent occurrence of pathologies associated with early processes involving an unsatisfied need to share; these needs often demand to be acknowledged, recognised and worked through well before the stages in which the Oedipus is identified and faced take on any real consistency.

Similarly, greater attention continues to be paid to the environment of relationships (both actual and oneiric) in which the analysis unfolds; in this regard, see the reflections in Viederman (1991)[2] on the 'climate' and 'atmosphere' of the treatment, and those of Borgogno (1992) on a consequent model of "personalised communication, imbued with naturalness and non-grasping relational tension".

Naturally these introductory comments should not be taken as an idealisation of the psychoanalysts of today and of the present 'state of the art'; I am, however, convinced that there really has been a development in psychoanalytical technique, towards one that is more alive, better articulated and more complex, which has been only partially recognised in the literature, because it is hard – as we are painfully aware – to find words that adequately describe the most intensely true and transformative sequences of our day's work, and harder still to formulate the concepts that organise our observations at the theoretical level. There is a 'public' aspect and a 'private' aspect to psychoanalytical technique (Sandler, 1993).

One hypothesis that I feel able to advance and to develop is that one of the reasons why the descriptions in the literature fall considerably short of the richness of the practice resides in the fact that in much of the clinical material that could be reported the analyst is in fact at work in moments and in conjunctures that are clinically rather unattractive, as well as not slotting neatly into any theoretical framework. In other words, I am inclined to think that our modes of operation, and with the help of which we often do succeed in getting on the same wavelength as our patients, depend so little on our will, and are often out of kilter with the ideals that inspire and guide our analytic attitude, that the idea of giving colleagues an account of the actual procedures we adopted on a day-to-day basis, even if the result was good, does not fill us with wholehearted enthusiasm.

"Yes, the patient felt better and even thanked me. But what kind of analyst will people think I am, if I tell them how we really arrived at this clinical transformation?!?"

This chapter is based on experience of the way in which many authentic and difficult situations of sharing were made possible precisely when the analysts gave up orderliness, control, the fine style (without thereby lessening their love and respect for psychoanalysis), only to find themselves – despite their intentions, rather unexpectedly – thrust into the realm of experience-sharing.

The shared field can at times include areas that neither the analyst nor the patient suspected the existence of before having direct experience of them; at times, however, as we will see, the terrain on which one moves is already known, but what is new is the strength with which certain lived experiences demand to be re-sampled. In both cases one is presented with the specific trait of the unpredictability of psychoanalytical dialogue (Eiguer, 1993) and the element of surprise seems at times to become unavoidable, due to the unanticipated upsurge of insight in the psychoanalytical relationship (A. Reich, 1951; Faimberg and Corel, 1990; Smith, 1995).

I will try, with the help of clinical material, to give an account of the sense and the possible therapeutic developments of these situations. I will endeavour above all to bring out how "sharing" and "empathy" are not at all the same thing, by presenting a session in which the first of these phenomena occurs extensively, while the second is absent: this unyoking of these two kinds of experience is of great value to us now – *a posteriori* – as we work towards differentiation and conceptual clarification.

SARA, A CASE OF CONTAGIOUS DEFEATISM

Sara is a woman of forty-five. At one time she was a patient with a very serious condition; having been placed in a psychiatric hospital at the age of twenty-two with a diagnosis of 'major depression', she underwent a series of ten electroshock treatments, followed by drugs and supporting psychotherapy until her release.

At the age of twenty-eight she began a nine-year period of psychoanalytically-oriented psychotherapy, with a psychiatrist who helped her considerably and whom she remembers with genuine gratitude and affection, but who decided, together with her, to end the treatment because of an increasingly acute sense of the pointlessness of the sessions, despite the evident improvements achieved: Sara was working with sufficient regularity as a employee and her depressive crises had become less frequent, although they continued to be very serious and caused her terrible suffering.

When she was forty years old she began twice weekly sessions of psychotherapy with me, which after two years was transformed into analysis.

She is an intelligent, solitary woman, very hard on others and on herself; working with her, from the beginning I have had the sensation that she was asking far, far more from me than most other patients.

A SESSION WITH SARA

The patient begins the session with her habitual sullen and challenging silence, going on like this for about twenty minutes; a gloomy and overcharged atmosphere was created, which I associate with a dark grey colour.

Then Sara expresses the idea that the analysis must inevitably be curtailed, an idea that re-presents itself every two or three sessions: "You have never understood me; you've never had any real contact with me."

I am not unduly disturbed. I reflect that she has been telling me these things for five years; five years in which I have tried to work with her, patiently, listening and working through these fantasies; I think that this time too she will not break it off.

While Sara continues her indictment, calmly and with a firm voice, in my mind I consult my inner colleagues (as I tend to, when faced with the more difficult patients) and certain authors, drawing from them an exhortation to apply still more patience and to hold fast. I recap to myself how, after a couple of years dedicated in large part to being broadly receptive to the inclination towards abandonment that she was living through, I then applied myself also to an analysis aimed at particular traits in Sara, in the relationship with me and with the people in her environment, which had gradually emerged as specific and structural elements of her character: traits that it would be difficult to call by their real name (intransigence, rigidity, greed) without running the risk of wounding her self-esteem, for which reason the insight was put forward by indirect means, with a softening effect, and supported by attempts at a genetic reconstruction that would make it easier to understand and to accept the origins of those aspects that were so damaging to her way of relating to herself and to others.

I then intervene by telling her that I notice how a sequence already known to us is repeating itself, a message expressing misgivings that asks to be received and understood so that we can return to the path we were moving along together. All in all, until halfway through the session my theoretical-critical apparatus gives me adequate support; the patient attacks me, complains about my lack of understanding, considers me technically inexpert, but I continue to think that we have worked well enough, I make good use of consultations with my 'colleagues within', I would argue that Sara is not capable at the moment of remembering all that we have achieved together that is of value, but that I will not interrupt this time either.

Sara, in an unhurried way, states: "I notice that today you are not even getting annoyed: obviously you too have realised that we really coming to an end."

Somehow, roughly from that moment I lose my inner sense of security, and I find myself thinking once again – with some surprise – that perhaps this time she really could break off the analysis.

"It is not your fault, doctor, I know that you have done your best with me, but you were expecting to change me, or maybe only to help me; the problem is, simply, that you're not the right therapist for me."

Taken over by a growing sense of being constitutionally ill-suited, I start to see the situation as she does; I feel she is right, that it is true; I give up the struggle; the therapy is over, it ends here; I feel a deep pain, but I see that this really is how things are by now.

My thoughts, at this point, wander uneasily between concern for the patient, the narcissistic wound due to my failure at a technical level, and an impression of the futility of my efforts when faced with the forces overdetermining the repetition. And overlaying this suffering and anger come depression and resignation, to which I surrender. There is about one minute left before the end of the session.

Sara gives a sigh of relief, and says, "Now I feel better!"

In a few seconds, without my having been able to determine anything, there is a break in the clouds and the sun comes out, for me too. It is the end of the session; we say goodbye to each other with a smile, and Sara can be seen even smiling at herself a little. She goes away completely happy: the analysis is over.

One question remains: did the analysis "have to" go that way?

REFLECTIONS ON THE CASE

It is usual for the analyst to turn, in the course of self-critique, to some theoretical points of reference: for example, with material of this kind, to Rosenfeld and the concept of evacuative projective identification (1965), or to the 'desperate projective identification' theorised by Ahumada (1984) as an attempt at connection with the basic object; or else to Bollas (1987) and to the necessity of the process of self-experiencing, in line with the thinking of Winnicott and Masud Khan. Or again, with more specific reference to the content of the emotional states shared on this occasion, comfort can be found in the pages in Rupp (1954) on the desperation of the psychoanalyst, and in Farber's encouraging considerations (1958): "The therapist must be capable of feeling real desperation on behalf of another as well as on his own behalf; it is when we are bereft of every artifice and prop, of all the technical support our profession gives, that we are close as possible to reality."

But while I was closing the door of the studio behind Sara as she left in such a state of happiness, I was actually thinking: "And this, how could I ever tell my colleagues about it? ..."

I had let myself be carried away by the flow of emotions, like a beginner; and yet I was happy too, although it seemed to me obvious that I had lost any semblance of orderliness and control in the session. And so I found myself remembering the judo instructor who had unexpectedly kept us occupied for several months, we cocky young lads of the first level, at learning the art of falling; to the extent that we were not surprised, years later, in seeing a great Japanese master open his master class with a series of properly performed falls, alternated by appeals to humility. Falling, I had finished head over heels, without expecting it, in the inner world of Sara.

Leaving aside, for the time being, the narcissistic conflicts of the analyst with regard to his own psychoanalytic ideal, let's turn to the question of the overall meaning of this clinical sequence.

Sara treated me like a part of her that had been refused by another part; her mother treated her like that, just another link in the transgenerational chain that implacably perpetuated "the traditional trade in unhappiness between human beings", described with bitter wisdom by Money-Kyrle (1951). The psychoanalytical field accommodates the intrapsychic and the interpersonal, and brings them back into play in a condensed form.

I believe that in the reported session there are all the elements that characterise an enactment: a concept that is perhaps overused, but which in cases like this can be usefully taken up, with the result that a complex scene, full of condensed unconscious meanings, a scene which cannot be reduced simply to the excitatory discharge of 'acting out', and which relies on the involuntary participation of the analyst and patient for the manifest (although not conscious) re-actualisation of a 'deep' script seeking representation, remains accessible to reconsideration and hence analysable.

Now, working after the event, I think we can ask ourselves: when was it that Sara felt good? When I tried to get her to accept an explanation (one that was basically correct and not only cognitive but could also have a containing function) of what was happening in her and between us?

No. Sara felt better – and she repeated this to me forcefully at the next session – when she felt that I was hurt, a failure, embittered, as she was; when she felt that I had really given up. At that point, the experience of sharing seems to have conceded the possibility of passing from transference to relationship.

And beyond that, what did her 'feeling better' consist of? Can we think of it as a one-off, superficial, transitory change of conditions, or as a structural change in the patient? And what, if anything, could the analyst have done in order to pursue the work, to go deeper, be more incisive, more 'psychoanalytical' (if we suppose for the sake of argument that this was possible in that situation)?

I will attempt to reconstruct how things might have gone on from there and to supply a plausible way of interpreting the scenario. I am inclined to think that Sara's change of condition, after the evacuation into me of the deep contents painful to her, was linked to the occasion and transitory, but not shallow. To explain better what I mean, I will have recourse to that particular fantasy of the functioning of the mind in which it figures as a hollow organ endowed with smooth muscles, as is implied by the term 'evacuation', and in line with Bion's conceptions.

I believe that Sara actually did 'feel better' in the way that a patient may do when an abdominal colic has passed, and that her feeling better had to do with a profound suffering, and a need that was also deep-seated and not superficial at all, to void herself of something intrinsically unmanageable. I believe that a suffering that up to that point was not amenable to representation had left its mark on Sara's self, and called for an external container endowed with capacity for introjection and transformative functions.

The depth of Sara's proto-experiential wound can be appreciated, in my view, from the intensity and authenticity of the sensations transmitted to me, and from the strength demonstrated in 'eradicating' the order

I had achieved in the work, which, in itself, was not entirely without merit (the considerations that I had appealed to 'keep myself on my feet' were not inappropriate and on the whole I would still stand by them).

The 'transitory' nature of the change in Sara, or – if preferred – the legitimate doubt about the structural nature of a change in her on that specific occasion, can be invoked because it is not clear how far the analyst's ego and that of the patient may have re-transcribed, represented and formalised in a lasting form, precisely at the level of the ego, an experience that was lived through, played out and undergone by both of them mainly at the level of the self.

Referring once again to the metaphor of the colic, we could say that after a colic a patient obviously feels better than during the colic; but, before we can consider the patient cured, we would not only have to treat the symptoms with spasmolytics, but also to identify and deal with the pathogenetic causes of the spasm which in turn gave rise to the colic. In fact, the reality of the case in hand needs to be seen, I believe, in terms that are both more relative and more complex.

In the first place, it should be noted that the patient's ego restructures itself functionally and recovers a capacity for psychoanalytical work when the patient's self attains to experiential conditions that are easier to live with; we can detect this dynamic in the clinical notation that Sara, at the end of the session, "can be seen even smiling at herself a little": recovery of a measure – however modest – of the self-observing function of the ego, made possible by the post-evacuative release of tension.

In the second place, I would argue that it is likely that Sara's wound (and the need corresponding to it) was exactly that of having been unable to rely on a containing object which would 'teach' her by way of experience to contain and to transform; and if a single, occasional session of this kind cannot have changed her life (and indeed it did not change it), it is also true that over the course of many analyses the progressive and lasting change is produced by an ever less occasional and haphazard chain of sessions in which the analyst and the patient live and work through significant experiences like this one, month after month, year after year (and in fact Sara's analysis went on in this manner and has little by little produced structural changes; a brick does not make a house, but without individual bricks no houses could be built).

Thirdly: interpretation. I was able to supply Sara with an interpretation of what had happened only some time later. It was a reconstructive interpretation, along the lines of: I believe that you, on that day, unknowingly used me like this ... as you would have needed, one day, to ..., just like every time that ... This *a posteriori* interpretation was useful: it gave a comprehensible meaning to the occurrence, further clarified the needs at stake, supplied the ego with an orientation and a reading protocol, and positively 'fixed' a future capacity to understand any other similar events.

I believe, however, that it can be said that this valuable labour of *finissage* at the level of the ego did not constitute the deep transformative nucleus of this clinical sequence, which is to be found rather (in this specific case: I would like to stress that!) in the experience of sharing. Working on the self, more than working on the ego.

As regards the attitude of the therapist, in the reported session the element that I consider most specifically of interest from the psychoanalytical point of view consists in the willingness to accept what happened.

Kayak experts – the ones that venture into the most turbulent rapids – count on their ability to perform a certain manoeuvre sufficiently smoothly should the boat capsize; known as the 'eskimo', it consists of exploiting the kayak's rotational movement to re-emerge upright the other side. This manoeuvre, which does not oppose but follows the thrust of the immersion, enables them to regain their composure.

SHARING AS A THERAPEUTIC FACTOR

Sharing constitutes a necessary stage in the psychoanalytical process ("intender non la puo' chi non la pruova" [he who has not experienced it cannot understand it], says Dante) at various levels and in different ways specific to each case, with all patients that are living through a disturbance in their contact with themselves. With those persons, that is to say, who do not simply have a need to be informed about their inner life, but who must be helped to gain experience of it, utilising for this purpose the relationship and the mental dimension shared with the analyst.

In one sense, the very criterion of *ex adiuvantibus* convincingly suggests, as a genetic hypothesis about the underlying failure, that what is missing is first and foremost the constitutive function of a primary object capable of letting itself also be penetrated, and then of restoring the shared experiential elements in digestible form.

The analyst, in other words, should emerge as a person sufficiently capable of feeling and thinking together with another human being, and interested in initiating and nurturing in the other a rich mental life, respecting the originality of the other's development. But this deeper sharing of emotional experiences cannot 'be decided' by the analyst as a programmed point of departure: at most, he can only allow himself to be more or less alerted to the inevitability as well as to the unpredictability of such occurrences, and in relation to this greater or lesser awareness – which is rather harder to cultivate in oneself than is commonly supposed – he will be able to give himself the illusion, or not, of being able actively to assume the right stance for the purpose. The theory of technique and the narcissism of the analyst appear to confront each other, on this point, with some difficulty.

In the descriptions of the 'ideal psychoanalytical attitude', which are to be found in abundance in the literature, the risk of illusion and the 'rhetoric of sharing' are always in ambush; the splendid passages in Schafer (1983) on the analyst who feels able to present himself as empathic ("I've got rhythm! Who can ask for anything more?"), with their irony, are an example of refined self-critical consciousness in an expert author, who knows how to tolerate and, in the end, to appreciate the undecidability of 'one's own way of being in analysis'.

THE RELATIONSHIP BETWEEN SHARING AND EMPATHY

At the same time, neither can sharing be understood as the end point of the whole psychoanalytical process, inasmuch as it calls for additional elaboration, and allows of further developments. The relationship between the concept of sharing and that of empathy serves to clarify matters in this regard: for, in my view, when things go particularly well, the latter actually constitutes the integrating end result of a maturing process of understanding, the point when a harmonious, common pattern of feeling and thinking takes shape, of which sharing is the necessary basic premise, but is not the final product, nor still less – once again – the guarantee.

SHARING IS A PRECURSOR OF EMPATHETIC UNDERSTANDING

The sharing of an occasional emotion, just like the sharing of more lasting and organised states of the self, can be experienced by the patient and by the analyst herself too intensely, or so strongly imbued with conflicts and with such a upsurge of resistance (this too shared) that the lived content, in one or both of the members of the couple, loses the characteristics that would allow it to be thought through; this is the terrain from which misunderstandings often spring up.

If, therefore, we remain faithful to the (clinically-derived) concept of empathy as a privileged condition that enables the psycho-analyst to feel with the patient and to think about (and often with) the patient, we are inevitably led to the conclusion that sharing often does not coincide with empathy, on account of the quantity or the quality of the lived content, which in the case of sharing is at least temporarily unrepresentable.

Moreover, examining the evolution of these conditions, Strayer (1993), Feshbach (1982) and Bonino and Giordanengo (1993) have demonstrated that a good capacity for identifying emotions does not always entail their being shared; this induces Bonino, Lo Coco and Tani (1998) to argue more generally that "the theoretical perspective that identifies the recognition of the emotions with empathic sharing is not . . . tenable".

It is like saying that a person on the beach, standing there high and dry, can understand that other people are bathing in water that is too cold (understanding without sharing); or else, if this person is used to the cold water, he can go for a dip along with the others, who may not be used to the cold, so he does not feel the same sensation of coldness (sharing without understanding).

The two functions, in other words, may not coincide.

SHARING AND ITS VICISSITUDES

In ideal conditions the analyst achieves good emotional contact with himself and with the patient, and maintains an adequate level of technical control over the process; the sharing of the lived content of experiences occurs to an extent that is significant but partial, so that the ego functions of the analyst are not entirely taken over (Bolognini and Borghi, 1989).

This harmonious condition is more easily reached not only when the analyst is in a happily balanced personal state, but also when the psychoanalytic couple, in terms of the development of their relations, are passing through a sufficiently stable stage in which the field of consciousness is broadening and common access to the preconscious is increasingly unproblematic.

The initial period of treatment (when it conforms to the model of the 'honeymoon' period) and the final periods of the most successful analyses often create the conditions for a psychoanalytical climate of this kind; unfortunately, however, this is far from being the general rule. For in every analysis there are phases in which the analyst and the patient, resisting the pull of emotions, coast along on a sort of small, methodical and rather regular itinerary, in which the technical mastery of the process on the part of the analyst does not superficially appear to be put at risk (Bolognini, 1991). In this configuration both analyst and patient unwittingly set off in the direction of unexpected micro-traumas, constituted by the emergence of the unconscious relation; in trying to resist these emergent forces, they may at such times come up against misunderstandings, with atmospheric effects that may well call to mind the vicissitudes of Jaques Tati's Monsieur Hulot.

What comes into being, in other words, is the prevalent condition that marks defensive organisation in the couple: something of considerable interest clinically speaking, if observed from the outside or after the event, inasmuch as it is very likely that it repeats a specific and clearly marked intrapsychic defensive organisation of the patient's.

It will have been noted that I refer to a mainly unconscious form of sharing (which is also a paradoxical form: the unconscious sharing of an unconscious fear of sharing), which is also to pose an underlying problem: is sharing properly so called only when it is conscious, or not?

I prefer to consider shared also those things of which we are unaware, but which originate in the patient's inner world, so long as they are experienced by us in an authentic and intense manner, and are such as to produce some sort of effect in us; not the things about the patient that have been understood, but the things that have been experienced together with the patient, even if they have not been understood.

An increasingly frequent clinical situation is that of a prolonged sharing of states of suffering of the self: in this the analyst, together with the patient, goes through long periods with very strongly marked characteristics from the emotional point of view, experienced at length as being inevitable and unchangeable; in this circumstance the analyst is in contact with the patient (what is more, against his inclinations, because painful sensations are in play), but has the impression of having lost technical control of the process, given that the efficacy and impact of his active interventions reveal themselves to be virtually zero.

I remember, for example, the sessions experienced together with a patient who had reached a point where she was in contact with a radically deprived and devitalised area of her inner world. For nearly a year we ran over the paths of an analogous primary relationship, worn out by dozens of sessions characterised by an extreme poverty of associations, our senses barren of feeling, while her hard-won recounts often returned to descriptions of a journey she had taken across the desert to the Dead Sea: the only representation that was possible (and transmissible . . .) of that inner area. This experience will be discussed at greater length in Chapter 11.

In these crossings of states of the self, the analyst seems to be called upon to exercise above all the virtue of tenacity, while waiting for stages of the work that will be more gratifying from the point of view of his participation in the analysis at the technical level.

As Lucio Russo (2001) effectively observes, "the analyst thus takes on the load of the patient's unconscious. This 'taking on the load' is not to be understood in the classical sense of entering into a relationship through neutral benevolence and the use of interpretation of the transference. The analyst tolerates having to accommodate in his psychic inner space whatever cannot be analysed in the patient's unconscious. It is not a matter of a position constructed with artifice in accordance with a technique, but of a real phenomenon that inevitably occurs when the analyst stops using the parameters of classical analysis as a defence". I would even go a little beyond what Russo states, in the sense that, in my opinion, this phenomenon (sharing) occurs inevitably anyway; and in certain cases the analyst has more chance of acquiring some awareness of it if he ceases to use any theory as a defence. That is to say, when he does not expect preemptively to saturate the lived content with meaning the better to control and evacuate it, instead of experiencing it so as to translate it into words 'from inside'; the representational creativity of the analyst touches the patient when the latter senses its experiential authenticity, the true proof that the analyst has 'been there' with him.

When, on the contrary, the analyst succeeds in using the theory not as a defence, but as a natural complement completing the process, then the work tends to develop for the best, although this does not happen when one is in contact with the unthinkable.

1 This is my own personal use of the concept of 'field': when the appearance of an element is recorded, before its attribution to either analyst or patient, the possibility of talking about and dealing with it should be looked at, whilst the investigation into the origins of the element itself should be temporarily and voluntarily suspended.
2 Viederman (1991) distinguishes between the *climate of analysis,* i.e. predominating emotional tone of the relationship, partly created by the analyst, and the *atmosphere,* which is more closely reflects the usual transference vicissitudes.

10
THE 'KIND-HEARTED' VERSUS THE GOOD ANALYST: EMPATHY AND HATE IN COUNTERTRANSFERENCE

> It's easy to write prescriptions, but difficult to come to an understanding with people.
>
> F. Kafka, A Country Doctor

A few days ago, just as I was putting my thoughts together to write this piece, I came across some clinical notes from two years ago. To my delight, here is what I found:

> January 12th. I get up from my chair and kill a moth on the carpet: it had been circling the room for days during sessions, preventing me from reacting to its presence in any way. I clobbered it during the session with M. She has been coming to me for analysis for 7 years, having previously spent 10 years with Doctor F., who had helped her a lot. M. has been using the sessions parasitically. She is a patient whom I have treated with great care, and has changed greatly, but for some time has avoided making strides or taking any initiative towards objects outside the analysis. It is obvious that she opposes separation, while I accept this post-maturity of hers less and less.
>
> January 15th, We spoke about her 'keeping me there'. The same thing happened with her first analyst, who ended up having to close his practice to get rid of her! (But M. found out that he had reopened elsewhere...) Her strength is in the sense of guilt that she tends to impose

on others by means of her silence and obstinate facial expression. My association: I'd read somewhere that the Italian police had tried years ago to replace German shepherds with Neapolitan mastiffs. They were unsuccessful: the mastiffs wouldn't let go of their prey, either by command or whip. (The dogs' heads had to be dunked in water before they'd open their jaws.) Perhaps the association refers to a problem in M.'s weaning, in the same way that my conscious countertransference does: anyway, I'm exhausted!

I have reported my notes in their entirety, complete with clobberings, killings and Neapolitan mastiffs, to provide the sense of an overcharged clinical atmosphere. During the following sessions, I had found it helpful to check these notes again. That is how I avoided 'acting in' my negative countertransference (and my originally unconscious intolerance) towards the patient. With M. we spoke of memories, fears and of the distress of separation. In the meantime, as my hatred of the moth and of M.'s parasitism had become conscious, I noticed how what had been repressed was being converted, in a way, into technique. I was more active in bringing things to M.'s attention, as well as in my work of reconstruction and interpretation. And this handling of the analysis, I am sure, helped terminate the treatment a year later (albeit not without some protest on the part of the patient).

M. came to see me some time ago and appeared to be in good spirits. She was working, had a social life and had even learned how to swim and dive at her local pool. In other words, she had become "separate". When we retraced the way in which she managed not to let herself be separated, she smiled knowingly. The analysis of negative countertransference had been of great value to me and, aside from providing me with a useful technical approach to the problem, ultimately made for an empathic connection with the patient. Of course, the impression of a 'kind-hearted' analyst does not emerge from these notes of mine. Narcissistically, I must say, this is something I do regret slightly. Will I be able to find reassurance, and temper my regrets, in the papers and presentations of distinguished colleagues who have concerned themselves with these aspects of our work? I wonder...

In some of the more enjoyable parts of his letters to Edoardo Weiss (Weiss, 1970), Sigmund Freud, clearly relaxed and at his ease (he liked Weiss and since he was outside the 'scrimmage' of conflict among his pupils, he felt he could express himself more informally), makes no mystery of the negative resonance triggered off in him by certain specific patients.

One such patient is a certain Dr A. In a letter dated October 3, 1920,

Freud writes: "Since you are asking me today for a professional report on him, I shall not hesitate to give you my opinion. I believe it is a bad case, one particularly not suitable for free analysis. Two things are missing in him: first, a certain conflict of suffering between his ego and what his drives demand, for he is essentially very well satisfied with himself and suffers only from the antagonism of external conditions. Second, he is lacking a halfway normal character of the ego which could co-operate with the analyst. On the contrary he will always strive to mislead him and push him aside."

He then concludes quite frankly: "In the most unfavourable cases one ships such people, as Dr A., across the ocean, with some money let's say to South America, and let's them there to seek and find their destiny."

Here, Freud does not come across as 'kind-hearted': Dr A. was definitely not his cup of tea (for well-documented reasons). Neither did he particularly take to a young Slovene, discharged from the army after the First World War, who – as Weiss tells us – "had hoodwinked many people and had a very immoral ego."

On May 26 1922, Freud replied to his colleague without mincing his words: "The second patient, the Slovene, is obviously a scoundrel who is not worth your trouble. Our analytic art is powerless with these people, nor can our insight penetrate the dominant dynamic conditions of such cases. I do not answer him directly, I assume you will send him away."

In present-day psychoanalytic language, we would say that Freud had empathised (in the technical sense of the term) only too well with these patients' perverse and destructive components, identifying them with great precision[1]. In a word, he was no masochist and had no intention of indulging in fantasies of therapeutic omnipotence.

Fundamental help in maintaining a sincere and honest rapport with one's own feelings can be found in Winnicott's celebrated work *Hate in the Counter-Transference* (1947). Winnicott was chiefly concerned with distinguishing the analyst's subjective emotions (derived mainly from repressed aspects of his own personality and experiences, in which the analyst's transference originates) from the 'objective countertransference': that is to say, from the feelings of love and hate specifically aroused in him by a particular patient. The analyst should not deny the hatred he feels for the patient. Of course, through personal analysis, he should have already freed himself of the 'baggage' of unconscious hatred linked to his own internal conflicts. He must also be able to tolerate moments of stress and anger for a long time before the patient is able to recognise and modify his behaviour. This is particularly true in the analysis of psychotics. It is essential for the analyst to be aware of his internal reactions. According to Winnicott, in certain cases the patient actually insists on the analyst's hatred: if the patient seeks hatred which is objective and justified, he must be able to obtain it. Otherwise, he will not feel able to receive an objective expression of love. (It seems to me that this is to be understood with regards to both the *authenticity* of the emotions as well as to their *containment*. Further on, in fact, Winnicott points out that we cannot expect a psychotic in analysis to tolerate his hatred for the analyst as long as the analyst is incapable of hating the patient.)

Containment is a crucial factor, going as far back as the mother/child relationship. In fact, Winnicott points out how a mother who, for fear of an aggressive reaction, cannot accept feeling hatred towards the child who hurts her, will be forced to assume a masochistic position. He concludes with a few considerations on the problem of interpreting the analyst's hatred for the patient. This, of course, is a most difficult and even hazardous intervention, which calls for an adept sense of 'timing' and a similar ability to 'connect' with the patient. Without this intervention, however, an analysis risks remaining incomplete. The main problem, it would seem, is to shed light on the analyst's own ambiguity.

The theme of 'ambiguity' has been thoroughly explored by José Bleger (1967), who developed a theory of the analyst's need to transform his particular mix of ambivalent and unconscious emotions into a full awareness of its conflictual components. This point was taken up and further developed by Gino Zucchini (1989) who, in writing ". . . of knowing how to hate in order to love", reminds us that ambivalence is like "an indistinct blend, in which sugar and salt seemed to be mixed together in the same container. The result, of course, is that the coffee cannot be sweetened nor the risotto salted." I believe that a psychoanalyst, more than anyone else, ought to be able to distinguish between internal containers. It is especially important, moreover, that the one with salt in should be identified, for the simple reason that we analysts usually like to portray ourselves as generous dispensers of sugar.

Kernberg (1988) believes there may be a higher level of empathy which consists of tolerating the ambivalence of object relations, and the capacity to tolerate love and aggression in oneself and to integrate one's own concept of self and one's own concept of object.

Finally, of great interest is the chapter on further difficulties which may occur in containing projective identification in Rosenfeld's excellent work *Communication and Interpretation* (1987), published posthumously. In it, Rosenfeld reconstructs the meaning of a violent attack of anger felt by a colleague toward a patient (Charles), who had driven him to exasperation by criticising his way of working and comparing it with that of an idealised Alice Miller, deduced from a book he was reading. The therapist acted, thus placing it in doubt with the patient whether it was right to continue treatment. This triggered off a series of extremely lively reactions and counter-reactions in their dialogue. For reasons of space, I cannot go into more detail here but would refer the reader to Rosenfeld's text. Suffice it to say that, once the anger had exploded, the analyst suddenly managed to recover his ability to understand and function. Rosenfeld emphasises how essential it is for the analyst to clarify to himself his feelings towards the patient. The need to hide the fact that he felt overwhelmed by his resentment toward the patient had caused him to act and suddenly he realised to what extent Charles had idealised him. It is interesting that this did not cause the interruption of analysis. Rather, it enabled Dr A. to recover his therapeutic function and increase the co-operation between patient and analyst.

It was not the acting out which was therapeutic – and this should be made clear to avoid all possible misunderstandings – but the fact of having shed light (even at the cost of acting out) on the feelings of aggression which pervaded the analyst.

It is undoubtedly true that many patients, especially borderline ones, may induce a serious crisis in the therapist with sudden and violent outbursts of aggression. Gabbard (1990) suggests that, to increase one's capacity for containment, one should seek a point of empathic contact with the compulsive need of these patients to separate their bad representations of the self and the object by projecting externally in order to prevent them from destroying the good representations. By representing the patient's internal situation in this way, the analyst would improve his own tolerance of attacks and his containment function.

EMPATHY AND ADEQUATE NEGATIVE COUNTERTRANSFERENCE

Following his observations on 'empathising' as a complex cognitive activity, R. Schafer (1983) points out the risk that sentimentally may limit our understanding of empathy solely to emotional experiences which we consider 'good' to undergo in analysis. In this way, we avoid empathising, for example, with our patients' boundless pride, sociopathic tendencies, sadism, parasitical attitudes, etc[2]. For this reason Schafer claims, under certain clinical conditions, an analyst's aloofness can prove to be as empathically appropriate as compassion might be at other times. This a theme I would like to develop.

It is well-known that the term 'empathy' is often associated, in its more superficial meanings, with the idea of an analytic atmosphere that is blissful, cloying and fusional. In this sense, it is easily confused with the positive feelings we associate with the term 'sympathy' (*Mitgefühl*). I intend here to point out that, in certain cases, it is more realistic and profitable to tune in to the patient through an attitude of *partial* empathy. By this

I mean tuning in to those experiences and characteristics of the patient, which though overtly negative are predominant in his personality, at least at certain stages in the analysis. In this way, we will avoid projecting onto the patient the fantasies of the good, idealised parts of our own internal objects, while also avoiding securing for ourselves the comfort of a civilised atmosphere by denying reality. We shall see things as they are while remaining conscious, of course, that to accomplish the empathic process of attunement a certain degree of complexity is inevitable. For this our perceptive sensitivity will definitely have to receive, for example, the despair behind a patient's harshness; the anguish of inadequacy that lies behind his grandiosity; the confusion behind his falseness; and the trace of old scars behind his sadism. However, we should also be prepared not to have to 'love' the patient right away, as he appears to us. We should do so neither routinely nor out of any concession to civility, which is merely an attitude that lends itself to an idealised and unrealistic professional cliché.

It is one thing to have faith in a person's possibility to evolve on the basis of psychoanalytic experience and insights, to postulate the existence of a warm, relational and germinative nucleus in every human being beneath his protective armour and callused skin, and to trust in the possibility of developing a fruitful analysis. It is another matter entirely for an analyst to be armed with good-natured optimism and perceive one's patients as nothing but abandoned kittens in search of a long-lost mother. This is to establish and provide an analytic framework that is prematurely protective, rather than self-created and inventive. The lack of an accurate and realistic empathic perception of a patient's negative aspects can cause, as we well know, a state of unconscious collusion, of deadlock and escapism. Moreover, it also trivialises the relationship while helping to mask the distinction between aggression and hostility in the patient. [3]

It is likewise quite easy for the overly 'conforming' analyst to remain inadvertently trapped in relationship models which, on the level of fantasy, are perverted. Another risk is to compromise one's analytic stance by making unilateral advances aimed at engaging patients with a resilient narcissistic structure. These patients' emotional centre of gravity is such that they will, in fact, resist each and every offer of engagement with supreme immobility.

The eye of the analyst must be sufficiently disenchanted to detect realistically those forces and aspects of the patient's personality that will tenaciously oppose analysis. Sometimes, it will take a long time, and a lot of analytic work, to develop positive feelings for a patient. A part of this work will be ongoing within ourselves, in an attempt to understand the particular traits that render a patient unpleasant, hostile and seemingly alien. (Such negative feelings may also be due to disturbing analogies with traits, experiences or fantasies of our own, or belonging to our internal objects.) There will also be times, of course, when above and beyond our countertransference elaborations and adjustments (and barring our 'falling in love' with a patient), a realistic appreciation of the analytic situation will suffice to give us a sense of the task that lies ahead. To illustrate my argument better, I offer here some clinical material of mine.

The patient, a very ambitious young doctor with unrestrained phallic pride, arrived terribly upset at a session. It was during his third month of analysis and on this particular occasion he was furious, railing against a housewife whom he had hit with his car just fifteen minutes earlier near a street-market. After the collision, the patient had leapt out of the car to inspect the damage to the bodywork. He had heaped abuse and threats on the unfortunate woman – who had scratched the metallic paint on his new car with her handbag. The woman, meanwhile, was lying on the ground, all bruised and aching. The patient's outburst went on for the whole session, without any signs of letting up.

I thought that his reaction might unconsciously point to the possibility that the analysis could scratch and damage his air of self-sufficiency and narcissistic metallic finish. (The housewife returning home from market, her bags full of groceries, made for a striking maternal equivalent.) I reasoned that it would be best not to over-stimulate him in any way at that time. Still, I could not stop pondering over the fact that, with his car, he had run over the housewife/analysis. Two weeks later, the patient discontinued his sessions.

For a while I wondered about the meaning of the interruption, ready to beat my breast for my technical shortcomings. Ought I to have interpreted, perhaps, what had happened with the housewife during the session about the accident? Had I not 'made room' for the patient in my mind ? Had I not given priority, in my imagination during the session, to some self-representation of the patient as a person in need? a representation to which I ought to have tuned in, well-disposed, above and beyond any emotion aroused in me by him as a real person ? It seemed to me that there was some truth in all of these assumptions.

However, I soon began to reflect on other aspects of the problem as well. First of all, from the time of our very first meeting, the patient had never seemed aware of being unwell. We all know that behind many requests for analysis, motivated on the surface by a multitude of cultural reasons, there lies a hidden call for help by those often unaware of the depth of their pain and suffering. However, this patient's powerful investment in resisting had always appeared so persistent and so motivated by a kind of self-legitimising narcissism as to have me question from the beginning whether he was really ready for analysis. Would it have been better to make him wait and let him first develop a sense of need?

Secondly, it is with some embarrassment that I now recall having relished, in our very first session, the unmistakable pleasure of a challenge. That analysis must have seemed to me, from the start, a risky and perhaps impossible proposition. I mean 'impossible' in a literal sense, and not in the general and philosophical way that Freud used the word, when putting on a par the three tasks of education, control and analysis; rather, in the literal sense he had used when he weighed up Dr A. and the 'young Slovene' mentioned above in his letters to Weiss.

As an ambitious young analyst, I too certainly had a metallic narcissistic veneer to protect, and a residual illusion of therapeutic omnipotence to defend. I had taken my 'impossible' patient into analysis right away, without taking into account an accurate, though complex empathic perception of the patient's interior world. Had I done so, I would have better been able to envisage the times and stages of his eventual journey through psychoanalysis. And such a journey, I am sure, would have proven of much greater value.

Using this brief case-history as a guideline, I should like to make a short digression to examine a problem in the diagnosis of seriously ill patients who provoke such strong and negative countertransference feelings. We sometimes hear the phenomena of 'destructive narcissism' and 'archaic and sadistic super-ego' used as more or less equivalent terms. Rosenfeld (1971 and 1987), however, does not use them synonymously, but implies that the former is a direct consequence of the latter. There are few doubts about this pathogenetic sequence. Nevertheless, I want to emphasise a clinical difference between *two typical groups of patients*. The first consists of patients whom I believe are best typified by what I distinguish as their *'archaic and sadistic super-ego'*. In this group, identification with the primary bad object and with its resultant disturbed relationship seems to be, though intense, partial and relatively superficial. To the extent that this is so, a perceptible internal relationship persists between parts of the self, albeit of a strongly sadomasochistic kind. The libidinal parts are as if shackled, and dramatically abused, *but remain at least partly preserved in the person's psyche*. This is typical of hypercritical patients who are occasionally self-critical as well. A frequent unconscious attack on their own creativity is recognisable; moreover, in cases where the use of splitting is particularly pronounced, such attacks are sometimes directed against their own physical and psychic integrity.

These patients subject the analyst to continual and disturbing critical attacks, as they come in time to naturally reproduce, in the interpersonal relationship of the analysis, their intrapsychic conflicts. In these cases, of clinical significance is the fact that notwithstanding these attacks, the analyst usually manages to garner and preserve – spontaneously, and not by way of acculturation – good internal representations of both the sadistic and libidinal parts of the patient. As a result, the analyst will develop a countertransference that is likely to be multifaceted, and thus at least partially positive.

A case presented by A. Gambara (1990) is illustrative in this context. The analyst's notes on the patient who routinely gave the analyst a hard time – were always placed in a white folder. This was meaningful, since Gambara became aware of his tendency to use folders whose colour emotionally matched the tone and atmosphere of the sessions of any given patient. In particular, Gambara focuses on the emotional quality that marks a therapeutic relationship over long periods. The link, then, between his work and these observations of mine lies precisely in our both having identified, in hostile and rather destructive patients, deep-seated elements of the personality that resonate positively in treatment.

What I would like to emphasise here, from a clinical standpoint, is the *representability, in fantasy and within the mind of the analyst, of both the sadistic and libidinal parts of the patient*. The result is that a good chunk of the analysis becomes an undertaking *aimed at fostering individuation and helping the ego separate from a sadistic super-ego*. It is the countertransference contact that provides the actual starting point for this task. Indeed, the 'data' for this undertaking derive, for the most part, from the analyst's monitoring of his own Self-experiences in response to contact with the patient. The work that ensues then makes possible the representation of that same psychic 'data', as well as visualisation of a reality so deep-seated as to remain imperceptible to most other methods of clinical investigation.

The second typological group, in which I would include my 'metallic finish' patient, is best defined by the term 'destructive narcissism', as classically understood by Rosenfeld. In this group, patients' identifications with the bad object are far more profound and complete, and the vast majority of libidinal elements are split and projected. As a result, these patients present a very limited capacity for internal object relations. In point of fact, they manifest very little internal conflict, along with a smug and substantial ego-syntonic state. Conflicts, instead, are fully revealed in the interpersonal sphere. Indeed, experiences of triumph and contempt, as described by Klein, are frequent, the consequence of a projective depletion which both unburdens and impoverishes the self. Self-criticism is by-and-large scarce, whereas creativity is anything but nullified – it is perversely developed and cultivated in the service of a unidirectional, alloplastic destructiveness.

In my opinion, the clinical factor which distinguishes this second typology from the first is derived from the analyst's own 'inner laboratory', as it were: in fact, with this second group of patients, the process of imaginatively representing both the patient's sadistic *and* libidinal parts is a difficult one for the analyst.

In a countertransference atmosphere marked by inhumanity, hostility, coldness and even fear, the analyst ends up making something akin to an act of faith, in the sense of postulating that a libidinal part exists in such a patient. Thus, the *specific function of the analysis* – following on a lengthy period of containment, essential to establish an interior space – becomes one of *initiating a process of reintrojection*, into the self, of something that can be loved, from which the capacity to love can then originate. It goes without saying that, apart from idealising one's own professional role, the analyst that braves treatments of this type must be prepared for a frustrating and depriving experience. For this type of analytic journey involves the revisitation of a barren, dry and seemingly endless relational desert. Indeed, the few experiences I have had with such patients have taught me that this is a desert the analyst crosses not in a Jeep, but on foot, hand-in-hand with the patient in whose suffering he comes to share.

To conclude, I can only hope for a sincere and delusion-free perception of negative countertransference feelings in the course of our work. By ignoring or neglecting them, we will certainly not become better therapists. On the contrary, in so doing, we run the far more dangerous risk of acting out our reactions instead of recording and understanding them. All this, of course, in no way authorises the analyst – in the name of some mistaken 'spontaneity' – to behave in anything less than a civil and humane manner with patients. To quote La Rochefoucaud, it is not for analysts to "pass off as frankness their irrepressible brutality", nor to swell the ranks of those who do. What an analyst is called on to do, if consciously committed to self-analysis, is to tell himself the truth, beyond any idealisation and in the interests of his own patients. This is both our right, and our obligation.

1 I find the criteria of 'differential diagnoses' formulated by Simona Argentieri in *La malafede, nevrosi del nostro tempo* (1992) of particular interest, aiming at distinguishing specific mental attitudes. Argentieri writes: "In good faith there is total adhesion to one's own convictions; in cynical falsity one is aware of the deceit one practises on others; but in bad faith, on the other hand, the deceit is practised, to a certain extent, on oneself. We should distinguish cases of bad faith from those of doubt and ambivalence (which are potentially much healthier) in which we are aware of the difficulty and anxiety caused by having mixed feelings."

2 This position is shared by most psychologists of the self. Ruggiero (1996), for

example, states that through introspection and empathy, we perceive the loving self, the desiring self, the hating self, the destructive and hostile self, etc.

3   While aggression "ultimately aims at getting closer to the object, and at times even to enter into a relationship with it,... hostility, on the contrary, masks the intent to destroy, humiliate, and especially to triumph over the object" (Giannakoulas 1996).

11
EMPATHY AND 'EMPATHISM'

"There is an enormous difference between false empathy, facile and postured, and authentic empathy, struggled toward through miscues, misunderstanding, and deeply personal work
on the part of both analyst and patient".
   S.A. Mitchell, *Influence and Autonomy in Psychoanalysis* (p.52)

As we have seen in the first part of this volume, until the late 1950s and early 1960s, when the now historic contributions of Olden (1958), Schafer (1959), Kohut (1959) and Greenson (1960) appeared in quick succession, there was a dearth of material specifically devoted to the subject of empathy in the psychoanalytic literature. Since then the situation has gradually changed, with the topic currently experiencing an inflationary boom, and empathy has become the analyst's ideal goal, a kind of all-purpose philosopher's stone, potentially capable of resolving any clinical difficulty and of profoundly influencing the course of a variety of theoretical controversies – so that today, to judge from clinical reports, if the analyst 'empathises', his work would seem to be already half done.

The invasion of the concept of empathy is in my view largely due to the growing success of self-psychology based on Kohut's model (1959, 1971, 1977, 1984), which is too well known to require description here. I believe that we analysts owe a great deal to this model, because it often enables us, by performing the functions of a self-object, to increase our ability to receive and understand patients' archaic narcissistic needs, which might in many cases otherwise be over-hastily classified and treated

– an attitude that we tend to justify by the claim, where the patient is concerned, to be engaged in a process of recognition and adaptation taking place predominantly at ego level.

However, I believe that the conceptions of the self-psychologists, which usually respect the complexity of the subject (Kohut mentions 'vicarious introspection' aimed at perceiving 'complex psychic states'), but which are often unduly simplified by those who quote them summarily from the outside, have brought about a restriction and in some cases a distortion of the concept of empathy as commonly used, both theoretically and clinically; and this is the subject of this chapter.

The widespread theoretical tendency today is to qualify as an 'empathic' posture what it would be much more appropriate to define as 'concordant' (Deutsch, 1926) – as opposed to 'complementary' (Racker, 1958). On the clinical level, the idea that the analyst 'must', or at least 'must try to', be empathic towards the patient is coming to be equally widely accepted; here the self-psychologists carry a more direct and precise responsibility. These two points must in my opinion be considered thoroughly if we are not to simplify and impoverish the subtlety and range of the psychoanalytic instrument, acquired laboriously over the course of a century of experience, and also so that empathy – which is rightly desired and sought by every analyst – can retain its most realistic character as a goal rather than a method within the therapeutic process.

In this chapter, I shall be dealing with certain theoretical and clinical incongruences (which can in my view be attributed to residual narcissistic-omnipotent illusions) that may arise from the distortion and abuse of this concept, which thereby tends to degenerate into what could be called 'empathism'. I use this word to describe a situation in which, by an excess of intentionality and dogmatic overdetermination, the psychoanalyst claims to be empathic beyond the level of his involvement in the vicissitudes of the transference and countertransference, so that he runs the risk of losing his freedom to associate, neutrality of posture, and capacity for suspension and waiting with respect to the natural development of his internal and external relationship with the patient and with the psychoanalytic process as a whole.

THE EMPATHIC POSTURE BETWEEN 'CONCORDANCE' AND COMPLEMENTARITY

Berger (1987) distinguishes between empathy as an 'emotional state experienced by a therapist mutually with the patient as *subject*' and countertransference as 'an emotional state experienced mutually with an *object* in the patient's inner world'; it seems to me that, thus formulated, this distinction already reflects the theoretical tendency discussed in this chapter. Taking up Berger's distinction in a remarkable clinical contribution, Spacal (1990) describes the (internal and external) relations of two identical twin girls, X and Y, with Mrs Z, their mother. The relationship of the young X with mother was intensely fusional, characterised by perfectly harmonious acceptance and understanding of her subjective experiences, whereas her sister Y had been brought up at arm's length and seemed incapable of understanding, so that she in practice reproduced the mother's attitude of irritability and lack of identification towards her.

When the mother was depressed and miserable, which of the two twins could understand her better – X, who saw her as defenceless and needing to be looked after, or Y, who experienced her behaviour as aggressive? Spacal's view was that both, X and Y, only half-understood the mother: X identified with her ego-syntonic subjectivity and Y with her ego-dystonic aggressiveness and sense of persecution.

In my opinion, X was engaging in concordant 'empathic' immersion, but her cognitive identification was at least as incomplete as that of Y, whose experience was of a 'countertransference-type' persecutory reaction. Spacal's conclusion is as follows: 'What both lack is the mediating introspective function capable of filtering their experiences and modifying their chaotic feelings so that they may be combined in more rationally knowable form'.

I agree with Spacal that X's relationship with the mother was fusional, lacking the capacity for detachment, but would add that in my view empathy is something different (cf. Olden [1958], who showed that separateness is a necessary condition for empathic recognition). *Empathy to me is properly a condition of conscious and preconscious contact characterised by separateness, complexity and a linked structure,* a wide perceptual spectrum including every colour in the emotional palette, from the lightest to the darkest; above all, it constitutes *a progressive, shared and deep contact with the complementarity of the object, with the other's defensive ego and split off parts no less than with his ego-syntonic subjectivity.*

The risks of excess 'concordance' are at any rate well known: Schlesinger (1994) writes that, if we listen from too close a vantage point- that is, if we are too identified with a single aspect of the patient, we are liable to collude with his defences and resistance; the analyst's transference is mainly responsible for his lapsing into identification with one of the conflictual parts of the patient.

Kernberg (1993) notes that many analysts outside the self-psychology school consider that the analyst's receptivity must not be limited to the patient's 'central'-i.e. conscious and ego-syntonic-experience but must progressively extend to what the patient cannot tolerate in himself and tends to dissociate and project. He points out that, when working with seriously ill patients in whom verbal communication is often distorted for defensive purposes, the analyst may sometimes, in an effort to remain in empathic contact with the patient, adapt himself to the latter's style of functioning, thereby involuntarily reinforcing the resistance. In other cases, the analyst's complete absorption, aimed at understanding the patient's confused communication, may become dangerous in itself if it paralyses the analytic functions of association and interpretation. Widlöcher (2001) believes that "... empathy allows us to identify not only the conscious thought of the present and its affective charge, but also, and especially, the associative context in which this thought is embedded" (p. 256).[1]

Jogan (1991) mentions three subsidiary risks of excessive concordance: (a) such an attitude by the analyst may encourage the patient to want even more and to demand 'ever-increasing doses' like a drug addict; (b) mutual narcissistic seduction may create a stable split in the patient's mind, in which the analytic relationship remains idealised while other relationships are experienced as bad and persecutory; (c) the patient may more readily develop a negative reaction to the analyst when he becomes aware of his humiliating position of need, contrasting with that of the analyst as an omnipotent dispenser of 'empathic well-being'.

Although patients with severe, specific problems of cohesion of the self do benefit from a predominantly 'concordant' attitude in the analyst, it is important not to restrict the potential range of meanings of the concept; clinical considerations must dictate whether a primarily concordant attitude or a free and initially neutral receptivity is more appropriate for a given patient.

The problem arises specifically with patients such as psychotics and borderlines who resort massively and frequently to splitting and projective identification. According to Kernberg (1989), empathic listening is particularly difficult with these patients, whose intense communicative dissonance and divergence may give rise to confusion or psychic dissociation in an analyst intent on empathically following their experience. Kohut (1984), Goldberg (1978) and Spacal (1990), from different standpoints, agree that it is impossible to adopt an empathic attitude with such patients.

I share this view if 'empathic attitude' is defined as a posture concordant with the aspect that is most ego-syntonic at any given time. However, to me a concordant posture is not the same as empathy; I believe that the complementary countertransference, once recognised and sufficiently elaborated, is often essential if we are truly to attune ourselves to the climate of our patients' internal world, to share the quality and intensity of their relations with their internal objects, and to experience deep, complex states of the self or projective impoverishments and highly structured defensive bottlenecks.

I am not, of course, saying that countertransference and empathy are the same thing: empathy is the final harmonious result of a process, whereas countertransference experience is a stage that is often necessary but is not in itself sufficient for access to the empathic condition. What I do claim is that concordance and complementarity are usually both necessary for integrated 'feeling with the patient and thinking about the patient'. In my view, the tendency to equate empathy with concordance alone is attributable to the following precise factors: (1) the wish to simplify matters and avoid the pain and effort of cognitive work on the countertransference, and (2) the omnipotent hope of being able to become empathic 'by one's very attitude'. This tendency is encouraged by the common experience that empathy sometimes (albeit seldom) arises quickly, and occasionally even with the immediacy of intuition; this may fuel the illusion of a process of the type *cito, tuto et iucunde* [quickly, safely and agreeably]. Usually, however, empathy can be achieved only after prolonged and complex work.

The basis of all these considerations in technical theory is in fact the concept of neutrality. Understood not as unattuned coldness on the part of a detached and anaesthetised analyst but as the capacity to suspend judgement temporarily and to hold back from prematurely seizing on just one part of the patient, neutrality in an analyst aware of the complexity of the situation allows progressively increasing contact with both ego-syntonic and ego-dystonic aspects.

Although Kohut himself (1984) seems to have listened preferentially to the narcissistically wounded or deprived parts of his patients – *the homo tragicus* – at the expense of drive-related conflictuality or processes of splitting and projection, he nevertheless accepts that neutrality – in the sense of substantial *observational* availability – is fundamental to psychoanalytic empathy.

I shall now present a clinical vignette in which the structured perceptiveness of the analyst is attacked by a female patient who attempts to influence his attitude for defensive purposes and to induce him in various ways to adopt a concordant disposition; the analyst was here in danger (by virtue more of the patient's defensive strategies than of his own technical and theoretical orientation) of becoming 'empathistic' rather than empathic.

ALESSANDRA, A REFINED YOUNG LADY[2]

I shall describe the last session of a week in the second year of the analysis of Alessandra, a 26-year-old woman who came into treatment because of acute anxiety and a sense of personal failure (inability to complete her university course). She is intelligent, attractive and takes good care of her appearance, but seems somehow inauthentic.

Alessandra is normally alive to the slightest manifestation of my own, at the limit of the interpretable, and often compels me to adopt as neutral as possible an internal and external disposition and to listen with wary alertness and tense expectation – for she is immediately and sensitively aware of anything of me that 'shines through' (a state of mind, an interest in a particular detail, and so on) and tends to 'attune herself to it, striking up a collusive symphony whereby all the rest of her person can avoid contact with me and, in particular, with herself.

In this session, the patient came into the consulting room more demurely and haughtily than ever, taking off her coat and hanging it up with care, *comme il faut*; having accommodated her scarf and handbag in the same way, she finally lay down on the couch with the studied movements of a refined young lady.

After a short silence, in the tone of a person stating a problem, she said: "You know, doctor, I'm in a bit of a predicament about my brothers; my parents have said they will buy me the flat so that Michele and I can marry. Should I feel guilty?"

[The patient turns her head slightly towards me, with a collusive, childishly playful sidelong glance, as if powerfully soliciting my adherence in advance to something she has in her mind but which is not apparent. The appropriate syntonic reply to the part of herself she is offering me would, I feel, be: "Of course you must not feel guilty!", pronounced immediately and with an air of redeeming and reassuring absolution. I imagine that after a year and a half of analysis, Alessandra knows perfectly well that I shall not answer at once; yet she seems to have to invite a dialogue of this kind, in which I feel that she is presenting me with a superficial part of herself, while the whereabouts of her true self are anyone's guess. For the moment, I can find no trace of empathic consonance with her.]

"Just imagine! My aunt knows someone, a senior executive, who can find me a job in Milan, where Michele is already working . . . But she does not want to act and instead produces one excuse after another . . . I feel almost persecuted by my aunt: I think she doesn't really want me to marry! I need to get away from her, don't I? What do you think, doctor?"

[Again she turns her head sideways, again she pauses, with a sidelong glance, studying me and doing her best to elicit an answer; I feel a sense of pressure and difficulty, as if I am being manipulated. More specifically, however, Alessandra is behaving so *'comme il faut'* that it can only seem like a sign of ill-breeding and bad taste if I do not immediately reply: "But obviously! Of course you must get away from your aunt!" I notice this and then feel a certain annoyance: I have a sense of being recruited into a kind of drawing-room theatrical production, as well as of being invested with a kind of official authority – I am supposed to act as judge and agree with her – which I do not feel within myself at all now, and which I am supposed to exercise artfully under someone else's direction; meanwhile I am wondering 'where the patient is': I cannot feel her and the situation is anything but one of empathy!]

The session continues for a while longer in this register; listening to the irreproachable and rather persecuted Alessandra, you would think that everyone in her family wanted to help her get married and that she 'certainly ought not to feel guilty', that it hurt them all because she was going to leave, but she should certainly not let that stop her, and so and, and so on.

I have not yet said anything at all; I feel no inspiration to do so. I am, of course, thinking that what Alessandra says has to do with separation, this being the last session before the weekend; but I feel that if I were to emphasise this, it would be dogmatic and the timing would be wrong; it seems to me that the handle for grasping the material must be elsewhere, because something very important and particular seems to be coming between us and the experience of separation ... I also feel disturbed and confused by Alessandra's well-bred and 'convincing' request for concordance – so much so, indeed, that I am almost beginning to wonder whether perhaps I am the one who is making difficulties, being too critical of the patient's behaviour – but then I hear her say: "what is absolutely definite is that, once we are married, I shall demand one thing above all from my husband: *complicity!*" This is the demand I felt at the beginning of the session, which I was unable to focus and formulate clearly.

I ask her: "Why on earth do you say complicity and not, for example, solidarity or alliance?"

"Well, because solidarity and alliance are not enough, complicity is more. What I shall want from my husband is complicity."

I reflect that solidarity involves making use of the relationship between the two people concerned, who acknowledge the reasons for the bond between them as well as the human condition they can share. In an alliance, the emphasis shifts to the relationship between two people on the one hand and certain difficulties or external dangers on the other, the word is already closer to the persecutory dimension. In the case of complicity, there is no doubt: not only is the world about an 'accomplice' persecutory, but the accomplice is usually participating in some form of illicit, concealed activity, actively attacking something; complicity normally involves a third party who is harmed, and somehow has to do with perversion.

So I say to the patient: "I feel that today you are asking me for complicity and not for understanding". I then ask: "Why, what is it to do with?" By asking this, I am trying to show her that I am interested, but also to communicate a sense of personal distance, however slight. In other words, I am offering her solidarity, rather than complicity: closeness in separateness and not confusion.

We are both silent for a couple of minutes. Alessandra then answers that she is beginning to feel very cold. She is actually shivering, clasping herself in her arms, with a bewildered, anxious expression on her face. In the last minute or two, I feel that I have been observing an important change of scene: the affected, refined young lady is leaving the stage, and a confused and persecuted little girl is taking her place more or less simultaneously. Still shivering, she tells me that she feels a great need for intimate contact with someone; that she is afraid of remaining by herself; that she is afraid of getting married, of going to Milan, of having to enter the world of work, to leave her mother, father, siblings and aunt, and, sooner or later, me and the sessions as well, she is afraid of all this. She then begins to cry, sobbing, shaking all over, finally surrendering to open weeping and desperate wailing. At this point I *feel a state of deep empathy with the patient arising in me*, which allows me to understand and make more genuine contact with her.

Gone is the false self, which disavowed the fear of parting and projected it on to the aunt, denying the sense of guilt and anxiety bound up with separation, and experiencing emotional bonds as annoying external persecutors – they were actually parts 'coming back to roost' which were not recognised as her own, with which she would have preferred to have nothing more to do and which, when she had expelled them through the door, came back in through the window – and I now have a clear sense of having rediscovered Alessandra; fearful as she may be of the prospects of growth and life, and terrified by fantasies of abandonment, she is there, authentically, before me.

This is the person who is now prepared to experience fear and may perhaps find the courage to do so – precisely the person that I and her false self (the 'refined young lady') were supposed to take out of circulation and hide in the dungeons, like perfect accomplices.

The end of the session, after 'little-girl Alessandra' had been sufficiently recognised, welcomed and comforted, was taken up with her specific form of avoidance and defensive concealment: in a sense, this involved welcoming back – psychoanalytically – the 'refined young lady', having, of course, first deactivated her claim to invade, colonise and control the whole of Alessandra's self and the analyst as well.

In fact the patient had been trying with all her strength to evoke predetermined standard answers of the kind: 'Of course not! You must not feel guilty!' or: 'Obviously! Of course you must leave your parents!' – and she had done this so much in 'drawing-room fashion' and so convincingly that, at the point when I felt most invaded by her, I even found myself wondering whether I 'was not creating too many difficulties' towards her;

at this point I almost lost my way.

The crucial element then was analysis of the countertransference, encouraged by my feeling of being forced to attune myself, like a good accomplice, to her false self, I was then able to identify what it was that had been imposed on me intrusively.

The 'refined young lady', as the final associations showed, stemmed from the identification with a specific behaviour pattern of her mother's, characterised by a lack of emotional contact, the powerful expression of hysteria, and the ease of incorporability and proven social acceptability of this relational style. This mother had staked everything on work and, in the little time she had spent together with the child, had regularly forestalled her inevitable complaints and protests, resolutely imposing on her certain planned activities to be engaged in together (reading, tidying up the room) and in particular certain mental concealment devices intended to avoid contact.

The work of understanding the 'refined young lady' took up the subsequent months of Alessandra's analysis; it was a prolonged process and demanded a genuine *alliance* between her and myself. When, still later, Alessandra was able to reconstruct and understand her own mother's history and difficulties, the analytic climate was further transformed into a greater *solidarity* to be endured and shared.

'EMPATHISING' AS A TASK OR CLAIM

I often feel uncomfortable when I read or hear about postures towards empathy involving intention or will: an empathic 'attitude', 'empathising' listening, 'use' of empathy as an 'instrument' and so on. These tendencies are not confined to the Kohut school: Modell (1990, chapter 3), for example, categorically asserts that empathy is an act of will. My psychoanalytic training and experience have finally stripped away my *programmatic illusion of being able to decide actively and methodically to bring about an empathic situation.* It is perfectly natural and desirable for us to try to understand the patient's experience and to establish a good analytic working relationship with him, and this may entail active and intentional attempts at identification, but true empathy is not a gear that can be engaged at will. Other authors seem to agree; for instance, Schafer (1983), who has studied the subject in depth, shows a wry and humorous disenchantment in his discussion of the risks of implicitly presenting oneself as an 'empathic analyst' (and anyone who has the temerity to write about this topic is particularly exposed to this risk).

Along the same lines, Brunacci (1994) points out the risk of a certain 'complacency' which may reduce the analysis to a sort of 'running on the spot'. He writes: "I believe we must be very careful that heightened sensitivity and receptivity should not become at times a source of excessive complacency, pursued for its own sake, like an engine revving up in neutral, having no part in the logic of the dialogue, but being expressed and to an extent even acted out, regardless of the effective relationship and the patient's real needs. 'Mirror, mirror on the wall, who is the most sensitive analyst of them all.'"

The author who has made the most complete study of the subject to date, Berger (1987), notes how therapists today vie with each other in presenting themselves as empathic, in accordance with their patients' expectations. Beyond the irreducible internal ideals with which the professional periodically finds himself in conflictual negotiation (Abend, 1986), the problem of the 'decidability' or otherwise of an authentic and deep empathic posture can, I believe, be evaluated realistically by taking account of the complex interferences of the original transferences and countertransferences of, and of those mutually induced (Turillazzi Manfredi, 1994) by, the two members of the analytic couple during the development of the process; these interferences determine whether or not it is possible to achieve an empathic condition, in a continuous dialectic with the analyst's self-explorative capacity.

Even if the theoretical school of 'total countertransference' has made for confidence that the conscious and preconscious experiences of the transference can be perceived, elaborated and hence used as an irreplaceable cognitive instrument, the 'classical' school, by drawing attention to the difficulties presented by the unconscious components of the countertransference. seems equally justified in inviting analysts to adopt a cautious and less optimistic stance on its frequent, direct and problem-free use.

In my view, underestimation of the difficulties and complexities of the transference and countertransference may sometimes induce the analyst to seek to achieve empathic contact by force, turning it into a stereotyped task, a claim or a dogmatic posture.[3] Patients readily perceive the rigidity of such a posture and take advantage of it for the purposes of resistance, or represent it indirectly and unconsciously in their communications, as if they were sometimes afraid of thereby wounding the analyst, but never fail to draw attention to it.

For example, I recall a seminar in which a decidedly 'empathistic' therapist presented clinical material on a patient who constantly complained in her sessions about her boyfriend, as follows: 'When I was sad because we had not understood each other, what I feared most was that Giorgio might as usual try to comfort me by making love . . . ' It turned out that the therapist in question did indeed tend to 'stick' to the patient through his constant, forced attempts at identification, whose accuracy she was frequently called upon to confirm; the patient herself complained of this in her sessions through stories displaced on to external objects, showing that she experienced the empathistic pressure on her as, if anything, suffocating.[4]

Most analysts can actually tolerate not being in a state of empathy with many patients even for long periods, during which they do their best to understand why this should be, but basically remain in a trusting, receptive listening position. Empathic understanding is often achieved after a period of incomprehension or confusion (Simon, 1981).

The reasons for difficulties of empathic contact can be assigned (with some oversimplification) to three groups: (a) difficulties attributable predominantly to the patient and his characteristics; (b) difficulties attributable predominantly to the analyst; and (c) difficulties attributable to specific phases of the analysis.

Regarding the *patient-related difficulties*, Greenson (1960) and Semrad (1969), for example, have described how patients actively avoid empathic contact for fear of excessive suffering; Buie (1984) showed that many are much more afraid of the risk of being abandoned precisely after an experience of contact; while Pao (1984) reported on how psychotics and borderlines make and break contact while constantly experiencing the 'need-fear dilemma'.

It seems to me that this group also includes patients who, although diagnosable in widely differing categories, have in common the capacity to export into the analyst not individual elements or states of mind but entire complex defensive organisations; regardless of the severity of the pathology, these patients have a kind of unconscious knack and penetrating capacity, which may give rise to unconscious collusion, repression, or avoidance behaviour on the part of the therapist; this is by no means coincidental but reproduces in the analytic couple the unconscious defensive style of functioning of the patient's ego. Projective identification (Klein, 1946), induction (Kelman, 1987), tracking (Holmes, 1993) and prompting (Kiersky & Beebe, 1994) are some of the mechanisms that have been invoked to explain these induced transformations. At a relatively unrefined level, I believe that my patient Alessandra had a certain capacity of this kind, which she deployed in trying to make me defensively her 'accomplice'.

As regards the *analyst-related difficulties*, Brenner (1985) and Abend (1986) have given realistic descriptions of the multifactorial internal equilibrium that usually makes the analytic function possible and results from subtle and complex intrapsychic compromise formations. I would add that the analyst's deep availability, whereby he can achieve an effective empathic understanding, has nothing to do with tasks or claims but depends greatly on how *capable he happens to be of making internal contact with himself;* with his memories and affects and with mankind in general.

Schafer quotes Terence's famous phrase *homo sum, humani nil a me alienum puto* [I am a man and hold nothing human foreign to me], which seems to be perfectly applicable to the psychoanalytic situation in the sense of Greenson's (1960) comment that the psychoanalyst should be profoundly familiar with his own unconscious processes, so that he can humbly accept the idea that what is wrong with the patient may well have been, or still be, to some degree wrong with himself as well; this will enable him to understand the patient and to deal with the manifestations he observes from within or at least from close by.

In my opinion, an analyst who is intensely distressed, wounded or at any rate suffering without excessive defences, provided that he has achieved a good degree of separation and individuation, has excellent prospects of entering into empathic resonance with the patient in a manner consistent with the phases and vicissitudes of the ongoing analytic process, the same applies to an analyst who happens to be happy. However, an analyst who is detached from himself, in a state of neurotic depression or euphoria, can surely not easily put himself in a patient's shoes, if only because the contact with the patient would threaten to bring him close to what he is trying to avoid in himself.

As to *difficulties related to specific phases of the analysis,* all analysts are familiar with those arising in prolonged periods of negative transference or acute episodes of negative therapeutic reaction (which tend to be silent and deadly if due to envy, but noisier and more warlike if jealousy-based); in my opinion, however, two other recurring situations, which are typical if not particularly frequent, are less well known: (a) impermissible instances of falling in love, and (b) prolonged sharing of states of suffering of the self.

In cases of *'impermissible' transference related falling in* love – which are usually of the erotised and loving rather than the erotic type (Bolognini, 1994) – patients resolutely attack the analyst's capacity for empathic identification in order to distract him from intensely feared fantasies and emotional contents.

In *prolonged sharing of states of suffering of the self,* the patient induces in the analyst ongoing, pervasive countertransference states which remain for long periods relatively unrepresentable and unthinkable and correspond to similarly unthinkable areas of the patient's experience; the analyst involved in such sharing is usually disturbed or suffering and returns with his patient to scenes of absence and suffering, for a while experiencing with him the impossibility of elaborating the situation. What is happening here is a *sharing of experience,* which is not yet empathy because it lacks thinkability; the next stage, *elaborative sharing,* may lead to empathy.

I shall now present a case history involving both of these difficulties related to specific phases of the analysis (impermissible falling in love in the transference and prolonged sharing of states of the self), as well as a futile 'empathistic' attempt by me.

AN ANALYTIC JOURNEY: FROM EMOTIONAL DESERT TO EMPATHY

Ada was a single, good-looking, 32-year-old bank official who had come for treatment because she could not attain orgasm. After two years of analysis, the quality of her life had progressively deteriorated: she did not go out in the evenings; she had no boyfriends although she was not only goodlooking but also an interesting person; and by the end of this period she had less and less contact with her female friends, and even these contacts were increasingly unenthusiastic.

At this point I became worried; such a severe regressive involution in analysis seemed abnormal to me, and I made an effort of will to attune myself to her productions in the sessions, with extremely modest results. Ada became more and more depressed without knowing why; she had little to say in the sessions, and seemed grey, devoid of life and incredibly sad. We were like the two sailors in Conrad's *Shadow-Line,* becalmed in an ocean as smooth as a pond for the lack of the slightest breath of wind. What struck one most about Ada was precisely the absence of any sign of drive or desire, which had disappeared into the void; in the end her capacity to dream also seemed stifled.

Ada touched bottom during the summer break, spending her holiday on the shores of the Dead Sea, which, of course, lies in a depression and is devoid of life owing to its extremely high salinity.

Since she communicated depression rather than ideational contents and associations during the sessions, I had much time to reflect; and so I abandoned my efforts to reach out ideally and empathistically towards her and was eventually able to formulate in my mind a two-point hypothetical reading of the situation.

The first point was that the analysis was staging a repetition of a severe neonatal depression, in which I too was made to have the experience of desperate impotence, lack of contact and incomprehension, and to become acquainted with a 'desertified', arid state of the self. If that were so, the sharing of the experience would have been part of the treatment; however, it needed to be integrated with a restored feeling of its meaning.

The second point, which is not inconsistent with the first, led to a more dynamic technical approach. I had often thought of the axiom that a patient's silence frequently means that he is associating to something connected with the analyst, and decided to apply this to the whole of Ada's behaviour in the last year of the analysis, which I associated with two memories of hers that I had more than once recalled. One was a dream she had had at the age of 20: in a night-time atmosphere, she had wandered over the terraces and roofs of her maternal grandmother's country house, but when she had almost arrived 'where she wanted to go', she had encountered an obstacle she could not overcome: a step or low wall that was too high for her, on which a big, grown-up man, a lorry-driver, was sleeping. She had tried and tried again, but had not been able to reach her goal.

Thinking of the night-time, oneiric atmosphere of the dream itself, the difficulty of using mother-related structural elements (the maternal grandmother's house, where she could move about only on the outside), and the impossibility of contact with the drive-related aspects of the father (the big, sleeping lorry-driver), I felt that all these features had represented Ada's difficulty in adequately negotiating the Oedipus complex.

The other memory was even more significant: at her first party when she was 16, a rather forward boy had asked her to dance; although she would have liked to, she had said no. To persuade her, he had then begun to pull her by the arm, but she had resisted; the whole thing had finally become a distressing tug-of-war, which everyone had noticed.

But she had not danced.

I therefore postulated that she needed to be helped to agree symbolically to 'dance' and make another attempt to overcome the step in the dream. To achieve this, I too had to 'join in the dance' and change from being a witness (however attentive and involved) to a genuine (disavowed) object of the relationship. The innovative aspect of this hypothesis for me was that an important part of the transference was not repressed – in which case it could probably have appeared in dreams or other material – but very deeply split off, so that, much more seriously, it was unrepresentable and unthinkable.

In a less worrying analytic situation, I would have confined myself to registering in my mind that I had had these thoughts, as with other parts of the field, and to awaiting developments in the patient's productions. In this case, however, it seemed appropriate to give preference to the second track – the split-off Oedipus complex – and I spoke about it to Ada, commenting simply that it seemed odd to me that she never felt or said anything about the two of us.

This intervention was generated not by empathy with the patient but by good inner attunement to what I was feeling and thinking at the time. It did not have any immediate visible effect, but I was not discouraged because I now knew that Ada's time-scales were long. I made sure of giving her more cues of this kind in subsequent sessions, as if every night leaving a sweet at an anorexic's bedside to see if she would eat it.

A few weeks later she told me a secret. Some years before starting the analysis, she had attended a corporate training group led by an expert executive. She had fallen deeply in love with him without telling anyone, and from a particular point on, *she had never thought about him again!* She had in fact not thought of it until now, when she was telling me about it.

At this point I saw this as one of the classic cases when the patient responds to the analyst's stimuli and expectations by producing precisely the kind of material he is seeking. I shall not discuss the situation in theoretical and epistemological terms but shall confine myself to the clinical aspect.

In practice, it was all grist to the mill. The atmosphere slowly began to come alive, with references to the two of us, and a few little flowers appeared on the stony island that was our analysis, in the form of dreams of love with a partner having some feature that could be associated with me, which Ada herself easily recognised. In this case, it seemed to me that representation of the loving transference (not of the defensive erotic transference!) in dreams and symbols had been made possible not so much by literal adherence to the material produced by the patient (which had cost us a prolonged impasse) as by attention *to what the patient had systematically not produced*. The almost complete absence of relational references may, with a negative sign, have constituted the actual analytic material. At any rate, the sessions now became more and more alive and richly communicative, and the release of her libidinal and affective side soon extended to the extra-analytic relationships in her life.

In the dream she had at twenty, Ada was only able to approach the man, without really reaching him, given her relational immaturity. After which – and there is an element of 'due to this' since we are dealing with the primary process – she then passed *outside* the maternal structural elements (symbolised by her maternal grandmother's house). She could not reach that level (the terraces) passing through her mother's mind and body (the interior of the house), as would have been both natural and necessary.

I believe that this had its countertransference equivalent in my not feeling 'touched inside me' (*ein-pathein; ein-fühlung*) by her for a long time and in my not succeeding in communicating empathically with her until that point of breakthrough. Paradoxically, the breakthrough was the result of a pre-planned psychoanalytic tactic, rather than empathic perceptions.

In this case, empathy represented a goal more than a method; and my initial efforts to empathise may even have done more harm than good. Perhaps I was not so very different from the boy at the party who ended up pulling her by the arm when she had not felt like dancing. This is a fine example of 'empathism'! I did not have to make an effort to empathise actively; contact was achieved spontaneously when it was natural for it to occur. Quite often, a meeting of eyes at the end of the session would enable us to retravel our entire route, intensely consciously and with a deep sense of emotional understanding.

In my view, the course of this analysis shows how empathy can sometimes be the *fruit* rather than the *instrument* of complex analytic work.

To end this brief and admittedly incomplete review of the difficulties of empathic contact attributable to specific phases of analysis, it should be noted that there are also periods when some patients have a genuine need to be by themselves – at least on the intimate level-and do not want the analyst to enter too closely into their states of mind (Bollas, 1987). Some dogmatic followers of Kohut feel that they have a mission to 'empathise' stereotypically and by theoretical compulsion; they remind me of the story of the boy-scout who forces little old ladies to cross the road even when they do not need to do so. However, it is important to remember that Kohut (1984) drew attention to a similar danger within his own school, describing the risk of an 'empathic invasion' and noting that what the subject wants from the beginning of life is to be exposed to an attenuated empathy rather than a total and totalising empathy.

CONCLUSIONS

I have tried in this chapter to draw attention to the complexity, linked structure and depth of psychoanalytic empathy, as well as to the risk of dogmatic voluntarism and an excessively intentional and defensive attitude to 'empathising' by the psychoanalyst. I do not wish my comments to be misunderstood: I believe that some degree of identification and deliberate concordance are obviously necessary in our work, and that an extreme view of the 'undecidability' of empathy might lead to fatalism, a passive attitude and ultimately a dereliction of responsibility on the part of the analyst, all of which would, of course, be undesirable. My concern instead is with the maintenance of a structured receptivity in the analyst and the reduction of his residual narcissism and omnipotence, which might lead not to the felicitous and subtle achievement of empathy but to the decadent phenomenon of empathism, in which the analyst strains by force to make contact at all costs, under the illusion of controlling the process better.

I believe that effective and genuine empathy is the fruit of a set of valid concordant and complementary identifications that are thoroughly elaborated and integrated and that sharing is a precursor of empathy, of which it constitutes the necessary crude experiential premise, but not the end-product, still less the guarantee (Bolognim, 1995). I think that at some stages of the analytic process empathy may occur with relatively higher frequency (for example in the idealising, 'honeymoon' phase of the transference, during which the analyst too may temporarily and consciously enjoy a positive countertransference, and in the final, warm and realistic stage of a successful analysis). This genuine empathy can at any rate be facilitated by constant self-analytic monitoring on the part of the therapist, undertaken with a view to recognising the countertransference and intrusive elements and, in general, to maintaining good contact with his own internal world, so that the defensive ego's levels of closure and control are lowered.

Let me end with a metaphor: on weighing the anchor, every sailor must take with him the best possible technical and cultural equipment for coping with the perils of the sea, but the expert sailor knows that he must adapt his techniques to the sea and the weather and that every voyage will be to some extent unpredictable and at any rate different from its predecessors. It is precisely this awareness, no less than the skills acquired, that distinguishes his approach from the rigid illusions nurtured by the beginner.

1 In line with the French conceptual tradition, Widlöcher describes empathy through reference to the 'imaginative construction of the other's subjective experience', the founding element being the representation.

2 In *Mirror Image and Therapy* (2001), Gisela Schmidt, an art historian at Heidelberg University and trained psychoanalyst, interprets this case history as an example of *Janusian mirroring*, i.e. reflecting an image on the model of Janus, the two-headed deity, with one face toward the inner world and the other toward the outside world. Using the philosophical approach of Gadamer, she develops a method of *double interpretation* of the reflections in famous paintings in which mirrors are featured and in clinical material which presents analogous situations. Schmidt used this approach to investigate the case of Alessandra, comparing it with *Family Picture*, (1920) a work by the German painter Max Beckmann.

3 On this subject, Mitchell's (1993) comparative approach is interesting: "The traditional analyst cannot really be neutral. The self-psychological analyst cannot really be empathic. The developmentalist, no matter how hard she tries, cannot really reparent. The Lacanian cannot help being one who knows things. And the interpersonalist who might actually try to be authentic involves himself in the same contradiction in terms as the poor consumer of popular psychology who is trying to be spontaneous." p.191

4 The therapist's compulsive need to verify or rather expect to be in touch with the patient may lead to 'performance anxieties' or the inability to tolerate sep-

arateness. The combination of desire for success and the confusion between the self and the other may produce a painfully inadequate therapeutic situation, which one might describe through the words of Don Ottavio in Mozart's Don Giovanni: "Upon her peace of mind / Mine also depends; / What pleases her / Is what gives me life, / What displeases her / Is what gives me death. / If she sighs, / Then I, too, must sigh. /Her anger becomes my own, / Her tears belong to me. / And there can be no joy for me / If she is not happy"
(*Don Giovanni*, Act 1, aria 11).

12
EMPATHY AND THE UNCONSCIOUS

At first glance, the reader may find the title of this chapter somewhat puzzling. How can a logical connection exist between *empathy* – a concept based at least partially on personal experience, and one defined differently by various analysts of various orientations – and the *unconscious* – a more general, structural concept that underpins virtually all of psychoanalytic theory? Such an attempt at connection may seem annoying to a classically trained, Freudian analyst, who may undervalue empathy, which is, after all, a relational state. This attempted connection may not be appreciated by self psychologists either, who may find my definition of empathy less straightforward and more problematic than theirs. I see empathy as an event rather than a method and I do not view *homo tragicus* as a necessary identification for the analyst to adopt systematically.

In fact, I believe that the concepts of *empathy* and *unconscious* are not as dissimilar as they at first may appear. One might say that *gnosis* without an element of *pathos* is useless to the analyst, who would perhaps remain in a dimension of affective isolation or perhaps of schizoid splitting, if forced to disregard the latter. An analyst functioning in this way would undoubtedly be on the wrong track for the achievement of analytic understanding. The analyst who expects to work in a purely observing, protected manner, having absolutely no identification contact with the patient is living in a fool's paradise (Bolognini, 1991). Neither is it realistic to think that the analyst can simply 'decide to identify with the patient', since identification is hardly a 'decide-able' attitude, and such a stance can lead to the degenerative phenomenon of 'empathism'. Rather, the analyst uses knowledge of the usefulness of empathy to keep his identification with the patient under appropriate control. The issues entailed with identification lead us directly to topographical-structural aspects of the concept of empathy.

TOPOGRAPHICAL ASPECTS

As we saw in the first part of this book, the topographical location of empathic phenomena became the subject of focused attention toward the end of the 1950s, when ego psychoanalysis, with its meticulous, almost obsessive descriptions of the structures, substructures and functions of the mental apparatus rose to predominance within our field. Such attention also produced some benefits: its location somewhere between the conscious and preconscious, but more toward the latter (Schafer, 1959, 1968; Greenson, 1960) was seen to hold up well even in later years with the emergence of related concepts, including Kohut's (1971) 'vicarious introspection', Bion's (1970) 'reverie' and 'at-one-ment', Stern's (1985) 'attunement', Kelman's (1987) 'resonant cognition', Holmes's (1993) 'tracking', Kiersky and Beebe's (1994) 'prompting' and Widlöcher's (2001) 'co-thinking'. This wealth of interest served to sharpen our insights into the phenomena concerned, and in their various ways have had a profound influence on analytic work; and this is true whether the processes are methodically implemented, unexpectedly entered into, or even carried out *malgré soi* (Bolognini 1995).

Greenson, in particular, collocated empathy mostly in the preconscious, and, as we saw in Chapter 4, was also the first to distinguish empathy from identification clearly and unmistakably. He saw identification as a permanent, unconscious phenomenon whose aim was all too often the defensive avoidance of anxiety, guilt or object loss. Empathy, on the other hand, was for him the feeling that one *understands* these states, characterised by its transient nature and by limited proportions, in the sense that the self is not wholly invaded or replaced by the other's experience. Nonetheless, the idea of a close link between empathy and unconscious was recently also taken up by Emde (1999). Though the link is not well defined, it is difficult to disagree with Emde's general statement that the analyst's empathy presupposes a level of comfort with the unconscious affect aroused. More intriguing, from this point of view, are Rosenfeld's (1969) 'projective communicative identifications', which some scholars believe form the basis for every type of empathic communication. These benign communications, occurring on both preconscious and conscious levels, can be seen as having a sort of 'passport' or 'press pass' to various topographical levels, permitting them to traverse or bypass the subject's and the object's normal intrapsychic parameters. Such a 'passport' is instinctively 'issued' by the defensive ego, by virtue of the benign nature of the 'physiological' projective identification, as well as its ability to communicate "without taking possession and without subjection" (Pasquali 1997).

We can conclude by saying that empathy is not purely or even primarily an unconscious event; rather, it is a situation of connection between or among the various topographical levels of one, two, or more people. It is for this reason that empathy has a key role to play in the analyst's functioning and area of expertise, for analysis is not only the science of the deep, but also the science of the deeply shared path to the deep.

STRUCTURAL ASPECTS

The concept of the unconscious underwent an important descriptive evolution during Freud's theoretical explorations, particularly in the first quarter of the twentieth century. Topographically speaking, Freud (1899, 1915) specified the existence of three levels of consciousness (conscious, preconscious, and unconscious), each separate and sealed off from the others. From the structural viewpoint (Freud, 1922), he described the psychic apparatus as being composed of three agencies (ego, id and super-ego), interacting conflictually with one another and each partly conscious and partly unconscious.

The functioning of the unconscious defensive ego has come to be seen as a crucial factor in the dynamics of analytic treatment. Indeed, the portion of the ego that regulates defences presents the greatest challenge to effective analytic treatment, which aims to foster in the patient a continuing dialogue of internal communication, thereby providing the patient with the means not only to understand his or her own deepest mental contents, but also to construct a figurative path around them. In order for the analyst to help the patient liberate the 'prisoner' (repressed material), the analyst must somehow win over the 'warder' (the patient's defensive ego)[1] through a permanent opening of the channels. The empathic situation would appear to favour this process, in that the analyst's ability to feel what the 'warder' is feeling puts the analyst in an advantageous operational position, producing a loosening and relaxing effect on the patient's rigid defensiveness, greatly facilitated by the analyst's awareness of and temporary identification with specific defences.

The patient's unconscious self can then be observed, monitored, and reconstructed in an 'engineered' fashion by the analyst. For example, the analyst may find himself postulating something like the following: "Since I note that the patient invariably reacts that way to that particular kind of stimulus or situation, then I can deduce that his fear could relate to . . .," etc. Even more important, the analyst can then feel and experience the patient's mental and emotional functioning from the inside; the analyst may enter into an internal dialogue with himself along the lines of "I am feeling a strong tendency not to listen to the patient, to think about other things, and to withdraw into myself: What are we afraid of? And why?"

In order for the analyst to make use of such an experience as an empathic one, he must be able not only to feel, but also to depict a sensation with a representation *(Darstellbarkeit)*. The ability to transmit feelings and representations, i.e. to engage in empathic communication, fosters the two-way dimension of analytic interaction.

Antonino Ferro has provided us with some very effective descriptive representations of the workings of the defensive ego. Ferro, an excellent reporter of his patients' dreams (both the sleeping and waking varieties), describes how the most unlikely characters appear in them in various ways, in different positions, trying to sabotage the meeting, work and contact. They seem to fear dangers, some of which are simple and obvious, while others are bizarre.

Still on the subject of the defensive ego and its representability, I am reminded of a certain type of film in which someone with a gun, living in a persecutory mental dimension, takes hostages, usually a child or a group of innocent bystanders. In the ensuing battle of wits between the police and the desperate hostage-taker, a liaison is set up through a negotiator (sometimes a psychiatrist, sometimes the police chief). In some such films, the negotiations either fail completely or seem to work for only a short while; the outcome is then tragic and bloody, with raids, gunfire, snipers and so on. In other films, however, a long, laborious process of mutual understanding is set in motion by negotiation. This usually leads the hostage-taker to experience painful memories of previous traumatic events, after which he eventually surrenders. Though naturally the viewer identifies most strongly with the helpless hostages and hopes for their rescue, he also comes to observe the hostage-taker's state of mind from a more complete and humane standpoint.

Since the beginnings of psychoanalysis, analysts and patients have created a burgeoning wealth of scenarios and characters – most, but not all, anthropomorphic ones, whose function has been to represent the tendency to shut off or divert thought so as to avoid dangerous situations. Such personas include a terrorised child, an envious one, an omnipotent tyrant who forbids others freedom, and so on. When the traditional analytic interaction is enriched by the analyst's growing sense of empathy and an increased feeling of two-way participation, both analyst and patient can more easily recognise these internal personas, with ever-growing familiarity, and come to see them as facilitating access to previously hidden psychic depths. Invariably, such character configurations are connected with desires and fears, as pointed out by Sandler and Sandler (1987) in describing the classic modalities of the *present unconscious*. As they continue working together, analyst and patient come to agree on specific descriptions and functions of these fictional characters, creating a sort of common property that they can draw on in the course of analysis.

In other cases, the patient may initially reject the idea that such characters emerging from associations or dreams are really parts of him. For many reasons, the patient may fear knowing or understanding the etiology of the creation of such characters, and therefore opposes their integration into the self. The passage in Freud's *Letter to Groddeck* (Groddeck 1934) comes to mind: "The unconscious: that gentleman in the green loden coat whose face I cannot manage to see". An apt description of the unrecognisable self.

At times the analyst may be amazed at the degree to which the patient completely *becomes* an alternative character, evidenced by language, facial expressions, mannerisms, and even general physical appearance during certain phases of a session. A sulky child may appear, for example, or a jealous little girl, a callow youth, or a destructive and heartless despot. In such instances, the analyst can more easily become attuned with the character as it emerges from the patient's unconscious, and direct analytic work related to the persona is markedly facilitated. In my opinion, this aspect of analysis is as important as assisting the patient in the repair of damaged parts of the self (prevalent in the approach of Kohut [1971]), or as the perception of the vitality and cohesion of the "bottom of the self" (Correale 1999).

PROBLEM AREAS
Oversimplification

One might suspect that the recurrent expression *empathic attitude* may refer to a specific and intentional search for contact with ego-syntonic elements of the patient's conscious experience. Berger (1987) and Spacal (1990), while making excellent contributions to analytic literature in other ways, inadvertently fueled this misunderstanding by distinguishing *empathic orientation* (presented as a certain type of approach by the analyst) from *countertransference orientation* (the analyst's complementary identification with the patient's internal objects). Such comments oversimplify the concept of empathy and fail to take into account its meaning in psychoanalysis, in that they do not address the complexity of personality structures and interpersonal relationships.

I believe that the analyst's 'complementary' experience of the patient's internal objects, and the analyst's gaining familiarity with the climate, rhythms, and expressions that characterise these, are part of a process necessary to achieve true attunement with the patient. Although long and laborious, this process is also necessary to build the *network* that Pao (1984) considered to be the basis of empathy.

I agree with Orange (1995) that the experience of countertransference may lead to the achievement of empathy and I consider the *sharing* of past experience (both concordant and complementary) a precursor to empathy (Bolognini, 1995). The level of conscious elaboration needed for the analyst to "feel with the patient and to think about the patient" (Beres and Arlow 1974) is already present when empathy is a real factor in the analysis. I therefore propose the following definition of the term: *Empathy is a condition of conscious and preconscious contact characterised by separateness, complexity, and a linked structure, a wide perceptual spectrum including every colour in the emotional palette, from the lightest to the darkest; above all, it constitutes a progressive, shared, and deep contact with the complementarity of the object, with the other's defensive ego and split-off parts, no less than the other's ego-syntonic subjectivity* (Bolognini 1997b; see also Chapter 11 above)[2].

Am I asking too much of empathy? Perhaps. After all, in its everyday sense empathy may be a flash of intuition into the mood or intentions of a stranger in the street. But here, we are concerned with something altogether more demanding, intricate and complex: psychoanalytic empathy.

Superficialisation

The basic technical emphasis on the analyst's seeking contact with the patient's self and the condition of that self – of which self psychologists are the major proponents – raises doubts among some analysts. Their hesitation is based on a concern that almost exclusive focusing on the self can reduce the analyst's tolerance of silence and detachment, which, when the analyst waits patiently, can permit the recovery of the repressed or the reintegration of split and projective elements of the patient's psyche.

According to principles of self psychology, interpretation and reconstruction quite often play only minor roles in treatment, with the major working through taking place primarily in the patient's mind (though facilitated by the analyst's support), according to the rhythm of the patient's individual internal processes, and thus insights are sometimes achieved outside of sessions (Spacal 1990). However, I believe that this view of treatment deprives the patient of a deeper psychological knowledge that can only be gained through the analyst's interpretations, and that the analyst's contributions during sessions are necessary for successful working through to take place.

These differing views pose something of a technical dilemma: should a focus on the self and attendant empathy be prioritised over analytic exploration of the unconscious? Or should empathic attunement give way to neutral waiting, a 'hoped-for void'? At first, it may seem obvious that the answers to these questions lie in the individual factors present in each analysis, i.e. the needs and capabilities of each unique patient (which naturally vary from session to session and even within the same session), not to mention the character traits and personality style of each analyst. But we know that in practice, our decisions about technique are only partially based on the variability of such factors. When we choose whether to speak or remain silent, to display an attitude of empathy or neutrality, to be supportive or incisive, we are first drawing on our established theoretical beliefs and clinical experience, and then modifying these as appropriate for the situation at hand. Since we are 'only human', we sometimes tend to concretise our theories or reify our methods more than we realise. I basically agree with all this but with certain reserves of an epistemological intersubjective nature (see Renik (1993). But since I reject the axiom: concordance = empathy, I would also tend to disagree with this line of argument.

While few would dispute the need for the analyst to be able to 'tune in' to the patient in order to support the patient's negotiation of unconscious conflicts, most would also agree that the analyst must beware of over-investment in such concordance, lest he end up merely 'patting the patient on the back'. Conversely, in bypassing the patient's ego-syntonicity, the analyst's exclusive focus is on 'what lies behind', a phrase which conjures up 'looking over one's shoulder', or even 'watching one's back', implying a sense of persecution on the analyst's part. This may give rise to the analyst's losing contact with a vast part of the patient himself, the very part the analyst is negotiating for access to, the deeper, unexplored areas.

In short, we are most effective as analysts when we neither adhere completely and naively to the patient's conscious depiction of himself, nor remain constantly suspicious and methodically questioning of it. A balanced analytic technique is more complex and cannot be dictated, for when analytic empathy is present, it can produce unexpected pathways to the unconscious due to the loosening of the defensive ego, in turn leading to expansion of preconscious communication channels and greater retrieval from the deepest aspects of the psyche.

It is broadly recognized that the opening of a pathway to the unconscious can be facilitated by the establishment of trust in the analytic relationship, and also that the analyst should strive to prepare himself for empathic receptivity (Mitchell 1993). Nevertheless, in my opinion, no single approach[3] or theory within psychoanalysis adequately addresses the need for a balanced technique incorporating both empathy and a more traditional, "uncovering" approach.

Optimism

There is a risk attached to having too much faith: the school of total countertransference, in particular, locating the experience of countertransference chiefly in the conscious-preconscious, maintain that it can be used during the session as a direct source of empathy, as well as giving insights into the patient's inner world. The theoretical school of classical countertransference, on the other hand, argues that the experience of countertransference is mainly unconscious and consequently to be regarded as a potential obstacle. This 'dispute' between the two schools of thought has been going on for forty years or so and I would only mention here two outstanding contributions by Italian colleagues on this theme.

Antonio Di Benedetto in his *Sperimentare un pensiero che verrà* (1998) stressed the need for thorough work on countertransference as a steppingstone to empathy, and also formulated the concept of '*projective pro-identification*': (the contrary of projective counter-identification) "a spontaneous receptivity capable of receiving with ease the other's ... most intrusive and disturbing aspects". Through projective pro-identification, the analyst can profit from contact with the germinative preconscious layer of the patient's mental experience.

Alberto Semi (1998), while agreeing on the need for examination of countertransference, pointed out that a primary goal of countertransference is the preservation of the analyst's narcissistic integrity – similar to one of the functions of sleep, whereas a secondary goal is wish-fulfillment – similar to a function of dreaming. If countertransference is successful in achieving these two goals, the analyst will not notice it (or at least not immediately), just as successful sleep and dreaming leave no memories on waking.

Clearly, their views reflect two very different vantage points: Di Benedetto seems to place more trust in countertransference, whereas Semi shows more caution.

THE ANALYST'S GRATIFICATION

The risk here occurs when the gratification of the analyst's wishes and needs are concerned, rather than any benefits for the treatment or the patient's *psychoanalytic needs*. There is no danger attached to a situation of *psychoanalytic commensality* (figuratively sitting at the same table, eat-ing the same food), i.e. when good empathic contact provides advantages for the coherence, introspection and working through of both members of the analytic couple. Strictly speaking, this comment is redundant, since it is obvious that genuine empathy is beneficial for the analyst, the patient and the analysis.

Genuine empathy is one thing; 'bootlegged' empathy is another. For example, Turillazzi Manfredi (1994) has pointed out that concordant identification with the patient's infantile and suffering parts may be used by the analyst not to better understand the patient, but to rid the analyst of an infantile aspect of himself that cannot be tolerated. In true empathy, such gratification does not occur; instead, the various emotional contents are clearly recognized and tolerated in a humane way.

Once again, the topographical aspect proves to be the decisive one. On the unconscious level, empathy may be 'sold illegally', so to speak, with the involvement of such heavy interpersonal events as parasitical, evacuating identification. But, on another level where there is greater awareness, recognition of the self and the other leads to mutual respect.

ANNA WITH THE CLENCH-TOOTHED SMILE

Anna, a 38-year-old doctor, presented particularly poor mental activity in analysis: poor in thought, affect, and memories. In keeping with this presentation, her interpersonal relationships appeared impoverished, despite her physical good looks and professional success. She lived alone, did not have many friends and would often fall asleep in the evenings on the sofa, in front of the television, which allowed her to avoid facing the depressing reality of her empty bed. Her analysis proceeded in a rather laboured fashion from the beginning, roughly eighteen months prior to the sessions I will describe.

In essence, Anna seemed not to accept analytical asymmetry: she demanded reciprocal self-disclosure, asked that dialogue be initiated by the analyst, and that patient and analyst dine together ("Now that would be a situation of real contact between two people, not just this play-acting!"), and so on. In our sessions, she hindered comprehension by responding with silence or impatient huffs ("Phew! We really don't seem to understand each other!"), and on the whole, she made me feel frustrated and annoyed. I was unable to build an analytic method with her that would be mutually acceptable, and I experienced prolonged feelings of helplessness and of being at an impasse.

With the approach of the Christmas festivities, Anna asked if we could cut the number of sessions from four to two per week, since she was 'not seeing any results'. Perceiving the functional presence of a constant, perverse, 'self-legitimising' element in Anna's character – merely accentuated by the proximity of the Christmas separation – which allowed her to avoid coming to analysis and to dodge problematic issues, I decided to explore the situation with her directly. I told her that I viewed her request to reduce the number of sessions as an effort to skip therapy; that she was not fully accepting the task of working with me; and that if we were to understand better the motivations behind her request, it would be up to her alone to make up her mind whether to continue analysis or not. At this point, all other issues became of secondary importance and we parted with a certain amount of mutual tension.

In the following session, Anna was more talkative, more puzzled and conflictual. She said that she realised that, all in all, I was not altogether wrong about the situation. She did not know exactly what she should do. Given my resolute stance in the previous session, I limited myself to defending the normal rhythm of sessions as a necessary basis for our work, and this she accepted. When she left, I had the impression that she felt reassured, although she said nothing explicitly about this.

The patient came in for her next session with a tight-lipped smile on her face and said she 'wished to collaborate', making a specific reference to being a 'dishonourable collaborator' (in the sense of supplying the enemy with something and at the same time betraying oneself), rather than to positive co-operation . Although I could have asked specific questions about these enigmatic remarks, I was curious to learn more of what Anna was driving at, and decided to wait for more information about 'collaborationism' to emerge on its own. She related the following:

> I remember two events... This will make you happy!... [with a wide smile] I was with my brother once; we were about five or six. We were in my parents' bedroom, behind the bed – basically, the spot farthest from the door. We had decided to look at each other's private parts, with an agreement like "I'll show you mine if you show me yours." I don't know if we touched each other or if we were just looking... Anyway, all of a sudden, my father came in. He asked what we were doing there, told us off, and made us leave the room.

Silence followed; Anna stopped talking abruptly as though there were nothing more to tell.

It is obvious what a juicy morsel the analyst can find here, in reconstruction terms. There was a very probable relationship between the attitude of 'I'll show you mine if you show me yours,' exhibited by Anna with her brother, and her repeated requests for reciprocation of 'self-disclosure' during analysis. Furthermore, concealed behind the resistance and perversion, there could be an unconscious attempt to resume a process of understanding that was traumatically interrupted, and at the same time, actively to re-enact a wishful-traumatic frustration sequence. But during this session with Anna, I hesitated to voice such an interpretation to her; I did not 'feel' an appropriate point of entry for doing so.

I noted that she was displaying no visible emotions. I did not sense an argumentative opposition at this point, but rather an atmosphere devoid of thought or emotion, typical of my sessions with Anna; her inner exploration, as usual, soon came to a dead end. But I appreciated the fact that she had managed to retrieve the memory and share it with me, and I chose to comment on this.

> Analyst: It's useful that you have managed to tell me of that event. [pause] And what did you feel? Do you remember?

> Patient: [sounding a little tense] Well, nothing in particular... Emotions not connected to the situation itself... the discovery of the other sex...

I was surprised by her answer. In imagining the situation as she described it, I felt that her father's arrival must have provoked intense feelings. (She had been previously described her father as strict, surly and hard.) At this point in the patient's account, my association was to the biblical scene of banishment from the Garden of Eden, as painted by Massaccio.

> Analyst: Excuse me, but on being discovered there by your father, didn't you feel afraid? Or any emotion at all?

> Patient: [slightly distracted] Being discovered... [recovering a more even tone]... but not emotions particularly connected to sex!

> Analyst: Exactly. That wasn't the most disturbing aspect, I think.

> Patient: Yes, certainly. It was a rare moment of getting on with my brother... Generally, we never spoke to each other. But I don't remember any strong sexual emotion.

Anna was clearly unable to think about the real traumatic event, that is, that she was discovered and sent out of the room by her father, who had entered unexpectedly. She exhibited a kind of blindness to the emotional side of that experience. This induces me to be too 'active', giving her 'cues'. By showing my surprise at her not remembering her feelings, I convey to her what would have been normal for her to feel. Undoubtedly, I am not identifying with her defensive ego.

It was my belief that the problem was not so much that Anna did not manage to remember her emotions, but rather that she *managed not to remember* them,. This she did by concentrating on the sexual aspect of this event – an aspect that she denied having any emotions about, but that she continued to refer to and represent mentally as the 'chosen fact', hiding to cover up what happened immediately afterwards.

Much later, I thought about the analogy between her focusing on the sexuality of the scenario (to avoid the unpleasant recollection of being 'banished') and her more general insistence in analysis to have contact outside analysis (to avoid something else of an similarly unpleasant but unknown nature). But at the time, my ideas were still rather confused and I certainly did not feel empathy for the patient.

> Patient: I think it all happened by chance; we probably didn't even intend to do it.
>
> Analyst: But perhaps it was no accident that you were in your parents' room, in a 'couple's bedroom', as you described it, and in a place farthest from the door.

I then realised that I had been 'contaminated' by the patient's defensiveness: I was also focusing on the sexual aspect. Following this realization, I chose not to continue along the path of reconstructing this memory, since at best, we would glean from it only mundane information, not the recovering of an affective experience. I then began to be curious about Anna's defensive ego: for the moment, it was allowing the recovery of cognitive memories, but without affect, apparently in order to put me on the wrong track.

> Analyst: You told me that you remembered two events. Could you tell me about the second one?
>
> Patient: Oh, yes, I remember cracking an egg on a windowsill in my grandmother's living room, as an experiment. I was about five then, and I had locked myself in. I remember they ordered me to open the door, and then they smacked me while I let out dreadful screams. [She laughs nervously, through clenched teeth.] I'd made everything dirty . . .

Although Anna had again failed to describe her emotions during this event, I noted the adjective she had used to describe her screams: 'dreadful'. It was an attempt to portray her emotions and I found it significant. The defensive ego seemed to be allowing something to surface through the preconscious, but I did not understand why. I thought perhaps she was letting herself go because she thought I did not understand very much. I wondered whether her failure to recuperate emotions connected to this scene was indeed due to the need to avoid remembering feelings of fear, or whether there might be something else behind it.

> Analyst: You have told me of two memories with two factors in common: the period of your life – both occurring at about the age of five – and, more important, the experiencing of a kind of prohibited awareness, in secret, after which you were discovered, put to shame, and punished by grown-ups. Why is it that you don't remember the fear and humiliation that you must have felt?

As I said this, I found myself a little surprised by the way I was working; it was as though I were being irrationally insistent by asking her something that, at the moment, she could not know. It was as though I were suggesting what she should have felt – risking further triggering of her defences in doing so. But to my surprise, tight-lipped Anna with the clenched teeth suddenly revealed herself:

> Patient: Because of a part of my character I don't like: my repression. [after a pause] My parents' strictness has had negative consequences.

Here I am reporting the patient's exact words, and the reader will note that she stated her reply very clearly, yet in a way that hinted at underlying complexities. My answer, in retrospect, seems to have been similarly formulated.

> Analyst: Yes, but that's why so many people just rebel against repressive parents.

> Patient: Recognising how afraid I felt would have meant asking for pity; it's as if I didn't want to acknowledge something which has restricted me, because now I'd like to be the way I would be if I'd had a different childhood...

"Be careful!" I thought to myself. An aspect of Anna's defensive ego was speaking to me here, the part that gnashed and bared its teeth, that cried through clenched teeth, and I was beginning to uncover the narcissistic problem that led to Anna's closed and misleading behaviour. Her attempt to forget the fear she had felt was based on the wish not to represent herself as an unhappy child, unfortunate in having been brought up by emotionally incompetent parents who were unable to perceive their effect on their daughter, in the above-described two situations as well as in many others. It was injured pride that spoke to me, and the wound was two-fold: on top of Anna's humiliating memory lay the present humiliation of having to remember it in analysis and show me her scars.

> Patient: When we were between eight and ten, my brother and I were often locked in our rooms, from the outside, because there was a rule that we had to have a nap. My parents were harsh in that way. If it hadn't been for such repression, I would have been, and would be, different. How can I now be a spontaneous adult?

We had reached the end of the session and I felt that I understood Anna very well. Her closing words had at last been spoken with emotion.

DISCUSSION

I believe that this clinical material lends itself to many types of interpretation. Taking the relationship between empathy and the unconscious as a departure point, we notice two key points.

First, during much of the sequence described, neither analyst nor patient experienced empathy. My attempts to identify myself actively with what Anna might have experienced when her father came into the room constituted an undoubtedly useful and necessary natural transition. They were 'attention to what was missing in the picture' – to the repressed and the split-off. But they did not constitute empathy. Indeed, I cannot agree with Mitchell (1993), whilst at the same time appreciating his positive approach in 'attempting to...'. Empathy is not created by attempts to empathise, though this may prove useful in other ways. Empathy is something else.

On closer examination of the sessions described, however, we can identify flashes of empathy. One occurred when I firmly stated the choice the patient faced about whether or not to continue in analysis. This was made possible not only by my allegiance to the analytic process, but also by emerging evidence of the sabotaging portion of the patient's defensive ego. This goes to show that empathy should not be intended as cloying and fusional contact only with good parts of the patient which can be developed or parts in need of help (Schafer, 1983; Bolognini, 2001).

Another moment of empathy occurred at the end of the session, when

Anna came back into contact with herself. The crumbling of her internal defences stimulated a similar expansion of my own preconscious and conscious communication channels, and I was able to feel with her, to think about her, and indeed to 'see' her, without 'becoming' her. This was not perhaps a sensational, resounding experience of great empathy – but it was empathy nevertheless.

A second key point in the clinical material described is the abundance of rich unconscious material. Numerous unconscious fantasies on the patient's part emerged, and these lent themselves to what Sandler and Sandler (1987) called analytic 'construction' work. For example, the theme of understanding could be analysed through attention to fantasies of sexual exploration, mutual disclosure, and confrontation. Anal and genital elements came into play in the memory of the cracked egg on the windowsill.

Interestingly, Anna's memories of her parents' unexpected arrivals and their prohibition of her exploratory experiments do not appear to have constituted the crucial core of this session (though it is noteworthy that the parents may have served as a sort of 'anti-understanding' device in Anna's probable identification with the aggressor). Rather, the core of the session resided in the unveiling of the 'tight-lipped patient with clenched teeth', the one who criticised herself as a 'collaborationist' when, conflictually, she was ready to co-operate – indeed, the patient who had resisted the psychoanalytic process for a year and a half, by refusing to reveal herself.[4]

What had Anna been afraid of? Certainly, of showing her brother/analyst her narcissistic wound, perhaps the equivalent of a phallic mutilation in the role it played in her psyche. (Anna was a doctor, and we know how difficult it is for doctors to be patients.) Did she perhaps feel the need to ineffectively repeat an attempt to seduce the father/analyst, finding herself once again desperately alone on the analyst's couch/bed in an office, rather than happily partnered off in a double bed?

The difficult-to-separate mixture of sexual and narcissistic problems was also evident in this case material in my association to the banishment from the Garden of Eden, in which sexual guilt is equated with shame and depreciation of worth; Eve is typically depicted covering her face with her hand so as not to see or be seen.

What I wish to highlight here is the arduous clearing of a path toward a moment of sufficient empathy, facilitated by my curiosity about the functioning of Anna's defensive ego – and even more so by my 'irrational' questioning of her about the strangeness of her not having felt anything (by which I surprised even myself). This was a rather imprudent intervention, in theoretical and technical terms, but an effective one in this case – almost as though I had touched a piece of ripe fruit on a tree and felt it drop gently and naturally into my hands. What at first glance might have seemed an overly conscious and direct intervention – almost an invitation to the patient to reason with me in an analytically sterile manner, 'in the light of the ego,' initially struck me during the session as an unsettling, preconscious action that in a certain sense preceded my more appropriate reflections about Anna's dynamics. It was as though something within me, outside conscious awareness, had sized up the 'warder' – the patient's defensive ego – grasped how to deal with it, and had identified this as the right moment to intervene in a non-traditional way.

Let me clarify that I do not wish to idealise or overemphasise the value of spontaneity in analysis. But I have chosen this particular clinical material, in some respects relatively unelaborated though it is, in order to illustrate the complexity of the relationship existing between appropriate, effective analytic empathy and the unconscious. Provided that the observations and resulting conclusions I have described seem sufficiently well founded, we may logically conclude that, in the case material presented, a sense of conscious empathy shared by analyst and patient was reached once the patient's unconscious defensive ego was 'felt and contacted' by the analyst – most certainly from a non-conscious level, from an aspect of the analyst's psyche that was pushed out into the open spontaneously and without awareness.

I would label this specific event 'contact' rather than empathy, but that only goes to prove that we still have to agree on our terminology.

Taking a step back to get a broader view of the subject-matter, I would say that negotiation with the unconscious defensive ego is only one of the many aspects to be explored by those who concern themselves with the analytic concept of empathy. Which again goes to show the rich complexity of the field.

1 Freud (1915-17) Lecture 19 on *Repression and Resistance*: here Freud uses the well-known metaphor of the warder.

2 Schafer's general definition of what he calls generative empathy also respects the complexity of the concept and remains virtually unsurpassed to this day: 'Generative empathy may be defined as the inner experience of sharing in and comprehending the momentary psychological state of another person [in] a hierarchical organisation of desires, feelings, thoughts, defences, controls, superego pressures, capacities, self-representations and representations of real and fantasised personal relationships' Schafer 1959, p.345).

3 Wolf (cited in Basch, 1983) includes 'an intentionally constructed intellectual experiment' among the conditions conducive to empathy.

4 Post (1980), in a paper read at the IPA Conference in New York (1979), pointed out the advantages of contact with accessible, preconscious 'focal conflicts' in the session, before proceeding to psychoanalytic work on unconscious fantasies.

13

EMPATHY AND FUSION

I must forewarn the reader that, in treating this topic, I will take the broad approach: since it is a matter of exploring the issue of the great or lesser distinction between the self and the other, between the subject and the object, and in substance the limits of the individual and of the channels of the exchange of communication between persons, I wish to reduce the complexity of the question, at least, by first of all doing justice, on the plane of the knowledge of empathetic events, to a phenomenon (or more precisely a mechanism of defence) that would otherwise get in the way at every moment: namely, projection.

I will state immediately that, despite being fully aware that projection as an event is ubiquitous and 'normal', in the sense of within the statistical norm, and despite knowing the subtle studies reporting the work of reconstruction that many authors have carried out into the complex play of projections and re-introjections of projected elements and further re-projections of these re-introjected projections, and so forth, that develop in the mental life of every human being ... in short, despite awareness of all this, I wish to clearly state, unambiguously and without beating about the bush, that projection in itself and for itself, in addition to being a primitive defence mechanism (Laplanche and Pontalis, 1967), also and above all constitutes an obstacle to knowledge, a malfunctioning of the ego, and an intrusion that is completely disruptive of the possible attainment of empathetic situations.

Projection, just like non-communicative projective identification, prevents empathy.

In keeping with this conviction, I would like to cite a study of an extra-psychoanalytical context which, however, apparently reaches the same conclusions, and which seems to me decidedly interesting.

Bonino, Lo Coco and Tani (1998), carrying out some experimental research of considerable interest, were able to examine, with a certain degree of precision, the behaviour of two groups of subjects ('empathetic' and 'un-empathetic'), selected by means of a version, specially revised and adapted for adult subjects, of the questionnaire for the evaluation of empathy devised by Feshbach, Caprara and others (1991). Ten slides showing individuals with either 'neutral', 'positive' or 'negative' expressions were projected for the subjects. Before showing the slides, assessments were carried out of the present state of mind of each of the subjects ('positive', 'negative' or 'neutral' mood), after which they were asked to identify the state of mind represented in each slide. The subjects previously assessed as tending to be 'empathetic' correctly recognised the emotions expressed in 96 per cent of cases; the 'un-empathetic' ones in 65 per cent of cases. Moreover, the capacity for recognising further diminished in the 'un-empathetic' group when the expression to be examined is not neutral but is either positive or negative.

The hypothesis advanced by the researchers is that the 'empathetic' subjects are "not only more 'capable', but also more 'willing to see' the emotions of others and less inclined egocentrically to project their own state of mind onto others". They continue: "The projection of one's own emotional state onto others thus seems to be a process of crucial importance in obstructing the sharing of emotions".

Considerations of this kind, although derived from an experimental-cognitive line of research, prove to be of undoubted interest for us psychoanalysts too; how could we not endorse their conclusions from our own observation point: "A certain level of satisfaction of one's needs and of emotional well-being is necessary to be able to accept and share the negative emotions of others" (see Barnett, King and Howard, 1979; Underwood, Froming and Moore, 1977).

For a person to be disposed to go towards others, it seems to be necessary for them not to be absorbed by overly negative personal affective problem situations, that is to say, by something that, being experienced as unpleasant, tends to be projected, and which blocks possible avenues of introjection.

Assumptions of this sort have at times been formulated using a different theoretical language; for example, psychologists of the self maintain that the ego's level of functional efficiency directly depends on the degree of integration and the overall condition of the self; followers of Bion set store by the metabolic-transformative capacities of the 'alphascreen', without which there would be an accumulation of catabolytes-beta elements which would ultimately seek release via projection, and so forth.

But the substance of these considerations would surely be acceptable to all psychoanalysts, whatever school they belong to.

Not that this means that they are simply to be seen as taken for granted, especially if they are understood with a degree of subtlety; for example, by 'emotional well-being' we psychoanalysts could mean not only and not so much a state of happiness, but rather a more general 'good inner functioning'; which could mean that, in some cases, a therapist who is in pain or in some way wounded, but who is in contact with his own pain, is able to work, and even to work well, without an effect of distortion due to excessive projections.

This is an experience that, sooner or later, all therapists can have in their work, and store in their memory.

But what I am most concerned to stress here, in clear terms, is the confirmation – as if there were any need of it – of the dysfunctional character of projection in relational and knowledge-acquisition processes: something that cannot after all simply be assumed, if one thinks of the terminological imprecision revealed in the often confused references that are to be found to projection and projective identification.

With projection one does not know the other and one does not communicate with him; with projective identification, which is physiological, measured and introjectable on the part of the other, one has a communication 'outlet', that is, one can emit inner elements that may or may not be received by the other and supply the other with knowledge of oneself, once subjected to processing and subsequent representational integration on the part of our interlocutor.

But it is only with a certain, even minimal, level of introjection that we can know the other, which means that a certain amount of 'receptive' inner space has to be available, and there must not be too great a flow of projection, which would overlay the external situation and the objects with internal elements.

This also implies the presence of access routes to our inner spaces; and if a point of view that is rather distant from ours, that of the spiritualists, would find it difficult to imagine 'entrance gates' to the soul, we psychoanalysts, who are used to making our way between the symbolic and the concrete and recognising biological phylogenesis in psychic reality, may well find it rather natural to direct our thought at the parts of the body that relate our inner to the outer world.

And this brings us to the second point in the unfolding of my discussion. For, among the various avenues that – I am convinced – could be used to approach the core issues of the phenomenon of empathy, in this chapter I would like to privilege one which, historically, pertains to the classic phase of psychoanalytical conceptualisation: namely, that which invites us to recognise the roots of many psychological configurations and functions in the equivalent basic somatic relations to be found among human beings.

Since empathy has to do with contact, with an inner openness, with the preconscious exchange of sensory and representational content, with feeling and seeing (sources of experience and knowledge) that are co-experienced and shared to a greater or lesser extent, I will venture into the area of greatest interpersonal openness, taking the notion of fusion to be a kind of ridge from which one may view possible cognitive-experiential meeting points, without falling into the abyss of confusion.

We could set ourselves some questions about fundamental issues; for example, do humans have the possibility to achieve a good level of fusion without this leading to confusion? And do conditions of inner contact exist in which the reciprocal identities are not lost, distance is in some way overruled but separateness is at the same time maintained and recognised? And beyond that: are there situations, in life as in clinical experience, in which co-penetration does not amount to invasion, and in which commensality underpins the recognition of reciprocal needs as the common base of a shareable humanness?

As Fonda (2000) has observed, in a contribution of notable profundity on this subject, which I will refer to at several points, "it seems that fusion as such has aroused interest in some authors largely in respect of its pathological aspects or in any case in situations involving serious regression".

Few contributions on the other hand have explored the field of physiological fusion, especially in the life of adults. In a panel of 'historic' importance in Italian psychoanalysis on the subject of fusion [*fusionalità*] (1985; published in 1990 in Neri, Pallier et al.), Roberto Tagliacozzo described a fusional position ("F") which, he argued, precedes both schizoparanoid and depressive positions. More specifically, however, Lidia Pallier explored some natural aspects of the state of fusion, securing for them a not inconsiderable 'area of respect' in the physiology of life of relational processes between persons. It is true that Pallier, in her investigation, also bases herself on clinical experience: the difference between healthy states of fusion and confusion, the alternation between the capacity to achieve a good level of fusion and to re-emerge from the partial regressions that allow of this achievement — these aspects she studies on the basis of pathologies, that is to say, basing herself on phobic symptoms and the necessity for defensive avoidance that accompany difficulties and conflicts in attaining states of fusion.

Nevertheless, the conclusions that can be drawn from her contribution go beyond the study of abnormal forms: a healthy state is achieved when the individual is able to track backwards and forwards – both regressively and progressively – with a natural alternation between fusion and detachment, just as occurs between the primary and the secondary process.

This alternation, partial co-presence and complex integration of the lived experience of fusional states and of separateness, has also been described by Solan (1991), who in particular dealt with the vicissitudes of individual narcissism in the recognition of the otherness of the object.

It is clear that the consolidation of a healthy capacity for alternating fusion requires the progressive and concomitant acquisition of separateness: thus we return, as can be seen, to the field described in the historic contribution by Christine Olden (1958) on empathy (a discovery — at least for us Europeans — of which, I confess, I am still rather proud).

Transposed onto the plane of psychoanalytical work, this theme of the alternation of fusion and defusion was pursued in a sensitive and precise manner in the already cited development by Di Chiara (1982), which I will quote here in view of its pertinence: "In order for the analyst to be able to fulfil his function to the full, he must be capable of the maximum possible closeness and separateness. In more common language: capable of an intense understanding and intimacy, and together with this, of reserve; affectionate self-abandonment, and attentive discretion."

I have always found this line of observation very persuasive, partly because in my own assessments I like to take into account not only the various forms of pathology but also the modes of being of persons who are, overall, in a healthy state.

Taking precisely this terrain of observation as my starting point, I formulated the concept of the 'loss and/or opening of the benign border' (Bolognini, 1997b): an event that, on the interpersonal as well as on the intrapsychic plane, is conditioned by the activating or the relaxing of the defensive ego.

The '(partial) loss and/or opening of the benign border' constitutes "one of the deep aims of human life, since it allows access to primary fusion, to concrete and symbolic nutrition, to socialisation, to amorous coupling, to inner contact with parts of the self, to empathy" (ibid.). These developments are usually opposed by the defensive ego, by virtue of mnemic traces that signal situations of danger.

The corporeal equivalents of these benign and partial fusional situations are represented by instinctive and natural co-penetrations in areas in which mucous membranes and liquid secretions constitute the somatic parallel to the 'battle of the preconscious': an area of transit between the inside and the outside, of contact between 'temperatures' and 'moods', of acquaintance between the known and the unknown, of exchange between the I and the You, of pleasure and the constitution of the 'We'.

The experiential prototype is constituted by intrauterine containment, in the robust, adaptable, thermoregulated amniotic environment formed by the mucous membranes. Subsequently, the suction of the nutritional process, with the mucous surface of the mouth lubricated by salivation, when the milk-supplying nipple is introjected. In continuity with this, hygienic caring, with the cleansing of the anal and urethral membranes, in the course of which well-balanced parents affectionately 'celebrate' the success of the infant's excretions, unlike those who are not so well balanced, who experience it as a troubling problem, or the still more pathological ones, who reject it all as disturbingly unacceptable.

In adolescence, kissing re-unites the spaces of the mouth, intimate mucous areas, already inside yet visible, the real antechamber of the 'inside' that is deeper and invisible; then genital union completes the framework of a healthy and natural state of fusion, in which the mucous membranes and moods comprise the terrain of contact, exchange and culture for the culmination of relational co-penetration and for the origin of a new life.

All these concrete biological events give form, by way of metaphor, to psychobiological configurations; psychosexuality is transferred, through symbolic equivalences, into modes of mental functioning, and of patterns of relationship between people.

We are touching on a complex issue that has frequently been discussed by psychoanalysts, but which they cannot lay claim to as pertaining exclusively to their domain: the universe of discourse is full of metaphorical expressions that describe bodily conditions to refer to psychic and relational sharing. What I am arguing, more specifically, is that many of these metaphors seem to draw upon the function and characteristics of the mucous membranes, real 'transitional tissue' between the inside and the outside, with which the intimate exchange of life-enhancing elements between two human beings organises itself and takes effect, from suckling to genital contact (or, contrariwise, the death-promoting elements in pathologies, for example, in the perversions).

A communication, in common language, can, after all, be 'dry', 'poor', 'chilling', or on the contrary 'hot', 'rich', 'fluid'; a person can 'loosen up' or 'rigidify', or more simply 'open up' or 'be closed'; contact can be 'soft' and 'enveloping', or 'bristly' and generate 'friction'; thought can become 'flowing' or can 'dry up'. One could continue at some length with this series of examples, but although initially 'stimulating' (on the side of the life-enhancers), it could become 'over-exciting' (tending towards the manic), until it was actually 'irritating' (when the stimulation is too much an end in itself, and does not issue into something satisfying and conclusive).

What interests us here is to explore these equivalences: bodily contact, and emotional contact, mediated at the intrapsychic level as well by that pre-conscious area that would seem to be analogous in some ways to the 'interior but not totally invisible' spaces whose limits are formed by mucous membranes and are rendered more, or less, passable or occupiable, for whatever is introjected, by the fluidity of the humours; the releasing of blocks and muscle spasms, and the dissolving of the throttlehold of the defensive ego; the acts of looking and recognising between the mother and the suckling baby (who, in Winnicott's reading, 'creates' the breast), between the male and the female, the master and the pupil — their seeing, being seen, and the "perceiving" of their relationship, integrating experience and the recognition of it, opening the way to gratitude and overcoming envy: all these components are integrated, at times, in the little intrapsychic and relational miracle of empathy.

A rare and privileged condition, a flower that opens, a fruit that ripens.

Something that certainly has not been invented by us psychoanalysts, modest gardeners that we are, trying with a great deal of patience and effort, at best to supply the right terrain, temperature and light in our hothouses for this small miracle to be repeated from time to time: in our own way, we do what we can to make it happen.

In his work *La fusionalità e i rapporti oggettuali* [States of fusion and object relations] (2000), Paolo Fonda discusses 'partial fusions', which he includes very definitely among the normal and physiological aspects of mature adult mental life. Starting from the well known passage in *Group Psychology and the Analysis of the Ego* (1921, p. 107) in which Freud speaks at some length of Einfühlung: "One ego has perceived a significant analogy with another upon one point – in our example upon openness to a similar emotion; an identification is thereupon constructed on this point, and, under the influence of the pathogenic situation, is displaced on to the symptom which the one ego has produced. The identification by means of the symptom has thus become the mark of a point of coincidence between the two egos which has to be kept repressed."

Fonda proposes an additional formulation: "When an ego perceives a meaningful analogy with an object at a precise point, at that point the borders of the self become attenuated to such a degree that they may disappear, and a undifferentiated-fusional zone comes to be created."

He adds that, with such a phenomenon, rather than there being a dissolution of the boundaries of the self, what occurs in that they extend to englobe the 'coinciding' parts of the object, which are perceived as various degrees of the self, with a wide range of situations in which the 'coefficient of separateness' can vary greatly. In the lived experience of empathy, fusion is considered to be involved only in certain ideo-affective complexes relating to some circumscribed zones of the self.

Referring to Fairbairn's (view of the) search for the object, Fonda hypothesises the constitution of 'common mental spaces', limited areas of fusion allowing free transit of mental contents between subject and object: an exceedingly common phenomenon in adolescence, in the process of falling in love, in the primary preoccupation of the mother, in analysis, and in social rites involving song, dance, communal meals and other elements where experiences coincide.

I am absolutely in agreement with Fonda; referring back to my 1997 work, and hoping not to offend the purists, I will limit myself to adding to this list of situations the relationship with dogs, as well as noting the way these phenomena extend to a dimension of inner contact between parts of the self, which can procure effects on the intrapsychic plane not unlike those of 'coinciding fusional experiences' between separate individuals.[1]

A strong point of Fonda's study (which finds good allies in Schafer and Solan) is his conviction concerning the well-balanced, properly evolved and mature aspect of the interaction between fusional experiences and experiences of separateness in the inter-exchange of human beings.

He schematically posits three levels of possible states of fusion, from the most primitive to the most mature: a level of indistinction (the 'fusional' level proper) between subject and object, without any boundary between the two selves; a level of fragmentary separateness, in which the intermediate space is not yet well constituted and the exchanges between the subjects — thanks to a similarly incomplete and fragmentary distinction between inside and outside, between subject and object — take place above all by way of projective and introjective identifications (this would be the level at which the process of containment described by Bion would take place); and lastly, a level of definite separation, with the boundaries of the self reasonably stable, and which sees the constitution of the potential intermediate space that makes exchanges at the symbolic level possible.

The three levels interact among themselves for the whole of one's life, and the aspect that for me is most interesting in this work by Fonda, in addition to the part on the 'places of coinciding experience' and the selectivity of fusional states, is that relating to communicational corollaries: both in what the patient transmits to the psychoanalyst and in what the psychoanalyst transmits to the patient, starting with the interpretations themselves, the mix of symbolic elements (pertaining to the 3rd level) and of concrete-fusional elements (pertaining to the first two levels), can be very varied. For example, says Fonda, if the symbolic interpretations (based on separateness) are excessive in relation to the fusional ones, the interpretation will emerge as 'rational', not 'attuned'; interpretations that are, overly-'attuned', too fusional, on the other hand, will tend to dissolve the borders and to cause the contents to be penetrated with concreteness, rather than 'knocking' at the boundaries to elicit the formation of adequate symbolic representations.

This 'chemistry' of communication is fully consistent with what I sought to propose, in slightly different terms, in Chapter Seven: in essence, it is a matter of understanding what is exchanged, how much and how exchange takes place between human beings; through which channels, whether receptive or communicative; and how all this takes effect in events involving empathy.

Like myself, Fonda also positions himself in the Freudian tradition that places particular emphasis on the relational importance of the erogenous zones; but while Freud was more concerned with considering them in relation to the vicissitudes of the drives and the 'pleasure/displeasure' axis, and many subsequent writers (such as Bouvet [1956] or Erikson [1963]) have dealt with them in terms of object relations or relational style, our respective observations are directed rather at the issue of the exchange of contents, in more or less well developed regimes of partial states of fusion.

LEOPOLDO'S RAGE

At times, in the course of a single session it happens that one may witness important changes of framework, involving very sharply marked stages. It is possible to witness them, but also to assist them, if one finds oneself in the right inner condition. Here is a brief example.

Leopoldo is a young narcissist with perverse traits and a strong conflict with regard to dependence; he has been under treatment for about two years. He asked for four sessions a week, and generally speaking he manages to attend them, but in a strongly ambivalent mood that often gives way to open contestation of the setting and of my actions.

Basically, he seems to be engaged in a titanic effort to demonstrate his self-sufficiency, and indeed, to build up megalomaniac fantasies of omnipotence, according to which I am supposed to be more than anything else a 'trainer' able to let him unleash from himself a store of repressed power which – so he says – he feels is in him and which requires only to be freed from constrictions.

My general impression is that, contrary to all this, it would be a very good thing for him if he managed to stay a little calmer, to accept his own limits, and to do what he is capable of; I feel, however, that this view of mine of how things stand cannot, at present, be proposed to him, and that he is driven on by an inner pressure that, for the moment, does not allow of treatment, except that of waiting and containment, in the hope of useful developments.

Leopoldo arrives at Monday's session (the last one was on Thursday) five minutes late, and subjects me to a shake of the hand that is deliberately excessive, violent, worthy of a keen practitioner of the martial arts such as himself.

His face is pallid and drawn, and I notice a false smile on it that is really a contraction of the muscles of the jaw, his lips thin and tightly pressed together.

His first utterance from the couch, delivered in a fatuous tone, with a touch of the schizo-maniacal about it, is: "Why do I always arrive five minutes late? Eh? Why, why?!? ... let's see if you are clever enough to understand why! ... Eh?!? ..."

I feel I am being blown over by a powerful surge of anger, and I have the sensation that he is provoking me directly into a fight.

His tone is such that I feel that there is no way I can even make some anodyne statement like: "Let's see if we can work this out together"; or, more specifically, ask him if something has disturbed him.

I feel that 'it is not just air': there is too much inner pressure, and to say a single word would be like striking a match in a room full of gas. I should add, though, that I feel not only blown over by but also blown up with a powerful charge of anger (in the sense that I experience it).

Humanly speaking, I had done nothing to him; I find myself thinking that I have a job to do as a psychoanalyst, and that if the patient has attacked me and has got it in for me precisely on that score, there must be some reason for it; I can only wait.

Leopoldo, after a short pause, again takes up the cudgels: "Mike Bongiorno [a TV presenter for over fifty years and still there] is a revolting character. Fifty years he's been there, with that jacket and tie ...".

Naturally I think that this Mike Bongiorno is me.

But why has he got it in for me?

Leopoldo gnashes his teeth, his jaws contracted; he is furious and envious; I sense that he would not accept anything from me at this moment.

I believe he is struggling against the perception and the recognition of something very painful and which infuriates him.

For my part, I have to be very careful not to react against him.

I open a mental window on the history of this thirty-year-old, searching for elements that might help in understanding the 'here and now'.

His father left his mother and more or less completely disappeared from the family scene when the patient was three years old. The little boy, left with his mother, who was hysterical and whose behaviour knew no limits, accustomed himself triumphantly to living without his father, like a wild foal.

At the same time he suffered terribly from his loss, but without ever being aware of it; in place of feeling, he would repeatedly act it out in terms that were grandiose and maniacal, giving representational form to (or perhaps it would be more correct to say, dramatising) his conflict, between feeling and not feeling the need for his father, between desiring and refusing his return in some shape and form. In various fields – in his study, in sport, and even in some experiences of sexual perversion – he first found and then regularly castrated several 'masters' of various sorts.

I thought he was trying to do as much with me too, in this first part of the analysis in general and in this session in particular: he would provoke me to make me nervous, thereby to neutralise me and castrate me as a psychoanalyst.

I have written "I thought" and not "I felt" because this is a view of things that I reached by means of reconstructive reasoning more than anything else; at the time I had feelings of anger, I feel attacked and 'sullied' by him (". . . let's see if you are clever enough . . .").

After a further perceptibly tense and conflict-riven pause, he finally relates something of certain unrealistic commercial ventures of his which were supposed to have allowed him to earn some money – ventures that unfortunately came to nothing.

After this, as if he had spat out what was bothering him, there was a progressive general relaxation in him, sensed and experienced by me too. It seemed like the end of an attack of colic, like after the expulsion of a gall-stone brought about by a visceral spasm.

Leopoldo then continues by fantasising reciprocal penetrations of his anus and that of his fiancée, with their respective hands; it can be understood that there is still a quota of violence in this scene, a need to force natural closures and to annul 'exclusions', of whatever type, from the inside of the object, which he wants to control himself.

I think that the interruption of the sessions from Thursday to Monday was an exclusion that he was scarcely able to tolerate, and which generated pain, anger and the wish to deny it by 'going against the flow' (the forcing and the upward probing of the anal channel, whereas its natural functions would involve only evacuative flows from the inside towards the outside).

At the same time, in the scene evoked with the anal penetrations with his girlfriend/analyst/basic object there is also a compensatory fantasy with respect to the financial failure: the fantasy of being able to gain access, without limits, to a fabulous, inexhaustible private reserve of faeces-money.

It is, in other words, a scene that condenses multiple levels, and which corresponds to the various repressed needs of this patient.

His mother, a hysteric inclined towards eroticisation, inhabiting with her son an atmosphere where incestuousness was always just under the surface, had shown during Leopoldo's childhood a limited capacity for containing and transforming: their outbursts of excessive anger were reciprocally and furiously 'flung back' from one to the other, to the point where normally the two of them had to physically separate themselves from each other. Nor, when they came back together each time, did they make mention of what had happened: the approach was to 'turn the event into a non-occurrence'.

Let's return to our session: the atmosphere progressively became fusional. Leopoldo recounted 'incidentally', without making any apparent link, that Saturday he had met a fellow university student, that they had recognised each other, had embraced each other and had 'gone to have a drink together'.

The session ends in a peaceful and calm atmosphere, which I feel able to share in with my body too, by stretching my legs; the patient is no longer tense and he concludes with a fantasy of a return to the womb ("I want to go home and get some sleep").

At the moment of parting he seemed to have got back his colour and was calm. After all, I found myself thinking, what he needed apparently was help in 'getting it out of his system'. Then, after he had gone, I thought that it was not that simple.

In a session of this kind a number of very complex lines of development are interwoven. I was for him an absent/excluding mother for the weekend; a mother who refused the faeces-anger, ready to pay him back in his own kind with interest; a rich and enviable Mike Bongiorno father-figure, 'always there' (transformation into the opposite of a reality made up of absence), 'disgusting' (that is to say: inadmissibly desired, because still necessary for the constitutive stages of a deep identity and for the construction of a limit in relation to the eroticising mother), whom he had initially counteracted with a provocative phallic defence (starting from the 'martial' style, crushing hand shake), which I had experienced difficulty in not reacting against in the session.

And I believe I was also, in passing, once the preceding reefs had been negotiated, the 'willing girlfriend'/mirror-object of the self (the reciprocal penetrations), useful in confirming for him a certain sense of self, for clearly this had been in crisis after the various blows that he had had to endure to his narcissism, the worst of which being the premonition he was beginning to feel of his own dependence on the object, his own reliance on the analysis.

It was, looked at in theoretical terms, a reverse progression, as far as the stages of development were concerned, especially if we remember that the endpoint consisted of a reconciliatory settling down, after so much battling, into a welcoming womb that would allow of a withdrawal and restoration of the narcissistic forces ("I'm going to get some sleep") within the original object, without him having to go on opposing this with maniacal demonstrations of being busy.

But, it will be said: what of the interpretation?

The interpretation, as can be inferred from the account of the session, I did not communicate to the patient. I considered it best, in this case, not to distract him from the experience that he was undergoing and which was difficult and out of the ordinary for him, as I perceived clearly enough that if I had expected him to start on the work of recognition at the level of the conscious ego, in those moments, I would have disturbed an important process that was getting underway, happily enough and in the midst of many difficulties, at the level of the self.

I felt that it would not have been the right thing to do: there would be time and opportunities to complete the work, to confirm and to stabilise, with suitable and properly documented formulations, the comprehensible sense of these processes and the connection with the personal history of the patient.

But at that point it was necessary, before all else, to make it possible for experiential development to occur, without prematurely reactivating the defensive ego.

In short, I privileged, as Bonamino (1993) puts it, "a configuration of the analyst's contribution, the nature of which consists essentially in putting oneself at the service of a process that happens in the patient and which concerns only the patient".[2]

I want to stress the fact that, after having started out kicking and biting, and after having evacuated himself of part of his inner negativity, the patient succeeded in attaining a level of fusion, the need for which he had both sensed and refused with equal intensity.

This partial, temporary, necessary, circumscribed and beneficial state of fusion was the hard-won fruit of an arduous and troubled therapeutic experience, and not of some easy route through prevention and defence designed to avoid difficulties.

Perhaps, falling back on the psycho-biological language to which I have had recourse, one could say that when the patient occasionally reached a condition of satisfactory openness, trust, relaxation and acceptance of his own need and of the availability of the object, he reached a point of being 'able to drink in' the transformed introjected contents, as if they had been easily digestible milk: he had no need to examine them and modify them by means of explanation or to 'cook' them by interpretation.

In this way, on these privileged occasions, a direct channel of communication between the patient and the inside of the psychoanalyst was created; one that does not necessarily bypass the conscious ego of each, just as it does not necessarily call forth its functions of control: the conscious ego functions as a tolerant 'third party' or even one that is uplifted and pleased, but respectful.

Just like a good father calmly and protectively present at the domestic scene of the infant receiving milk, as is right, vital, 'sacrosanct'.

1   In the same work (*Empatia e patologie gravi*, 1997b), I posed myself the question: as regards our predisposition toward empathic sharing, what is it that

many parents, loving couples and even certain dogs have in common with psychoanalysts? The answer: "There are undoubtedly some fundamental elements: a good basic affective disposition, meticulous attention to everything that develops in the relationship, loving care for the fate of the object, and living together at close quarters (or at least intense periods of close proximity), a prerequisite for mutual understanding."

2   Bonaminio (2001) goes on to deal with the analyst's 'non-interpretation' and clearly states: "I refer specifically to that technical tradition – with which I agree – which places tolerance of the patient's regression and refraining from interpretation on a level with, and in opposition to interpretation as a transforming agent for psychic change."

14

NATURAL EMPATHY AND PSYCHOANALYTICAL EMPATHY

In one of his inspired vignettes, with a flash of insight that reveals rich and rather complex layers of meaning, the French cartoonist Sempé depicts the following scene.

In the foreground, viewed from the inside, is the wide-open window on the first floor of a detached suburban house with a garden; at the right-hand end of the window-sill sits a cat, looking out – it is seen from the back, and one notices that it has its head and neck slightly stretched to the left, as if to observe something better; from its position, the cat looks vaguely ill at ease, perhaps even a little down in the mouth; one also understands that it is concentrating on whatever it is observing outside.

But what is it watching? At the centre of the frame formed by the window, but twenty metres away, on the front lawn, the owner of the house and his dog are romping around: the man is throwing a ball with an air of sneakily playful challenge, and the dog is already lurching forward eagerly to catch it.

To just the same extent that the cat is still and perplexed, the two outside are active and taken up in this stimulating game of theirs that gives them dynamism and puts them in close relation to each other, in an explosion of vitality.

At the left-hand edge of the window, from inside, the house-owner's wife looks at the cat discretely, appealing to it with an air that is serious and protective at the same time, and says: "Ne t'inquiète pas. Ils ne s'amusent pas, il font semblant!" ("Don't worry, they are not enjoying themselves – they're just pretending!")

The vignette makes us laugh, but not because the fact that the woman imagines that the cat is experiencing exclusion, suffering, jealousy and envy comes across as incongruous and unlikely, and that the woman is thus projecting on to the unwitting and probably dozy feline a complex and typically human set of reactions: no.

It makes us laugh, on the contrary, because it is evident – thanks to the priceless and masterly touch of a Sempé – that the woman has simply got it right, that the cat really is experiencing those sensations, and that as a result the soothing import and the serious and respectful tone of the woman's message are completely in keeping and likely to be beneficial, given the situation.

We do not laugh at the woman behind her back. If anything, one feels a sense of disorientation at the thought that, for a moment, one has allowed onself to consider her to be a visionary.

More deeply, the real fact of the matter, the one that has a bearing on us, is that the cat, that put-upon and slightly skewed creature gazing out from the window-sill, is really us.

We, we children faced with others who pair off, have fun, exclude us; we who, caught between disbelief, dismay and the irremediable feeling of 'being left out of things', we feel the need for a soft parental voice that will reassure us, that will deny the existence of a reality that is tragically evident and unfavourable to us, and will protect us from the pain it brings: more or less the role of the father played by Roberto Benigni in the film *Life is Beautiful* in relation to his little son in the concentration camp.

In an obscure way, the laugh is thus the outcome of a release of tension: for an instant we are saddened and shocked to recognise ourselves unconsciously in that cat, on the verge of trauma, but then we think, it's not true, it cannot be true, we are not that cat, and in any case cats do not 'reason' like us, and so it is all made up, and so on.

So far so good: the analysis of the cartoon could be continued, but I will stop here because the level in it that serves the present purpose is this: that woman, who presumably is not a psychoanalyst, has understood what is being experienced by a creature that does have the power of speech.

It is this that occurs (quite frequently, luckily) in the case of little children; nevertheless, perhaps even more frequently, it does not happen – projections prevail, and the mental development of human beings seems to proceed in so many cases in spite of deaf and harmful interactions that, in some cases, leave a mark and in others, rather inexplicably, much less of a mark.

Nevertheless, natural empathy exists – I have allowed myself the indulgence of illustrating its workings through the inventiveness of a cartoonist – and it is a common experience (again, I must add, luckily for us) to be able to find signs of it on the way, as we follow our various paths in everyday life: in schools, in the hospitals, on the bus, in the workplace, and so on.

On the subject of buses: one must carefully distinguish the various possible senses of apparently similar gestures. A young man may give up his seat to an elderly person for fear of criticism by other travellers (persecutory version of courtesy), just as it can happen that someone may perform the same action as a result of a sensation experienced by putting themselves in the position of an old and doddery person who finds it hard to remain standing with all those sudden stops and rapid starts.

And something of the kind can also occur in our profession: it happens sometimes that one may hear some erudite therapist reel off an impressive-sounding stream of quotations of texts and authors (those held to be sacred) in order to justify a choice, an interpretation, or a procedure that is not apparently the result of having understood the conditions of the other, in a reasonably convincing way, by means of even a minimum effort to put oneself in their situation; rather, the impression is of rigorous applications of a technical manual that has been painstakingly studied and learned *ab externo*.

An example – to me unforgettable – of this form of behaviour occurred during the period of specialisation in psychiatry. It concerns a colleague in torment because of a fixed idea he had about 'restitution': "… and in this way, at the end of the session, 'I restored it all to him'!", he would announce triumphantly at the end of his psychotherapy reports. And from the tone of straightforward listing of assignments completed, of due observance of procedural norms, with which he reported, as the never failing epilogue to every session, the completed 'restitution' to the patient of any notable contents expressed during the encounter, it was apparent that the patient was expected to store away these blessed restored goods and take them home with him, whether he wanted to or not, because he was required to do so by someone else.

In reality I have made the acquaintance, as everyone has, of persons more capable than others of understanding those around them; at times these were persons of high cultural standing, at other times very simple and perhaps fairly uneducated people who nevertheless were endowed with real humanity.

Is it possible to sketch a general framework of requisites, or at least of favourable factors, which, if present, increase the likelihood of an individual's active participation in situations calling for an empathetic response? An attempt can be made to do this on the basis of the material reviewed in the previous pages.

Thus: the possibility to live through situations involving empathy is undoubtedly greater in persons who have developed and consolidated a good sense of individuation and of separateness between self and other, but who have also kept the capacity to 'shuttle' alternately between regressions 'in the service of the ego' and progressions towards the more mature levels of mental functioning.

Those persons who are able to occupy common transitional areas without the expectation of invading the other and without, at the other extreme, the strenuous defence of narcissistic withdrawal, are at an advantage in this respect, and a fundamental requisite also seems to be that of being able to rely upon a sufficiently well-regulated inner environment, such that the perception of the outside world is not obscured by projections, and that a space of containment can be made available, which the introjected contents can be taken into, accommodating them, learning about them, sharing them.

The possibility of experiencing partial, temporary and purposeful fusions, through relations based on matching needs – whether nutritional, to do with caring, or genital – is very conducive to the setting up of empathetic situations, and of exchanges 'from inside to inside'.

And if it is true that such situations can come about unexpectedly, even with people we do not know, especially in particular kinds of situations in which the usual systems of defence are likely to be working to more relaxed standards or are totally inoperative, it is also true that certain basic factors (those mentioned earlier: good basic affective disposition; very close attention to whatever develops in the relationship; loving consideration for what befalls the object; periodic, intense closeness) contribute strongly to the achievement of moments of empathy.

For this reason it is more likely to be situations involving protracted periods of living together and based on a willingness to work through experiences that will allow of such developments.

In some ways this may appear to be a sort of identikit of psychoanalysts. Are we really so well placed in this direction, we psychoanalysts?

In a previous piece (Bolognini, 1997b) I used a meteorological metaphor, likening the non-programmable nature of empathy to that of days of fine weather:

It could be said that clear, bright days should be enjoyed and appreciated, they can certainly be wished for, but they cannot in any case be planned and brought into being on command.

In effect, the metaphor of the undecidedness of weather conditions, in my view applicable to the highest peaks of genuine empathy, cannot be considered completely satisfactory when it comes to the analyst's inner regulation: for this a certain degree of reliability and functional stability is required, superior by a reasonable margin to that of the average person.

One could perhaps say that a psychoanalyst who has passed through a regular and complex training programme should be taken to be comparable to a person who has moved to a region with a particularly favourable climate, the variability of which, although naturally non-eliminable, manifests itself within determined and rather restricted limits, especially when compared with the region from which the move was made.

I realise that I could be accused of corporatism, or at least of a certain idealisation of the category; but I really do believe that the training experience and the day to day practice of psychoanalysis confer additional resources on practitioners.

I would like to express myself on this point using language tied to daily life: psychoanalysts, for the most part, know how to listen (most people tend to interrupt the speech of others); they tend not to form an idea immediately of what the other is saying, and they do not hurry to give advice, as would be the case with ninety per cent of people when faced with problematical communication; they get the measure of the atmosphere that is created in the meeting, carefully take note of it and reflect on it, whereas most would react to it and try to modify it with the aim of changing it immediately into another that is considered 'better'; they try to keep the process of 'thinking' active alongside 'feeling', maintaining links and setting up connections between things that are apparently distant and dissociated; they are not ashamed to be in contact with sensations, thoughts and fantasies of all kinds, such as may pass through them in the session (indeed, *"homo sum, nihil umani mihi alienum puto"* [I am human, I consider nothing that is human to be alien to me]), confiding in the hope of being able to make use of them in due course to give a sense to things; they have sufficient recollections of their own childhood and adolescence, and an image of themselves with little idealisation in it, but which is rather robust and well-defined, for which reason they are able to stand up to the projective distortions of the patient; as they know that they often, unfortunately, make mistakes, they usually know how to apologise; they are precise; they have a certain capacity for imagination, and they manage, a little at a time, to represent to themselves the things that the patients speak of; and, last but not least, they have a sense of the complexity of mental life.

This last point is the most specific one: psychoanalysts, unlike ordinary people, are trained to keep their minds 'open to complexity', always to leave a part of their mental screen unsaturated, to be able to make room, in a representative way, for new developments in a situation and other points of view.

Here is a small example of what I mean. A candidate presented to me a session with an agoraphobic patient with whom he had worked for many months in analysis. He was trying to extricate her from a complicated tangle consisting of the combination of the difficulties relating to the patient's internal integration, on the one hand, and the patient's own reluctance to abandon some of the secondary advantages of the illness, on the other. Basically, it was a question of losing sight neither of the patient's genuine insecurity (at the idea of leaving home alone, she perceived her own effective pseudo-maturity towards separating, establishing her own identity and being her own person), nor of a retinue of fixed pleasures which she had little intention of giving up, connected to being able/having to be accompanied everywhere by her husband (who was like a brother to her) or by her father (who was, to some extent – in her mind – like a husband to her). The patient's father, an authoritarian type with a strong personality, emerged as symbiotic and hypercritical at the same time, and this made him hypersensitive, in the transference, to every communication by the psychoanalyst. My young colleague managed to focus rather well on the concomitant presence of these factors and therefore the complexity of the problem.

During supervision we had many opportunities to reflect, partly by means of the patient's direct responses or associations prompted by his interventions, on whether the latter were on target and useable, or the contrary.

For example, the psychoanalyst had occasion to point out to the patient the way she hung on to fusional pleasures associated with expectations of maintaining control over the object, which she recognised as having been developed and encouraged although they were not indispensable, and which she gave him support for. At other times, on the other hand, the patient had seen him as being unfairly distrustful towards her and had shown him, in one way or another, that he had not really taken note of her very real, deep incapacity.

My colleague reported an interesting event which took place after a week of sessions, during which there had been clashes between analyst and patient more or less about this dilemma: "how much is difficulty and how much is the pleasure of having control?" The patient was out on the balcony of her house together with her husband, intent on watching the people passing by on the street below.

On the other side of the road, a mother went into a greengrocer's, leaving her four-year-old girl to play outside the shop.

The patient recognised the woman. She knew that she lived nearby, also had a little boy, that there was a lot of tension in the home and that she was on the verge of getting separated. Suddenly, the little girl knelt down on the ground and deliberately wiped the knees of her tights to make them dirty. Then she limped in to see her mother.

The patient and her husband watched this scene from the balcony and were moved by it. The patient's father, who had joined them from behind in the meantime and had also witnessed the scene, commented with a sarcastic sneer: "Well, what a cunning little thing she is!..".

The patient told the psychoanalyst that at the time she felt intense sorrow and sadness.

Commenting on this scene, my colleague observed that it was highly significant on several levels. The patient was seen to be capable of considerable empathetic identification with the child; she understood that both the child's simulation and her sufferings were real, but most of all, that in this case the simulation was a consequence of the suffering. The little girl felt that her internal suffering did not reach the others' attention and ingenuously attempted to propose to the mother another type of suffering that was more concrete and less avoidable.

The patient, but also her husband, showed they were capable of putting themselves in the child's place and reconstructing it in terms of a somewhat complex inner logic. Moreover, they shared the emotion and thoughts connected to this episode. We might say that, though they are not experts in this field, they showed extraordinary psychological sensitivity. Of course, the analytical work carried out so far made the patient more perceptive and observant of mental life.

My colleague, moreover, quite appropriately, went beyond the patient's point of view, which he greatly appreciated however, and added to it with an interpretation: through her account, she had brought the analyst's attention to her own genuine deep suffering, which he had underestimated over the preceding days.

The patient was rather surprised and replied that it was true. Here the session ended with an encouraging feeling that something had been stated, had reached the addressee and that they had managed to understand each other.

I asked my colleague what he thought of the father's remark, a restrictive and distrustful comment on the simulation/request for help by the little girl. I also pointed out to him that the father had made his comment from behind, coming up on them unexpectedly. The candidate thought that the father represented him (the analyst) as well as the real father, and the negative paternal fantasy, hypercritical and heavily incumbent, had been rendered almost tangible the previous week in his somewhat excessive insistence on analysing her expectations of control, without enough attention and therapeutic effort being given to both facets of the patient's inner world (the needs versus the regressive and fixed desires).

In any case, this sequence supplied him with some useful indications. I told him that in my opinion even the patient's sharing this comprehension and emotion with her husband was a continuation of the work he and the patient were carrying out.

We thus continued our work of reflection; pursuing a chain of development through various 'windows' (the greengrocer's shop-window, the patient's balcony, my colleague's studio and the supervision) could in turn generate new ideas.

I will not go further into the analysis of this material. I merely want to draw the reader's attention to the comparison of two different capacities for contact and articulate thought, that of the patient and that of my young colleague. I chose this scene because I see in it the modus operandi of two people with a gift of sensitivity and the ability to identify themselves with others, at least on this specific occasion.

The reader will certainly have noticed the open-mindedness – open specifically to complexity – of the psychoanalyst; it is this open-minded attitude, derived from training and method, that facilitates access to the articulation, further development and multi-layered interpretation of the scenes presented in sessions.

This is a very special feature which belongs to us as psychoanalysts and which, despite our many faults, characterises those who share our training.

CONCLUSION

My first thought in writing these conclusions is gratitude to the reader who has had the intellectual curiosity and patience to follow me throughout this long, but I hope useful journey of exploration. We set off together way back, with the enthusiastic impulsiveness of the poets and philosophers of the German Romanticism and the closely connected medical environment; we then entered the great scenario proposed by Sigmund Freud and his colleagues in the early twentieth century. With a leap, we reached the 1950s and 60s and the burgeoning of studies on the specific subject of empathy – especially in the United States – as well as the parallel development of Kleinian contributions, extending into the decades that followed.

In the second part of the book, I offered my views on certain issues connected with empathy and its rapport with other interrelated concepts. In so doing I also made considerable use of the contributions of many colleagues who over the past twenty years have investigated this vast, fascinating but also highly delicate terrain.

Why 'delicate'? For a number of reasons. The concept of empathy may conjure up both fears and illusions in the same measure. Scholars concerned with the scientific study of psychoanalysis may fear a conceptual and theoretical *reductio ad unum*. For this reason, I should like to state in no uncertain terms that I regard empathy as just *one of the multiplicity of aspects, planes and sectors on which the theory and practice of psychoanalysis is based*. On the other hand, younger members of the profession might delude themselves that empathy enables them to lay their hands on the magic formula to successful treatment. It might also titillate secret fantasies of omnipotence, the belief that a magical natural gift could allow one to skip the lengthy and toilsome theoretical training required of every psychoanalyst worthy of the name. This is clearly an illusion; things are by no means so simple. It is my hope that I have rendered some idea of the beauty but also the complexity of our field of study and work. To use an image drawn from photography, we have to learn to focus through different but interchangeable lenses: the zoom lens enlarges the details, whilst the wide-angle produces a broader overall vision.

But, to my mind, the 'delicacy' of the concept of empathy should be seen in two other ways. One concerns its fleeting and impromptu nature, the fact that it can neither be fixed nor reproduced *in vitro*. In this it is like a rainbow or rays of sunlight between swiftly moving clouds, children's games or the 'togetherness' of a string quartet on a good night, or even the trusting and totally unambiguous look a dog reserves for his master.

It is also true, however, that for the play of light, we should have our camera ready; children play willingly if we create the right conditions; members of a string quartet harmonise better after frequent rehearsals; to understand a dog's expression you need to live alongside him. In a word, our senses can grasp the beauty or goodness of these occasions if we have lovingly cultivated within us an idea of their precious value.

The other aspect of 'delicacy' concerns the way moments of empathy are dealt with and experienced. Sometimes, empathy should be kept in reserve: some patients cannot bear to be understood at the beginning of treatment. Their paranoid experience of being 'seen through', 'unmasked' or 'found out' by another, seen as omnipotent and persecutory, sets up resistance and jeopardises the psychoanalytic functions of the therapist. The patient tends to attack the psychoanalytic tie (which is at the same time both feared and desired as potentially empathic) when he is defending himself against internal contact with parts of himself, which a deep understanding with the analyst might facilitate. On other occasions, deep interpersonal contact is specifically attacked or avoided: the fantasy of coupling, on various levels, provokes violent feelings of hatred and danger. All such problems are worked on in analysis.

The psychoanalyst should most definitely avoid behaving like the legendary boy-scout who helps little old ladies across roads they have no need or desire to cross at that moment. And here we return to the risks attached to 'empathism'. An understanding based on overlooking the obstacles to understanding is not true understanding.

These observations only serve once more to confirm that in our field it is far easier to describe what not to do than what should be done. It is the umpteenth affront to our professional narcissism but it should not lead us into scientific relativism.

On these lines, with a somewhat complex case history, I intend to conclude this long exploration of the concept of empathy. This time I will deliberately leave the theoretical interpretation of the case open to favour the 'long wave' of internal resonance when you close the pages of this book. I would only point out that this episode inevitably contains a small affront to the analyst's narcissism and at the same time a tribute to the largely impromptu originality of the psychoanalytic process.

MR P'S LEAVE-TAKING

Mr P. had been in analysis with me for a number of years. At the beginning of treatment, everything about him seemed to provoke feelings of hostility. Rich and successful himself, he was scornful and sadistically hypercritical toward the rest of mankind, not hesitating to exploit others' weaknesses to his own advantage. Toward analysis, his attitude was one of mockery and, with a caustic blend of sarcasm, mistrust, pedantry and neglect, he had in effect prevented me from working on his analysis for a couple of years. The few things I had been allowed to say were regularly 'chewed up and spat out' as if they were worthless. Yet, in another sense he had forced me to work, causing me to experience, at first hand and for a considerable time, the unhappiness of his libidinal self, projected into the other and there attacked, vilified and suffocated.

He had sought treatment when he realised that though his way of being was of great advantage in his work, it made it impossible for him to have warm human relationships in general (but this was of little concern to him), and in particular it made him cold and irritable toward his children, whom he experienced as strangers. These initial glimmerings of awareness had been traumatic; it was almost a re-enactment of the myth of King Midas. He had told me this with a certain apparent nonchalance, while allowing me a glimpse into his desperation, enough to convince me to accept him as my patient.

The session I shall report came at the end of several years of hard work. Mr P. had by this time changed considerably. Whilst retaining many of his characteristics, he had re-constructed many of his more human attributes and gradually allowed himself more confidence, sincerity and familiarity in analysis, which brought him similar changes and benefits at home with his family. Analytically speaking, I would say that we had become quite good friends. I had also learnt a great deal from him since he knew much more about certain things than I did. In short, I had just begun to like him when he proposed we should agree to terminate analysis the following summer. At which, apart from the satisfaction of a good job well done, I also felt a pang of displeasure. However, in the session in question, we seemed to have returned to our initial climate.

A SESSION WITH MR P.

Mr P. was extremely vexed by a contractual disagreement with a firm whose company name had something to do with 'Bologna'. One of the two contracting parties would have to lose out and it was a matter of deciding which. My patient was absolutely convinced that he was right and was particularly annoyed with his wife, who had suggested a way out which would solve the problem to neither party's detriment. She had not understood his anger and sense of narcissistic defeat. At the time, I did not grasp the unconscious reference to the two different levels of our relationship: anxiety for the psychoanalytic separation by which someone would inevitably lose out (the action against the 'Bologna' company) and my presence as a 'deaf' and rather uncomprehending consultant (corresponding to his wife's advice, lacking as it was in 'psychology'). My mind dulled over for a good half hour as the patient worked himself up against his wife and the company and I began to find him annoying, spiteful, nasty and even disappointing. Then, he paused and changed the subject.

He began to tell me how for business reasons the previous evening he had dined alone in a half-empty restaurant in another city. A German couple were dining at another table some distance from his. He could only see the girl's back and the strange thing was that one of her feet was out of its shoe. Mr P. was a little bothered by this. The girl then began to move her toes around and Mr P. – who was sipping his soup – became seriously indignant; he was about to call the waiter.

As he was telling me this story, I could just imagine the scene and I felt like laughing. Knowing how demanding and fussy he was, I found it all irresistibly amusing and, to an extent, I was getting my revenge for the previous half hour of analytic tedium. But I made absolutely sure that not a whimper was to be heard.

Then, Mr P. stopped talking a moment, turned to me with great seriousness and said: "At this point the woman picked up the glass with her foot and lifted it to her lips. In doing so, she had to turn slightly towards me. She had no arms."

There was dead silence for a minute or so. I felt terrible and deeply ashamed of having laughed up my sleeve.

Then he said: "I know you were laughing up your sleeve just now. But then you were left thunderstruck. Just like me. I think we understand each other you and me. You see, doctor, how easy it is to misjudge an apparently offensive gesture if you don't know the situation properly."

I was left speechless, but not just speechless; I was astounded, dumbfounded and utterly thunderstruck. Then my mind cleared. I realised that he was not just talking about the poor handicapped girl, but also about himself. He it was who had had no arms to embrace his loved ones, to shake my hand, to touch and feel things properly. And he it was who had not been seen as he really was for such a long time. Indeed, that very day I must have been defending myself – just as he was – against the displeasure of our forthcoming separation and had not 'seen' his difficulty in terminating analysis. I had judged him rather harshly, just as once his parents had done, so blind and deaf to him, and symbolically without arms to embrace him. And he too had been hard on himself, misreading, scorning and sneering at his own humanity.

But those years of analysis had not been in vain: Mr P. had not attempted to evacuate his trauma totally on to me. He had carefully sought and brought about the sharing of those 'dumbfounding' elements with me, when he led me to 'jump in my seat' as the girl turned round. I was very ashamed of myself as I said before. But nevertheless experienced a strong sense of deep empathy with the patient, for whom I felt great esteem, genuine respect and a sense of brotherliness.

And my thoughts turned to our profession, so strange and unpredictable that we can hardly ever decide what is ours to experience next.

BIBLIOGRAPHY

Abbagnano N., Dizionario di filosofia, Utet, Torino 1993.
Abend S., Countertransference, Empathy and the Analytic Ideal: the Impact of Life Stresses on Analytic Capability, Psychoanal. Q., vol. 55, 363–75 (1986).
Ahumada J. L., Sobre la vivencia inconciente del analista como "base", Psicoanálisis, vol. 6, 585–604 (1984).
Albarella C. e Donadio M. (a cura di), Il controtransfert, Liguori, Napoli 1986.
Argentieri S., La malafede, nevrosi del nostro tempo, Micromega, N. 2, 226–34 (1992).
Arlow J. A., Some Technical Problems of Countertransference, Psychoanal. Q., vol. 54, 164–74 (1985).
Baranès J.-J. and Sacco F. (eds.), Inventer en psychanalyse, Dunod, Paris 2002.
Baranger M., The Mind of the Analyst: from Listening to Interpretation, Int. J. Psycho-Anal., vol. 74, 15–24 (1993).
Barnett M. A., King L. M. and Howard J. A., Inducing Affect about Self or Other Effects on Generosity in Children, Dev. Psychol., vol. 15, 164–67 (1979).
Basch M. F., Empathic Understanding. A Review of the Concept and Some Theoretical Considerations, J. am. psychoanal. Ass., vol. 31, 101–25 (1983).
Beres D. and Arlow J. A., Fantasy and Identification in Empathy, Psychoanal. Q., vol. 43, 26–50 (1974).
Berger D. M., Clinical Empathy, Northvale, NJ and London: Jason Aronson 1987.
Berlincioni V. and Petrella F., Notes on "Per la critica della psicoanalisi" di Karl Jaspers, Atque, N. 22 (May 2001).
Berti Ceroni G., Molteplicità delle funzioni dello psicoanalista nella relazione analitica, in Correale e Rinaldi (1997).
Bertolini G., Giannakoulas A., Hernandez M. and Molino T. (ed.), Squiggle and Spaces, Rebus Press, London 1997.
Bezoari M. and Ferro A., Percorsi nel campo bipersonale dell'analisi, Riv. Psicoanal., vol. 37, 5–47 (1991).

BIBLIOGRAPHY

Bion W. R., Attacks on Links, Int. J. Psycho-Anal., vol. 40 (1959).
- Learning from Experience, Heinemann, London 1962.
- Second Thoughts, Heinemann, London 1967.
- Attention and Interpretation: a Scientific Approach to Insight in Psycho-Analysis and Groups, Tavistock, London 1970.

Bleger J., Simbiosis y Ambiguedad. Estudio psicoanalítico, Paidós, Buenos Aires 1967.

Bollas C., The Shadow of the Object, Free Association Books, London 1987.

Bolognini S., Empatia. Read at the Centro Veneto di Psicoanalisi (10 April 1984).
- L'interpretazione partecipata: aspetti integrativi della relazione analista-paziente, Gli Argonauti, N. 35, 289–99 (1987).
- Modi tipici di funzionare psicoanaliticamente, Riv. Psicoanal., vol. 36, 607–37 (1990).
- Gli affetti dell'analista: analisi con l'Io e analisi col Sé, Riv. Psicoanal., vol. 37, 339–71 (1991).
- Transference: Erotized, Erotic, Loving, Affectionate, Int. J. Psycho-Anal., vol. 75, 73–86 (1994a).
- Il focolare analitico, Psiche, vol. 3, 349–52 (1994b).
- Condivisione e fraintendimento, Riv. Psicoanal., vol. 41, 565–82 (1995).
- Empatia e differenza (1997a), in Sacerdoti e Racalbuto (1997).
- Empatia e patologie gravi (1997b), in Correale e Rinaldi (1997).
- Empaty and Empathism, Int. J. Psycho-Anal., vol. 78, 279–93 (1997c).
- The 'Kind-Hearted' versus the 'Good' Analyst: Empathy and Hatred in Countertransference (1997d), in Bertolini, Giannakoulas, Hernandez and Molino (1997).
- Compartir y malentender (1998).
- A Look at the Analyst's Emotions. Obstacle and Asset. Read at the 41st Conference IPA, Santiago, Chile, July 1999a.
- (ed.), Il sogno cento anni dopo, Bollati Boringhieri, Torino 1999b.
- L'Io precario di fine secolo, Leggendaria, N. 17, 4–6 (1999c).
- Tenere insieme la mente e il cervello (2000a), in Borrelli (2000).
- Vicissitudini contemporanee nell'uso di modelli psicoanalitici. Read at the International Congress "Quale psicoanalisi per la coppia e per la famiglia?", Naples, 1 December 2000b.
- Super-io fisiologico e sue vicissitudini contemporanee. Read at Italian Argentine Congress "Insegnare e curare", Pavia 9 February 2001.
- The Analyst at Work: Two Sessions with Alba, Int. J. Psycho-Anal. (2002a).
- Dé-construire (2002b), in Baranès and Sacco (2002).
- and Borghi L., Nota storico-critica: empatia, Riv. Psicoanal., vol. 35, 1077–99 (1989).

Bonaminio V., Del non interpretare, Riv. Psicoanal., vol. 3, 453–77 (1993).
- The Analyst as a Person. Read at the 1st British-Italian Scientific Dialogue, London 4 March 2001.

Bonino S., Lo Coco A. and Tani F., Empatia. I processi di condivisione delle emozioni, Giunti, Firenze 1998.
  – and Giordanengo B., L'empatia: condividere, ma non troppo, Ric. Psicol., vol. 17, N. 3, 101–16 (1993).
Borgogno F., Evoluzione della tecnica psicoanalitica. Un omaggio a Paula Heimann, Riv. Psicoanal., vol. 38, 1047–72 (1992), in Borgogno (1999).
  – L'elasticità della tecnica come progetto e percorso analitico di Sándor Ferenczi, Riv. Psicoanal., vol. 44, N. 4, 769–88 (1998), in Borgogno (1999).
  – Psicoanalisi come percorso, Bollati Boringhieri, Torino 1999.
Borrelli F. (a cura di), Pensare l'inconscio, Edizioni "Il Manifesto", Roma 2000.
Bourguignon A. e altri, Traduire Freud, Presses Universitaires de France, Paris 1989.
Bouvet M., La clinica psicoanalitica. La relazione oggettuale (1956), in A che punto è la psicoanalisi, Casini, Roma 1969.
Brenner C., Countertransference as Compromise Formation, Psychoanal. Q., vol. 53, 155–63 (1985).
Brunacci R., Discussion of the work of S. Bolognini, Condivisione e fraintendimento, 10th National Congress SPI, Rimini 1994.
Buie D. H., Empathy, Its Nature and Limitations, J. am. psychoanal. Ass., vol. 29, 281–307 (1981).
Carloni G., Tatto, contatto e tattica, Riv. Psicoanal., vol. 30, N. 2, 191–205 (1984).
  – Sándor Ferenczi e la scuola ungherese (1988), in Semi (1988a).
  – Lo stile materno, Riv. Psicoanal., vol. 44, N. 4, 753–67 (1998).
Chianese D., Costruzioni e campo analitico. Storia, scene e destino, Borla, Roma 1997.
Cisotti V., Introduction to 'Inni alla notte' by Novalis, Mondadori, Milan 1982.
Correale A., Empatia e fondo psichico, St. junghiani, vol. 5, N. 1, 27–45 (1999).
  – and Rinaldi G. (ed.), Quale psicoanalisi per le psicosi?, Cortina, Milan 1997.
De Benedetti Gaddini R., Ambiente di nascita e sviluppo dell'empatia. Read at the conference 'Il trauma della nascita', Milan 1984.
Deutsch H., Occult Processes Occuring during Psychoanalysis (1926), in Devereux (1953).
Devereux G. (ed.), Psychoanalysis and the Occult, International Universities Press, New York 1953.
Di Benedetto A., Controtransfert: sentire, ricreare, capire, Riv. Psicoanal., vol. 37, 94–131 (1991).
  – Empatia e controtransfert. Read at the Centro Psicoanalitico di Bologna (21 June1996).
  – Sperimentare un pensiero che verrà, Riv. Psicoanal., vol. 44, 5–22 (1998).
  – Prima della parola, Angeli, Milan 2002.
Di Chiara G., L'assetto mentale dello psicoanalista quale invariante tra terapia e conoscenza. Read at the 5th National Congress of Società Psicoanalitica Italiana, Rome 1982.
  – La tolleranza tra l'integrazioe e la disintegrazione, in Sacerdoti and Racalbuto (1995).

Egidi Morpurgo V., Alla ricerca dell'empatia psicoanalitica. Precursori e affini. Simpatia, compassione, affinità, imitazione, identificazione. Read at the 33rd Multiple Seminar Conference of SPI, Bologna 2 June 2001.

Eiguer A., Un des traits spécifiques du dialogue analytique: l'imprévisibilité, Psychanal. Europe, N. 41, 20–29 (1993).

Eisenberg E. (ed.), The Development of Prosocial Behavior, Academic Press, New York 1982.

Emde R., Moving a Head: Integrating Influences of Affective Processes for Development and for Psychoanalysis, Int. J. Psycho-Anal., vol. 80, 317–40 (1999).

Engelhardt D. von, Der metaphysische Krankeitsbegriff des deutschen Idealismus. Schellings und Hegels naturphilosophische Grundlegung, in Seidler (1984).
– L'etica medica nell'Ottocento tedesco, Kos, vol. 76, 34–41 (1992).

Erikson E. H., "Identity and the life cycle". Psychological Issues Monograph 1. Int. Univ. Press, New York.

Childhood and Society, Norton, New York 1963.

Faimberg H. and Corel A., Repetition and Surprise: a Clinical Approach to the Necessity of Construction and Its Validation, Int. J. Psycho-Anal., vol. 71, 411–20 (1990).

Farber L. H., The Therapeutic Despair, Psychiat. J. St. interpers. Proc., vol. 21, 15–20 (1958).

Fenichel O., Psychoanalytic Theory of Neurosis, Norton, New York 1945.

Ferenczi S., Tecnica psicoanalitica (1918), in Fondamenti di psicoanalisi, vol. 2, Guaraldi, Rimini 1974.
– L'elasticità della tecnica psicoanalitica (1928), in Fondamenti di psicoanalisi, vol. 3, Guaraldi, Rimini 1974.

Ferro A., La tecnica della psicoanalisi infantile, Cortina, Milan 1992.
– Nella stanza d'analisi, Cortina, Milan 1996.
– La psicoanalisi come letteratura e come terapia, Cortina, Milan 1999.
– Fattori di malattia, fattori di guarigione, Cortina, Milan 2002.

Feshbach N., Sex Differences in Empathy and Social Behavior in Children, in Eisenberg (1982).
– Caprara G. V., Lo Coco A., Pastorelli C., Manna G. and Menzes T., Empathy and Its Correlates: Cross-Cultural Data from Italy. Read at the 11th Biennal Meeting of the International Society for the Study of Behavioral Development, Minneapolis 1991.

Filippini S. and Ponsi M., Enactment, Riv. Psicoanal., vol. 39, 51–16 (1993).

Fine R., A History of Psychoanalysis, Columbia University Press, New York 1979.

Fliess R., The Metapsychology of the Analyst, Psychoanal. Q., vol. 11, 211–27 (1942).
– Countertransference and Counteridentification, J. am. psychoanal. Ass., vol. 1, 268–84 (1953).

Fonda P., La fusionalità e i rapporti oggettuali, Riv. Psicoanal., N. 3, 429–49 (2000).

Freud A. The Ego and the Mechanisms of Defence, Hogarth Press, London, 1937

Freud S.
- Studies on Hysteria (with J. Breuer) (1895). Standard Edition vol. 2
- The Interpretation of Dreams (1900). Standard Edition vols. 4 and 5.
- Jokes and their Relation to the Unconscious (1905). Standard Edition vol. 8.
- Delusions and Dreams in Jensen's 'Gradiva' (1907). Standard Edition vol. 9.
- The future prospects of psycho-analytic therapy (1910). Standard Edition vol. 11.
- Recommendations to physicians practising psycho-analysis (1912). Standard Edition vol. 12.
- Totem and Taboo (1913). Standard Edition vol. 13.
- On beginning the treatment (1913). Standard Edition vol. 12.
- Observations on Transference Love (1915). Standard Edition vol. 12.
- Papers on Metapsychology (1915). Standard Edition vol. 14.
- Introductory Lectures on Psycho- Analysis (1916). Standard Edition vols. 15 and 16.
- Group Psychology and the Analysis of the Ego (1921). Standard Edition vol. 18.
- The Ego and the Id (1923). Standard Edition vol. 19.
- Inhibitions, Symptoms and Anxiety (1926). Standard Edition vol. 20.
- New Introductory Lectures on Psycho-Analysis (1932). Standard Edition vol. 22.
- Letter to Groddeck (1934). Standard Edition vol. 22.
- Analysis Terminable and Interminable (1937). Standard Edition vol. 23.
- Lettere a Wilhelm Fliess 1887-1904, Bollati Boringhieri, Torino 1991.
- Lettere tra Freud e Jung, Bollati Boringhieri, Torino 1991.

Fries M. E., Problems of Communication between Therapist and Patients with Archaic Ego Functions, J. Hillside Hosp., vol. 41, 136–60 (1968).

Gabbard, G. (1990). Psychodynamic Psychiatry in Clinical Practice, Amer.Psychiatric Press Washington, DC/London.Gaddini E., On Imitation, Int. J. Psycho-Anal., vol. 50, 475–84 (1969).

Gambara A., Stati affettivi perduranti nell'analista: la "situazione globale" del controtransfert. Read at the 9th National Conference SPI, Saint Vincent 1990.

Giaconia G., Pellizzari G. and Rossi P., Nuovi fondamenti per la tecnica psicoanalitica, Borla, Roma 1997.

Giannakoulas A., Il paziente difficile. The Borderline Engagement. Read at Centro Psicoanalitico di Bologna (27 February 1996).
- Empatia. Considerazioni cliniche. Read at the AIPSI Seminar, Rome 20 January 2002.

Gitelson M., The Emotional Position of the Analyst in the Psychoanalytic Situation, Int. J. Psycho-Anal., vol. 33, 1–10 (1952).

Goldberg A., The Psychology of the Self. A Casebook, International Universities Press, New York 1978.

Greenson R. R., The Struggle against Identification (1954).

- Empathy and Its Vicissitudes (1960).
- That 'Impossible' Profession (1966).
- Transference: Freud or Klein? (1974).
- Explorations in Psychoanalysis, International Universities Press, New York 1978.

Grinberg L., Sor D. and Tabak de Bianchedi E., (1975), Introduction to the Work of Bion, Karnac Books, London.

Groddeck G., Carteggio Freud-Groddeck, 1917–1934, Adelphi, Milan 1973.

Grotstein J., Splitting and Projective Identification., New York: Aronson.

- Projective Identification and Countertransference. Brief Commentary on the Relationship, Contemp. Psychoanal., vol. 30, 578–92 (1994).

Heimann P., On Countertransference, Int. J. Psycho-Anal., vol. 31, 81–84 (1950).

- About Children and Children no-longer, Tavistock-Routledge, London 1989.

Hinshelwood R. D., Dictionary of Kleinian Thought (1989), Free Association Books London.

Holmes J., John Bowlby and Attachment Theory, Routledge, London 1993.

Hufeland C. W., Über Sympathie (1811), in Engelhardt (1984).

Jaspers K., Allgemeine Psychopathologie (1913).

Jogan E., Commento allo scritto di S. Spacal 'Empatia e controtransfert come parti costitutive della comprensione analitica'. Read at the Centro Veneto di Psicoanalisi (12 October 1990).

Jones E., The Life and Work of Sigmund Freud, 3 voll., Basic Books, New York 1957.

Kamla H., Novalis Hymnen an die Nacht (1945), in Cisotti (1982).

Kelman H., On Resonant Cognition, Int. Rev. Psychoanal., vol. 14, 111–24 (1987).

Kernberg O. F., Borderline Syndromes and Pathological Narcissism (1975).

- Projection, Identification, Projective Identification, in Sandler J. (ed) (1988) Karnac Books, London.
- Psychodynamic Psychotherapy of Borderline Patients, Basic Books, New York 1989.
- Convergences and Divergences in Contemporary Psychoanalytic Technique, Int. J. Psycho-Anal., vol. 14, 659–73 (1993).

Kiersky S. e Beebe B., The Reconstruction of Early Nonverbal Relatedness in the Treatment of Difficult Patients: a Special Form of Empathy, Psychoanal. Dialogues, vol. 4, 389–498 (1994).

Klein M., Notes on Some Schizoid Mechanisms, in M.Klein et al. (eds.), Developments in Psychoanalysis, Hogarth Press, London (1952).

- On Identification.
- Klein, M.. Our Adult World and Other Essays, (1963): Heinemann Medical Books, London.
- Scritti 1921–1958, Boringhieri, Torino 1978.
- Heimann P. and Money-Kyrle R. (eds.), New Directions in Psycho-Analysis, Tavistock, London 1955.

Kohut H., Introspection, Empathy and Psychoanalysis: an Examination of the Relationship between Mode of Observation and Theory (1959) In P.H. Ornstein (Ed.), The Search for the Self (Vol. 1, pp. 205-232), International Universities Press, New York.
– The Analysis of the Self, International Universities Press, New York 1971.
– The Restoration of the Self, International Universities Press, New York 1977.
– How Does Analysis Cure?, University of Chicago Press, Chicago 1984.

Kris E., Ricerche psicoanalitiche sull'arte (1952), Einaudi, Torino 1973.

Laplanche J. and Pontalis J.-B., Vocabulaire de la psychanalyse, Presses Universitaires de France, Paris 1967.

Lichtenberg J. D., Lachmann F. M. and Fosshage J. L., Self and Motivational Systems: toward a Theory of Psychoanalytic Technique, Analytic Press, Hillsdale 1992.

Lipps T., Das Wissen from fremden Ichen, Psychol. Unt., vol. 4, 494–722 (1905).
– Aesthetik: Psychologie des Schönen und der Kunst, vol. 2, Die aesthetische Betrachtung und die bildende Kunst, Voss, Hamburg 1906.

Lopez D., Al di là della follia, al di là della saggezza, Guaraldi, Firenze 1976.

McDougall J., Winnicott Fifty Years ago. Read at the International Conference 'Winnicott in 2000', Università di Milano-Bicocca, 18 November 2000.

Milella M., Autorappresentazione: autoreferenzialità ed incontro. Read at the 9th Colloquio italo-francese, Bologna 24 November 2001.

Milner M., 'The Role of Illusion in Symbol-Formation' (1955), in New Directions in Psychoanalysis, ed. M. Klein et al.; republished in Milner (1987), pp. 83-113

Mitchell S. A., Influence and Autonomy in Psychoanalysis, Analytic Press, Hillsdale 1993.
– and Aron L. (ed.), Relational Psychoanalysis: the Emergence of a Tradition, Analytic Press, Hillsdale 1999.

Modell A. H., Other Times, Other Realities. Toward a Theory of Psychoanalytic Treatment, Harvard University Press, Cambridge, Mass. 1990.

Money-Kyrle R., Psychoanalysis and Politics, Duckworth, London 1951.
– Normal Countertransference and Some of Its Deviations (1956).
– Cognitive Development (1968).
– Papers 1927–1977, Clunie Press, Perthshire 1978.

Muller J. P., Beyond the Psychoanalytic Dyad, Routledge, New York 1996.

Neri C., Pallier L., Petacchi G., Soavi G. C. and Tagliacozzo R., Fusionalità, Borla, Roma 1990.

Novalis (F. C. von Hardenberg), The Novices of Sais. Sixty Drawings by Paul Klee. Preface by Stephen Spender. Translation from the German original by Ralph Manheim. (1949) Published by Curt Valentin. New York.

Olden C., Notes on the Development of Empathy, Psychoanal. St. Child, vol. 13, 505–18 (1958).

Orange D., Emotional Understanding, Guilford, New York 1995.

Pao P. N., Schizophrenic Disorders, International Universities Press, New York 1979.

– Therapeutic Empathy in the Schizophrenic. Empathy II, Analytic Press, Hillsdale 1984.

Pasquali G., L'empatia e la clinica. Read at the International Conference 'Lo psichesoma', Milan April 1997.

Petrella F., Percezione endopsichica/fenomeno funzionale, Riv. Psicoanal., vol. 39, 101–20 (1993).

Pick I., Working-through in the Countertransference, Int. J. Psycho-Anal., vol. 66, 157–66 (1985).

Pigman G. W., Freud and the History of Empathy, Int. J. Psycho-Anal., vol. 76, 237–54 (1995).

Post S. L., Origins, Elements and Functions of Therapeutic Empathy, Int. J. Psycho-Anal., vol. 61, 277–93 (1980).

Racalbuto A., Tra il fare e il dire. L'esperienza dell'inconscio e del non verbale in psicoanalisi, Cortina, Milan 1994.

Racker H., A Contribution to the Problem of Countertransference, Int. J. Psycho-Anal., vol. 34, 313–24 (1953).

– The meanings and uses of countertransference (1957), Psychoanalytic Quarterly. 26, 303-357.

– Countertransference and Interpretation, J. am. psychoanal. Ass., vol. 6, 215–21 (1958).

– Transference and Countertransference, International Universities Press, New York 1968.

Reich A., On Countertransference (1951).

– On Countertransference, Int. J. Psycho-Anal., vol. 41, 389–95 (1960).

Renik O., Analytic Interaction: Conceptualizing Technique in Light of the Analyst's Irreducible Subjectivity, Psychoanal. Q., vol. 62, 553–71 (1993).

Riolo F., Sogno e teoria della conoscenza in psicoanalisi, Riv. Psicoanal., vol. 29, N. 3 (1983).

Rosenfeld H., Psychotic States (1965).

– The Importance of Projective Identification in the Ego Structure and the Object Relations of the Psychotic States. Read at the International Colloquium on Psychoses, Montreal November 1969.

– A Clinical Approach to the Psychoanalytic Theory of the Life and Death Instincts: an Investigation into the Aggressive Aspects of Narcissism, Int. J. Psycho-Anal., vol. 52, 169–78 (1971).

– A Discussion of the Paper by Ralph Greenson on "Transference: Freud or Klein?", Int. J. Psycho-Anal., vol. 55 (1974).

– Impasse and Interpretation, Tavistock, London 1987.

Ruggiero L., Nevrosi e salute psichica. La nevrosi ossessiva e la psicologia del Sé, Lombardo, Roma 1996.

Rumi M., Sentire insieme. Evoluzione del concetto di empatia in psicoanalisi. Graduate thesis, University of Padua 2000.

– L'empatia psicoanalitica dalle origini ai nostri giorni, Psichiat. gen. Età evol.,

vol. 39, N. 1 (2002).
Rupp P., La disperazione dello psicoanalista (1954), Marsilio, Padova 1974.
Russo L., L'Io, il doppio, il rivale. Read at the 9th Colloquio italo-francese, Bologna 25 November 2001.
Sacerdoti G. and Racalbuto A. (eds), Tolleranza e intolleranza, Bollati Boringhieri, Torino 1995.
– (eds), Differenza, indifferenza, differimento, Dunod, Milan 1997.
Sandler J., Countertransference and role-responsiveness, (1976), Int. Rev. Psychoanal., 3:43-48.
– Projection, Identification, Projective Identification, International Universities Press, New York 1988.
– On Communication from Patient to Analyst: not everything Is Projective Identification, Int. J. Psycho-Anal., vol. 74, 1097–117 (1993).
– and Sandler A.-M., The Past Unconscious, the Present Unconscious, and the Vicissitudes of Guilt, Int. J. Psycho-Anal., vol. 68, 331–42 (1987).
Schafer R., Generative Empathy in the Treatment Situation, Psychoanal. Q., vol. 28, 342–73 (1959).
– Aspects of Internalization, International Universities Press, New York 1968.
– The Psychoanalytic Vision of Reality, in A New Language for Psychoanalysis, Yale University Press, New York 1970.
– The Analytic Attitude, Basic Books, New York 1983.
Schlesinger H. J., How the Analyst Listens: the Pre-Stage of Interpretation, Int. J. Psycho-Anal., vol. 75, 31–38 (1994).
Schmidt G., Mirror Image and Therapy, Peter Lang, Bern 2001.
Schubert G. H., Briefe über das Studium der Medizin (1805), in Engelhardt (1984).
Searles H. F., Countertransference and Related Subjects, International Universities Press, New York 1979.
Seidler E. (ed), Medizinische Anthropologie, Berlin 1984.
Semi A. A., Tecnica del colloquio, Cortina, Milan 1985.
– (ed), Trattato di psicoanalisi, vol. 1, Cortina, Milan 1988a.
– La funzione delle teorie e delle differenze teoriche in psicoanalisi (1988b), in Semi (1988a).
– Il transfert nell'ottica freudiana: una nota, Riv. Psicoanal., vol. 44, 319–28 (1998).
Semrad E. V., Teaching Psychotherapy of Psychotic Patients, Grune & Stratton, New York 1969.
Simon B., Confluence of Visual Image between Patient and Analyst: Communication of Failed Communication, Psychoanal. Inq., vol. 1 (1981).
Smith H. F., Analytic Listening and the Experience of Surprise, Int. J. Psycho-Anal., vol. 76, 67–78 (1995).
Solan R., "Jointness" as Integration of Merging and Separateness in Object Relations and Narcissism, Psychoanal. St. Child, vol. 46, 337–52 (1991).
Spacal S., Empatia e controtransfert come parti costitutive della comprensione psi-

coanalitica. Read at the Veneto-Emilia Psychoanalytic Meeting, 10 March 1990.

Spezzano C., The Triangle of Clinical Judgement, J. am. psychoanal. Ass., vol. 2, 365–88 (1998).

Stein E., On the Problem of Empathy, (1970), The Hague: Martinus Nijhoff. Trans. by Waltraut Stein of Zum Problem der Einfühlung [Originally published (1917)]

Stern D. N., The Interpersonal World of the Infant, Basic Books, New York 1985.

Strayer J., Children's Concordant Emotions and Cognitions in Response to Observed Emotions, Child Dev., vol. 64, 188–2001 (1993).

Strenger C., The Classic and the Romantic Vision in Psychoanalysis, Int. J. Psycho-Anal., vol. 70, 593–610 (1989).

Titchener E., Experimental Psychology of the Thought Processes, McMillan, New York 1909.

Tuch R. H., Beyond Empathy: Confronting Certain Complexities in Self Psychology Theory, Psychoanal. Q., vol. 66, 259–82 (1997).

Turillazzi Manfredi S., Le certezze perdute della psicoanalisi clinica, Cortina, Milan 1994.

Underwood B., Froming W. G. e Moore B. S., Mood, Attention and Altruism: a Search for Mediating Variables, Dev. Psychol., vol. 13, 541 sg. (1977).

Viederman M., The Real Person of the Analyst and His Role in the Process of Psychoanalytic Cure, J. am. psychoanal. Ass., vol. 39, 451–89 (1991).

Vischer T., Aesthetik oder Wissenschaft der Schönen (1846).

Wallerstein R. S., One Psychoanalysis or Many?, Int. J. Psycho-Anal., vol. 69, 5–21 (1988).

Weiss E., Sigmund Freud as a Consultant (1970) Basic Books, New York.

Widlöcher D., The Treatment of Affects: an Interdisciplinary Issue, Psychoanal. Q., vol. 70, 243–64 (2001).

Winnicott D. W., Hate in the Counter-Transference (1947) in Collected Papers Through paediatrics to psycho-analysis (1958) Tavistock Publications, London.
– From Paediatrics to Psycho-Analysis (1958) Tavistock Publications, London.
– The Maturational Processes and the Facilitating Environment, Hogarth Press, London 1965.
– Playing and Reality, Tavistock, London 1971.

Wisdom J. O., A Methodological Approach to the Problem of Hystery, Int. J. Psycho-Anal., vol. 42, 224–37 (1961).

Zucchini G., Psicoanalisi e sogno: clinica e teoria (1989).

INDEX

Abbagnano, N. 28
Abend, S. 84, 128
Ahumada, J. L. 99
Albarella, C. 34
Argentieri, Simona 116
Arlow, J. A. 92, 141

Baranger, M. 95
Barnett, M. A. 154
Basch, M. F. 151
Beckmann, Max 134
Benedetto, Antonio Di 58, 81, 84, 92–93, 143
Benigni, Roberto 168
Berger, D. M. 37, 59, 119, 127, 140
de Bianchedi, Tabak 56
Bion, W. R. 17, 52, 56–58, 137
Bleger, José 110
Bollas, C. 63, 77, 99
Bolognini, Stephano 9, 10, 12, 72, 83, 90, 93, 129, 133, 136–137, 141, 149, 157, 170
Bonaminio, V. 165, 166
Bonino, S. 83, 104, 154
Borgogno, F. 40, 56, 95
Bourguignon, A. 31
Brenner, C. 92, 128
Brunacci, R. 126
Buie, D. H. 128

Campbell, Donald 12
Carloni, G. 40, 80
Ceroni, Berti 21

Chianese, D. 71
Chiara, Giuseppe Di 17, 43, 80, 157
Cisotti, V. 26
Corel 96
Correale, A. 28, 140

Daninos, P. 71
Deutsch, Helene 36, 119

Eiguer, A. 96
Emde, R. 137
Engelhard, Von 27, 28

Faimberg, H. 96
Fenichel, O. 51
Ferenczi, Sándor 32, 37, 38
Ferro, Antonino 56, 139
Feshbach, N. 104, 154
Fine, Robert 33
Fliess, Robert 39, 92
Fonda, Paolo 156, 159, 160
Freud, S. 9, 17, 26, 28, 30–35, 50–51, 56, 74, 84, 108, 138, 151, 161, 175
Fries, M. E. 41
Fromm-Reichman, Frieda 51

Gabbard, G. 111
Gaddini, Eugenio 53
Gaddini, Renata de Benedetti 41
Gambara, A. 115
Giannakoulas, A. 21, 117
Gitelson, M. 92

INDEX

Goldberg, A. 62–64, 121
Greenson, R. R. 18, 42, 46, 47, 53, 75, 77, 118, 128, 137
Grinberg, L. 56
Groddeck, G. 140
Grotstein, J. 57-58

Heinmann, P. 92
Hinshelwood, R. D. 55
Holmes, J. 128
Hufeland, C. W. 27

Jogan, E. 121
Jones, Ernest 26, 47

Kamla, H. 27
Kelman, H. 77, 128, 137
Kernberg, O. F. 17, 47, 63, 110, 120–121
Kerner, Justinus 28
Khan, Masud 99
Kiersky, S. 128, 137
Klein, M. 17, 55–56, 58, 70, 115, 128
Kohut, H. 17, 48–50, 56, 63, 70, 118, 121-122, 133, 137, 140
Kohut, Heinz 42, 47
Kris, E. 46, 79

Laplanche, J. 153
Lichtenberg, J. D. 93
Lipps, Theodor 28, 31
Lo Coco, A. 83, 154
Lopez, D. 78

Manfredi, Stefania Turillazzi 43, 127, 144
McDougall, Joyce 17
Milella, M. 78
Miller, Alice 110
Milner, M. 72
Mitchell, S. A. 17, 81, 134, 142, 149
Modell, A. H. 126
Money-Kyrle, Roger 55, 56, 99
Morpurgo, Egidi 28

Neri, C. 156
Novalis, F. C. von Hardenberg 25–26

Olden, Christine 42–43, 45, 49, 53, 62, 118, 157
Orange, D. 93, 141

Pao, Ping-Nie 42, 51, 52, 92, 128
Pasquali, G. 138
Petrella, Fausto 35
Pick, I. 92
Pigman, G. W. 30–32
Pontalis 70, 153
Post, S. L. 152

Racalbuto, A. 81
Racker, H. A. 40, 92, 119
Reich, A. 92, 96
Renik, O. 142
Riolo, F. 38
Rosenfeld, H. 18, 40, 55, 62, 64, 110, 114, 137
Ruggiero, L. 116
Rumi, M. 26
Russo, Lucio 105

Sandler, J. 96, 140, 150
Schafer, Roy 33, 40, 42, 44, 45, 47, 49-50, 52-53, 77, 103, 111, 118, 129, 137, 149, 151
Schmidt, Gisela 134
Searles, H. F. 92
Semi, Alberto 18, 143
Semrad, E. V. 128
Smith, H. F. 96
Solan, R. 157
Spacal, Savo 59–60, 62–63, 65–66, 120–121, 140–141
Stein, Edith 28
Stern, D. N. 137
Strayer, J. 104
Sullivan, Harry Stack 51

Tagliacozzo, Roberto 156
Tani 83, 104, 154
Titchener, E. 25
Tuch, R. H. 85

Underwood, B. 154

Viederman, M. 95, 106
Vischer, Theodor 27

Weiss, Edoardo 108
Widlöcher, D. 121, 134, 137
Winnicott, D. W. 17, 29, 56, 71, 99, 109

Zucchini, Gino 16, 110